First Grade Thinking Skills and Key Concepts

TEACHER'S MANUAL

Thinking Skills and Key Concepts Series

📖 Kindergarten 📖 First Grade 📖 Second Grade

Written by
Howard Black
Sandra Parks

Early Childhood Education Consultant
Ellen O'Shaughnessy

Graphic Design by
Howard Black

© 2015
THE CRITICAL THINKING CO.™
www.CriticalThinking.com
Phone: 800-458-4849 • Fax: 541-756-1758
1991 Sherman Ave., Suite 200 • North Bend • OR 97459
ISBN 978-1-60144-700-5

FSC — MIX — Paper from responsible sources — FSC® C011935

Table of Contents

INTRODUCTION V

CHAPTER ONE - DESCRIBING SHAPES 1
    Describing Lines.. 1
    Describing Circles and Ovals.. 2
    Lines Make Angles and Shapes.. 4
    Finding Rectangles and Squares.. 5
    Describing Triangles... 6
    Describing Trapezoids.. 7
    Describing Hexagons.. 9
    Matching Picture, Color, and Name 10
    Shapes You Should Know..11
    Describing Shapes.. 12
    Describing Cubes and Spheres.. 13
    Describing Cylinders and Cones.. 14

CHAPTER TWO - THINKING ABOUT POSITION 16
    Describing Position - First to Last 17
    Describing Position - First, Second, Third, Fourth 18
    Describing Position - Left, Center, Right 20
    Describing Position - Above, Middle, Below... 22

CHAPTER THREE - SIMILARITIES AND DIFFERENCES – SHAPES 24
    Matching by Shape and Color... 24
    Which Shape Does Not Match?.. 25
    Comparing Shapes... 26
    Describing Differences.. 28
    Coloring One of Two Equal Parts... 29
    Dividing Shapes into Halves 30
    Coloring Fourths... 32
    Dividing Shapes Into Fourths... 33

CHAPTER FOUR - SEQUENCES OF SHAPES 34
    What Color Square/s Come/s Next? 35
    Which Comes Next? 36
    Describing Sequences 38

CHAPTER FIVE - GROUPS OF SHAPES 40
    Describing a Group of Shapes 40
    Which Shape Does Not Belong?... 43

CHAPTER SIX - THINKING ABOUT LAND FORMS AND BODIES OF WATER................. 46
    Describing Land Forms and Bodies of Water 46
    Kinds of Land and Water.. 54
    Similar Land or Water 55
    Comparing Land Forms and Bodies of Water 56

CHAPTER SEVEN - THINKING ABOUT LIVING AND NON-LIVING THINGS 58
    Describing Living and Non-living Things 59
    Kinds of Living Things 65
    Comparing Plants and Animals 67

CHAPTER EIGHT - THINKING ABOUT FOOD 69
    Describing Food.. 72
    Describing Parts of a Grape Vine... 81

Similar Foods 82
Similarities and Differences - Foods 85
Comparing food.. 87
Kinds of Food 89

CHAPTER NINE - THINKING ABOUT ANIMALS 94
Describing Animals 96
Describing Parts of a Bee 106
Kinds of Animals... 107
Similar Animals... 110
Similarities and Differences - Animals 112
Comparing Animals 114
Kinds of Animals... 116
Classifying Animals 119

CHAPTER TEN - THINKING ABOUT FAMILY MEMBERS 122
Naming Family Members 123
Describing Family Members 124
Similar Family Members.. 128
Similarities and Differences - Family Members 130
Comparing Family Members 132
Groups of Family Members 133
A Different Family Member... 134
Classifying Family Members 136

CHAPTER ELEVEN - THINKING ABOUT JOBS...................................... 137
Describing Jobs 138
Similar Jobs... 145
Similarities and Differences - Jobs 147
Comparing Jobs 148
Kinds of Jobs.. 150
Classifying Jobs 152

CHAPTER TWELVE - THINKING ABOUT VEHICLES 154
Describing Vehicles 156
Parts of a Dump Truck 161
Similar Vehicles.. 162
Similarities and Differences - Vehicles 164
Comparing Vehicles 166
Kinds of Vehicles.. 168
Classifying Vehicles 171
Match Drivers to Their Vehicle 173

CHAPTER THIRTEEN - THINKING ABOUT PLACES 175
Describing Places 176
Parts of a Farm 181
Similar Places 182
Similarities and Differences - Places... 184
Comparing Places.. 186
Kinds of Places 188
Classifying Places 190
Match the Job and Vehicle to the Places 193
Finding Places on a Map.. 194
Finding Distances on a Map.. 195

APPENDIX 196

THINKING SKILLS AND KEY CONCEPTS

GOALS/STUDENT OUTCOMES

- Improve young children's vocabulary development and observation skills
- Clarify thinking processes required for content learning (identifying similarities and differences, sequencing, and classifying)
- Improve students' understanding of mathematics, social studies and science concepts taught in the primary grades

THINKING SKILLS INSTRUCTION

FIGURAL SKILLS
Describing Shapes
Naming shapes, finding shapes to match a description, describing characteristics of a shape
Figural Similarities and Differences
Matching shapes, producing equal figures, figure completion
Figural Sequences
Recognizing and producing the next figure in a sequence
Figural Classification
Classifying by shape and/or color, forming classes.
Describing Things
Matching a picture to a description, describing people or objects shown in pictures, describing parts of a whole
Verbal Similarities and Differences
Selecting similar family members, occupations, food, animals, vehicles, and places and explaining how they are alike or different
Verbal Sequences
Ranking objects or people by a significant characteristic
Verbal Classifications
Explaining characteristics of a class, exceptions, and sorting objects or people into classes

CONTENT OBJECTIVES

MATHEMATICS OBJECTIVES
Properties of polygons & solids
Names, sides, angles
Reading and Writing Mathematical Terms
Geometry terms, ordinal numbers, positional words
Pattern Recognition
Recognizing sequential patterns

SOCIAL STUDIES CONCEPTS
Family members
Age, gender, relationships
Occupations
Activities, consumer/producer, goods/services
Places
Residence, government, storage, education, business
Vehicles
Personal, public transportation, recreation, emergency
Map directions

SCIENCE CONCEPTS
Land forms and bodies of water
Living and non-living things
Food
Plant or animal products, preparation, dairy, meat, vegetable, grain, part of the plant we eat (root, stem, leaf, fruit)
Animals
Type of animal (fish, bird, mammal, amphibian, reptile), habitat, locomotion, reproduction, and skin covering

METHODS TO IMPROVE THINKING AND LEARNING

DIRECT INSTRUCTION
Prior knowledge, clear objectives, practice, metacognition, application
DEVELOPMENTAL FORMS
Concrete (pictures), semi-concrete (student book), abstract (discussion)
COOPERATIVE LEARNING
Paired problem solving, and think/pair/share
GRAPHIC ORGANIZERS
Graphics to show thinking (description, compare/contrast, order, class relationships)
WHOLE SENTENCE RESPONDING
In both thinking skills activities and in general instruction, students and teachers speak and write in whole sentences
MENTAL MODELS
Graphics show key characteristics of mathematical, social studies, and science concepts
LANGUAGE INTEGRATION ACTIVITIES
Developmental activities supplement vocabulary acquisition and include drawing activities, creating big books, story telling, writing, and discussing picture books

PROGRAM EVALUATION

- Student performance on language proficiency and cognitive abilities tests
- Student performance on normed-referenced or criterion-referenced achievement tests
- Improved student writing
- Number of students placed in advanced academic classes, including gifted programs, and subsequent successful performance in such classes

INTRODUCTION

PROGRAM DESIGN

Rationale

Thinking Skills & Key Concepts is a program is designed to:

- Develop thinking processes that underlie content learning (describing/defining, identifying similarities and differences, sequencing, and classifying)

- Improve young children's observation and description skills

- Improve students' understanding of mathematics, social studies and science concepts taught in first grade

- Develop academic vocabulary

In *First Grade Thinking Skills & Key Concepts* lessons, students describe the properties of geometric shapes, living and non-living things, land forms/bodies of water, family members, occupations, animals, food, vehicles, and places. Students clarify their thinking by peer and class discussion of richly detailed photographs.

Thinking Skills

The thinking skills developed in this program include describing, defining, finding similarities and differences, sequencing, and classifying. These processes were selected because of their frequency in academic disciplines, particularly mathematics and science instruction. Students must be proficient in these thinking skills because most first grade curricula, particularly those based on the Common Core State Standards, emphasize concept development and reading comprehension.

These thinking processes are commonly featured on objective tests. Since improved school performance is an important goal of thinking skills instruction, many variations of each of these thinking skills are featured in *Thinking Skills & Key Concepts* exercises.

Within each chapter these thinking skills are sequenced in the order in which a child develops intellectually. A learner first describes objects, recognizes their characteristics, and distinguishes similarities and differences between them. Describing, comparing, and contrasting are necessary to put objects or events in order and to group objects by class.

To transfer thinking skills to other contexts, students must remember the steps in their own thinking. They practice metacognition of the thinking skill in each lesson. In each chapter lessons feature the same thinking processes, giving students many transfer examples. This repetition builds students' confidence and competence as thinkers and learners.

Academic Vocabulary Development

Students discuss detailed photographs in order to develop key mathematics, science, and social studies terms. Through peer discussion learners with limited vocabulary hear and express the properties of key academic concepts.

Common Core State Standards promote increased use of non-fiction books to improve reading comprehension and background in science and social studies. They also emphasize writing as a technique for improved content learning. *Thinking Skills & Key Concepts* features numerous activities for listening, speaking, and writing to accomplish these goals.

INSTRUCTIONAL METHODS

Direct Instruction

Each chapter features direct instruction for each thinking process. When introducing a skill, the teacher identifies a school-related or nonacademic example in which the learner has used that thinking process, cueing the learner that he or she already has some experience and competence with that skill.

Stating the lesson objective clarifies both

the content and the thinking skill. Modeling the thinking task teaches students the language of thinking and shows them how to do the thinking process skillfully. Guided and independent practice promote mastery.

The Thinking About Thinking section of each lesson reminds students of the thinking process practiced in the lesson. Research on thinking process instruction indicates that, without metacognition, subsequent transfer is less likely. Metacognition is fostered by peer discussion and class discussion. The learner then identifies other contexts in which he or she has used this skill. This association with past personal experience increases the learner's confidence in his or her thinking and encourages transfer of the skill.

Developmental Forms

Picture books and photographs depict the significant details that illustrate examples of key concepts. Peer and class discussion clarify concepts and promote vocabulary.

Listening and speaking employ different learning styles, allowing students to recognize different ways to describe an object. Discussion reinforces the learner's memory of the thinking process, promotes transfer to similar tasks, and enhances the learner's confidence and willingness to participate in class.

Students trace and copy mathematics, science, and social studies terms as they begin to express them in model sentences.

Cooperative Learning

Peer discussion significantly enhances language acquisition, particularly for second-language learners. Through conversation each student hears and expresses both the thinking process and the content. Before students learn to read (an in-put process), they first listen (a more basic in-put process). Before students write (an out-put process), they first speak (a more basic out-put process).

Many students of poverty have limited experience listening or speaking for a sustained period. Peer discussion promotes the quality and accuracy of students' responses. Evaluation of thinking skills instruction shows that young children, particularly bilingual students, gain confidence and willingness to participate in class discussion when they have had an opportunity to "rehearse" their comments with a partner.

Whole-Sentence Responding

In *Thinking Skills & Key Concepts* lessons, students and teachers respond in whole sentences. Teachers who have used this technique report that this practice is so significant in promoting students' language proficiency that it should be considered an essential element of instruction.

Mental Models

A mental model is a framework that features the key characteristics that a student must know to understand a concept. A mental model helps a learner to:
- Find what one needs to know to understand a new concept
- Remember the characteristics
- State clear definitions or adequate descriptions
- Explain a concept to someone else

By the end of each chapter, first grade students should know the significant characteristics of each of the following concepts. Teachers should use picture books or actual objects, when possible, to illustrate the key characteristics shown below.

CONCEPT	KEY CHARACTERISTICS
Polygon	Lines (curved or straight), sides (equal or unequal), number of sides, size of angle
Solids	Number of faces, what shape is seen from each side
Patterns	Describing color, size, and shape, color/size/shape sequences
Land Forms/ Water Forms	Size, shape, height/depth, fresh/ salt, relationship to land or bodies of water

Living/Non-living things	Growth, food, reproduction, plants/animals
Family	Relationship, age, gender, role in the family
Food (animals)	Color, liquid or solid, how we eat them, taste, how prepared
Food (plants)	Type (vegetables, fruit, grain, seed), part of plant we eat (leaf, root, stem, fruit), kind of plant (vine, bush, tree), taste, color/shape/size, how prepared
Animals	Type (mammals, birds, fish, reptiles, insects), live birth/hatch from eggs, size shape/color, appearance, habitat, how it moves (fast, slow), protection
Jobs	Types of jobs (provides goods or services, emergency workers, health care workers), equipment, special clothing, building where they work, training
Vehicles	Types of vehicles (emergency, personal, work, public transportation, recreation), size, number of passengers, where it travels (land/sea/air), speed
Places	Types of places (residences, government buildings, education, businesses, storage), size, number of people who live there, what is sold or stored there, special features, finding buildings on a map

Language integration activities

Language acquisition research suggests several strategies to help young children develop and express new or partially-conceived concepts. *Thinking Skills & Key Concepts* lesson plans include drawing activities, using portfolio assessment, creating big books, story telling, and writing exercises.

• **Drawing activities-** Students depict details of concepts explored in the *Thinking Skills & Key Concepts* program (family members, jobs, food, vehicles, animals, and buildings).

• **Creating "big books"-** Drawings are collected to form individual or class "big books" to show students' understanding and growth.

• **Story telling-** Personal narratives and imaginative stories extend concept development in the *Thinking Skills & Key Concepts* program

• **Writing-** Students create sentences, definitions, paragraphs, and full stories about concepts featured in the *Thinking Skills & Key Concepts lessons*.

• **Picture Book Extension-** Fiction and nonfiction books for first grade students depict and explain important concepts. Common Core State Standards emphasize using non-fiction books to promote reading comprehension and to teach science and social studies objectives. Consult your school librarian to identify appropriate books, particularly picture books that show multicultural diversity.

DESCRIPTION OF CHAPTERS

Describing Shapes

Students name polygons, observe the sides and angles, and write about the properties of common geometric figures and three-dimensional objects. They identify shapes within common objects and describe the color of examples.

Thinking About Position

Students identify and write about various positions (first/last, first through fourth, left/right, above/below)

Similarities and Differences - Shapes

Chapter 3 features activities to develop visual discrimination skills (size, shape, and color). They divide shapes into halves and fourths.

Sequences of Shapes

In Chapter 4 students evaluate, produce, and write about a variety of sequences involving color and shape.

Groups of Shapes

In figural classification exercises students identify and write about common characteristics and group geometric figures by class.

Thinking About Land Forms and Bodies of Water

Students identify, describe, and write about various land forms and bodies of water.

Thinking About Living and Non-Living Things

Students identify, describe, and write about various living and non-living things. They identify whether various objects grow, need food, or reproduce themselves. They distinguish between plants and animals.

Thinking About Food

Students describe, compare and contrast, classify and write about food. They discuss whether food is a plant or animal product, its appearance and taste, and how it is prepared across cultures. To describe food products from plants, students identify the parts of a plant: root, stem, leaf, fruit, and/or seed.

Thinking About Animals

Students describe, compare and contrast, rank, classify and write about animals. They discuss whether various animals are cold-blooded or warm-blooded, give live birth or lay eggs, have a backbone, appearance (color, size, body covering), where it lives, how it protects itself, and how it moves. Students learn types of animals: insects/fish/birds/reptiles/mammals.

Thinking About Family Members

Students describe family members, compare and contrast them, and classify and write about them. They discuss age, gender, relationship to other family members, roles, and interests or experiences that make various family members special.

Thinking About Occupations

Students describe, compare and contrast, rank, classify and write about occupations. They discuss whether jobs provide goods or services, how much training is required, the activities of various professions, and the equipment and uniforms associated with the profession. They learn types of jobs: producers, health workers, government workers, construction, banking, retail workers and service providers.

Thinking About Vehicles

Students describe, compare and contrast, rank, classify, and write about vehicles. They discuss the size and purpose of various vehicles, where they are driven, their appearance, their ownership, and the kind of equipment they contain.

Thinking About Places

Students describe, compare and contrast, classify, and write about places. They discuss the size, purpose, construction, design, materials, location of various places, as well as who lives or works there, and who owns it.

EVALUATING THINKING SKILLS INSTRUCTION

Thinking skills instruction has been evaluated using many assessment procedures:
- Student performance on cognitive abilities tests
- Student performance on normed-referenced achievement tests
- Student performance on criterion-referenced achievement tests
- Student performance on language proficiency tests

- Number of students placed in heterogeneous grouped classes, or advanced academic programs, as well as students' subsequent successful performance in gifted or academic excellence classes

Cognitive Abilities Tests

The figural and verbal subtests of cognitive abilities tests are closely correlated to *Thinking Skills & Key Concepts* goals and activities.

The following cognitive abilities tests have been used in program effectiveness evaluation of thinking instruction using the *Thinking Skills & Key Concepts* series:

- Cognitive Abilities Test (Woodcock-Johnson)
  Riverside Publishing Company
  425 Spring Lake Dr.
  Itasa, IL 60143
  800-323-9540 • 312-693-0325 (fax)

- Developing Cognitive Abilities Test
  American College Testronics (formerly American Testronics)
  P.O. Box 2270
  Iowa City, IA 52244
  800-533-0030 • 319-337-1578 (fax)

- Test of Cognitive Skills
  CTB-McGraw Hill
  P.O. Box 150
  Monterey, CA 93942-0150
  800-538-9547 • 800-282-0266 (fax)

Norm-referenced Achievement Tests

Composite scores on norm-referenced achievement tests are generally poor indicators of improved thinking skills. Some subtests do reflect the thinking skills addressed in *Thinking Skills & Key Concepts* instruction. Program evaluation using this series has indicated substantial gains in subtests which measure reading comprehension and mathematics concepts.

If achievement test information is used to report the effectiveness of *Thinking Skills & Key Concepts* instruction, only those subtests should be reported.

Language Proficiency Tests

Program evaluation of *Thinking Skills & Key Concepts* shows substantial gains on locally designated assessment in vocabulary, reading comprehension, and mathematics. Anecdotal data, and students' drawings show unusual conceptualization of primary science and social studies concepts. Students using *Thinking Skills & Key Concepts* are found to be well prepared for second grade instruction in science and social studies, which is commonly measured by state and local assessments.

Because one goal of the *Thinking Skills & Key Concepts* program is language development, increased vocabulary can be shown on a variety of language tests. Tests commonly used to evaluate the effect of thinking instruction on language development include the following:

- Peabody Picture Vocabulary Test
- ESOL proficiency tests

Inclusion and Performance in Mainstream or Advanced Academic Classes

The *Thinking Skills & Key Concepts* series is commonly used to promote access to academic excellence programs or to prepare special education students to be successful in mainstream classes. This program has been successful in Chapter 1 classes, bilingual programs, ESOL classes, special education classes, and remedial programs. School districts evaluate this goal by the number of students who gain access to more advanced programs, the speed with which the transition is accomplished, and the students' level of achievement when included in general or advanced classes.

INSTRUCTIONAL RECOMMENDATIONS

- **Do description and similarities and differences exercises first.** These two processes are required for sequencing and classifying.

- **Encourage peer discussion.** The quality of student responses and their attentiveness significantly improve when peers discuss their answers before class discussion. Peer discussion is particularly effective in special education, bilingual, and Title I classes.

- **Conduct short exercises.** Each page is usually takes one 20-30 minute session in order to have time for the "Thinking About Thinking" and "Personal Application". Discuss a few exercises with ample time for students to explain their thinking, rather than conducting additional lessons.

- **Identify and use students' background knowledge.** Use these lessons to diagnose students' prior knowledge. Remember the language that students use in their descriptions. Use the same words to remind students of the thinking processes in subsequent social studies and science lessons.

- **Use Thinking Skills & Key Concepts lessons before or after social studies or science activities.** Possible responses in each lesson plan exceed the answers commonly expected from students in first grade. Continue accepting students comments until key characteristics have been mentioned.

- **Teach other mathematics, science, and social studies concepts using the same thinking processes.** Use correct terms for the thinking process to cue students to transfer the thinking process to other contexts. Use the same methods (peer and class discussion, observation of pictures or objects, etc.) in other lessons.

- **Insist that students use complete sentences when responding.** Students whose language proficiency is underdeveloped are inclined to answer in single words or phrases. To realize the language acquisition benefits of these lessons, students should answer in complete sentences, expressing whole thoughts that are grammatically correct.

- **Lessons should not be given as homework assignments or as independent activities.** The lessons in *Thinking Skills & Key Concepts* are designed to enhance cognitive development through discussion and observation. Exercises from the student book should not be used as a substitute for class discussion.

- **Use non-fiction picture books to introduce concepts.** Before each lesson read non-fiction picture books about food, animals, jobs, vehicles, or buildings that are featured in the lesson.

- **Check students' understanding of mental models.** At the end of each chapter discuss an example of food, animals, jobs, vehicles, or buildings not featured in the lesson. Check whether students have internalized the mental model sufficiently so that they can identify the key characteristics without prompting.

VOCABULARY AND SYNONYMS

Reinforce the language of thinking in thinking skills activities and in other lessons. The following list includes terms that teachers and students can use in *Thinking Skills & Key Concepts* lessons, content lessons, and personal applications. Students may create a "thinking thesaurus" of the words and idioms that they use to describe their thinking. Encourage them to express their thinking using the terms below.

WORD	SYNONYMS
Arrange	place, assemble, organize, put together, gather, build
Category	class, group, kind, type
Class	group, category, kind, type
Classify	arrange, group
Compare	match, find similarities
Contrasts	differs, is unlike
Decrease	lessen, shrink, become smaller
Definition	meaning, explanation, description
Describe	explain, give details
Detail	part, piece
Differences	unlike, contrasts, not like
Discuss	talk about, describe, explain
Eliminate	remove, take out, erase, end
Equal	same, matching, same size
Examine	find the details, look at
Explain	make sure, show, tell
False	not true, not real, untrue, unreal
Figural	drawn, geometric
Figure	shape, diagram, drawing
Geometric	figural, having shape
Identify	find, recognize, pick out, show
Locate	identify, place, find
Location	place, position
Matching	equal, making an equal pair
Member	belongs to a group or class
Observe	pay attention to, examine, look at carefully
Order	rank, sequence
Part	piece, detail
Pattern	arrangement, design
Prepare	produce, create, ready, plan
Produce	make, create, assemble
Recognize	identify, be familiar with
Relationship	connection, how related or similar
Select	pick out, identify, locate, decide
Sequence	steps, order, rank, change
Shape	figure, pattern, drawing
Significant	important, basic
Similarity	likeness, sameness
Sort	group, classify, organize
True	real
Verbal	spoken, said in words
Whole	entire, complete, total

GUIDE TO USING THE LESSON PLANS

LESSON TITLE

CURRICULUM APPLICATIONS
Lists content objectives which feature the skill or require it as a prerequisite.

TEACHING SUGGESTIONS
Alerts the teacher to special vocabulary or concepts in the lesson. Identifies materials or special concerns when conducting the lessons.

LESSON

Introduction
- Provides information that the student may not have previously learned or indicates when he or she has used similar thinking. This step reassures students that they are prepared for the lesson and establishes the pattern of using prior knowledge.

Stating the Objective
Teacher Comment: Explains to the student what he or she will learn in the lesson. This step previews the directions that the teacher gives when conducting the lesson.

Conducting the Lesson
- Provides a sample dialog to emphasize both the content and the thinking process.
  Teacher Comment: **Bold type shows suggested dialogue for teachers.**
    Student Response: Sample student answers.

THINKING ABOUT THINKING
Helps the student clarify and verbalize the thinking process (metacognition).

PERSONAL APPLICATION
Relates the skill to the learner's experience and cues the learner regarding possible future uses of the skill.

CHAPTER ONE – DESCRIBING SHAPES (Pages 2-13)

GENERAL INTRODUCTION

ACTIVITIES TO INTRODUCE AND REINFORCE THE CONCEPT OF SHAPE

Ask students to cut out pictures of objects that are good examples of the shapes discussed in this chapter. Organize their pictures into a bulletin board display, grouping and labeling the objects by shape.

TEACHING SUGGESTIONS

- Ask students to discuss and explain their answers in complete sentences. When asked "How many sides does a square have?" a student may correctly answer "four." If the student responds, "A square has four sides," he or she has named the shape and its characteristics, imprinting the term for its shape and stating its properties. This practice seems artificial at first, but it is essential for young children, especially second-language learners.

- Ask students to name the object as they discuss it and explain their answers.

- Integrate these shape terms into your language arts program by discussing picture books which emphasize shape.

- In many of these lessons the teacher directions to students include language that shows order (first ..., next ..., last; first ..., second ..., third ..., last). Many young students may not be familiar with these terms in the kind of directions used in school. Repetition of these sequences and consequently hearing them in student responses models the language patterns that students will need in primary level writing tasks.

CURRICULUM APPLICATIONS

Language Arts: Visual discrimination for reading readiness
Mathematics: Naming geometric shapes
Science: Recognizing shapes of leaves, insects, or shells
Social Studies: Recognizing geographic features on map puzzles
Enrichment Areas: Recognizing shapes of road signs; describing patterns in art

Page 2 - DESCRIBING LINES: STRAIGHT, CURVED, LONG, SHORT

LESSON

Introduction

Teacher Comment: **Lines are thin marks that can be any color. Some lines are long. Some lines are short. Some lines are straight. Some lines are curved.**

Stating the Objective

Teacher Comment: **In this lesson we will identify lines and color them.**

Conducting the Lesson

Teacher Comment: **Look at the box at the top of the page. Some of the lines are long and some are short. Color the long lines red.**
Teacher Comment: **Now color the short lines green.**

• Check students' work.

> Teacher Comment: **Look at the lines in the bottom box. What do you notice?**
>> Student Response: Some of the lines are straight and some are wiggly.
>
> Teacher Comment: **Color the straight lines red. Color the curved lines blue.**

• Check students' work.

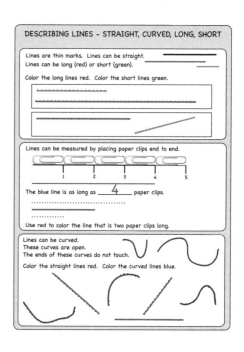

Thinking About Thinking

> Teacher Comment: **What did you think about when you colored the curved or straight lines?**
>> Student Response:
>> 1. I looked for straight lines and decided which were curved.
>> 2. I checked how the lines looked and how it feels to draw a straight or a curved line.

Personal Application

> Teacher Comment: **When do you need to draw straight or curved lines?**
>> Student Response: I need to draw straight or curved lines when I write letters or draw pictures.

Page 3 - DESCRIBING SHAPES - CIRCLES AND OVALS

LESSON

Introduction
• Hold up a circle.

> Teacher Comment: **A circle is a closed curve. (Run a finger around the circle to show that it is closed.) It has no beginning or end and looks the same from any side. (Rotate the circle to show that its appearance does not change.) Trace the word "circle." What objects are shaped like a circle?**
>> • Answers will vary.

• Hold up an oval.

> Teacher Comment: **An oval is also a closed curve. (Run a finger around the oval.) It looks like a flattened circle. (Rotate the oval to a vertical position.) In one position it looks tall. (Rotate the oval to a horizontal position.) Now it looks short. Trace the word "oval."**

Stating the Objective
> Teacher Comment: **In this lesson you will trace and color circles and ovals.**

Conducting the Lesson

Teacher Comment: **Look at the second box. Is the first shape in the row a circle or an oval?**

Student Response: The first shape is an oval.

Teacher Comment: **Color the oval blue.**

Teacher Comment: **Is the next shape a circle or an oval?**

Student Response: That shape is a circle.

Teacher Comment: **Color the circle red.**

Teacher Comment: **Color the rest of the circles red and color the ovals blue.**

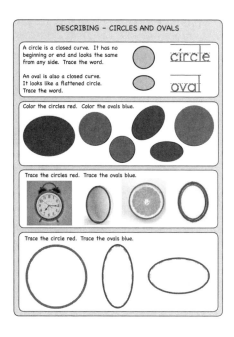

• Check students' work.

Teacher Comment: **Look at the objects in the next box. Name the objects in the pictures.**

Student Response: The objects are a clock, an egg, an orange, and a picture frame.

Teacher Comment: **Look for a circle or an oval in each picture. Trace the circles red. Trace the ovals blue.**

• Check students' work.

Teacher Comment: **In the bottom box trace the circle red. Trace the ovals blue.**

Thinking About Thinking

Teacher Comment: **What did you think about when you traced and colored circles and ovals?**

Student Response:

1. I looked for a closed curved line that had no beginning or end and looks like an "O" from all sides.
2. I looked for a closed curved line that looks like a flat "O" and looks tall or short from different sides.
3. I paid attention to how it feels to color and trace a circle and how it feels different to trace and color an oval.

Personal Application

Teacher Comment: **When do you need to find circles?**

Student Response: I look for circles to draw things or to find or describe items.

Page 4 - LINES MAKE ANGLES AND SHAPES

LESSON

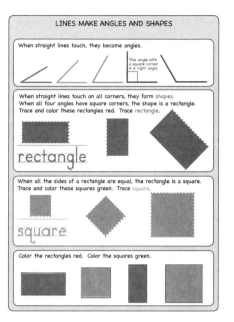

Introduction

- Use a folding ruler to make the angles and shapes in this lesson. Fold the ruler to make an acute angle like the red one.
  Teacher Comment: **When straight lines touch, they become an angle. (Hold up the acute angle and run your finger along the two sides to show the angle.) Sometimes the angle makes a sharp point like the red one in the book.**

- Open the ruler slightly.
  Teacher Comment: **Sometimes the angle is not so sharp like the orange one.**

- Open the ruler wider.
  Teacher Comment: **Sometimes the top line is almost straight up like the green angle.**

- Open the ruler to make the top line completely vertical, making a right angle.
  Teacher Comment: **When the top line is straight up it makes a square corner like the blue angle. You could draw a little square inside it. This square corner is called a right angle.**

- Open the ruler wider to make an obtuse angle.
  Teacher Comment: **Sometimes the top line can make an angle that is wider than a corner like the purple one. Whether the angle is sharp, square, or wide, anytime two lines touch they make an angle.**

- Find some examples of sharp, right, or wide angles in objects in the classroom.

Stating the Objective

Teacher Comment: **In this lesson you will find lines that touch to make angles.**

Conducting the Lesson

- Use a second folding ruler, make both folding rulers into right angles, each with two longer sides.
  Teacher Comment: **When straight lines touch on all corners, they form shapes.**

- Hold up the first right angle and move the second one into position to form a rectangle.
  Teacher Comment: **When straight lines touch on all corners, they form shapes. When all four angles have square corners, the shape is a rectangle. Trace and color the rectangles red. Use your red marker to trace the word "rectangle."**

- Fold the rulers so that all sides are equal.
  Teacher Comment: **When all sides of a rectangle are equal, the rectangle is called a "square." Trace and color the squares green. Use your green marker to trace the word "square."**

- Check students' work.

Teacher Comment: **In the bottom box color the rectangles red and the squares green.**

Thinking About Thinking

Teacher Comment: **What did you think about to show which shape are rectangles and which are squares?**

Student Response:
1. I looked for lines that make square corners.
2. I checked whether all four sides are equal or whether two sides are longer.
3. I picked the colors to show whether the shape is a rectangle or square.
4. I paid attention to how it feels to trace and color a rectangle or a square.

Personal Application

Teacher Comment: **When do you need to find rectangles and squares?**

Student Response: I need to find rectangles and squares when I draw objects such as boxes, doors, windows, etc.

Page 5 - FINDING RECTANGLES AND SQUARES

LESSON

Introduction

Teacher Comment: **In the last lesson you traced and colored rectangles and squares.**

Stating the Objective

Teacher Comment: **In this lesson you will find rectangles and squares in pictures.**

Conducting the Lesson

Teacher Comment: **Look at each picture. Trace the rectangles red. Trace the squares green.**

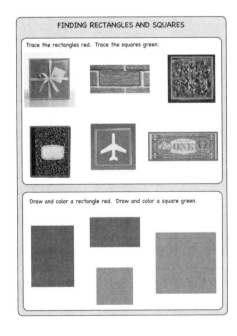

• Check students' work.

Teacher Comment: **Which objects are squares?**
Student response: The present, the picture frame, and the airport sign are squares.
Teacher Comment: **Which objects are rectangles?**
Student response: The brick, the book, and the dollar bill are rectangles.
Teacher Comment: **In the bottom box draw and color a rectangle red. Draw and color a square green.**

Thinking About Thinking

Teacher Comment: **What did you think about to show which shapes are rectangles and which are squares?**

Student Response:
1. I checked whether all four sides are equal or whether two sides are longer.
2. I picked the colors to show whether the shape is a rectangle or square.
3. I paid attention to how it feels to trace and color a rectangle or a square.

Personal Application

Teacher Comment: **When do you need to find rectangles and squares?**

Student response: I need to find rectangles and squares when I draw objects such as boxes, doors, windows, etc.

Page 6 - DESCRIBING TRIANGLES

LESSON

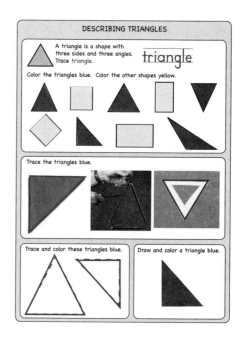

Introduction

• Use a folding ruler to make an equilateral triangle.

Teacher Comment: **When straight lines touch on three corners, they become a triangle.**

• Hold up the triangle and run your finger along all three sides, counting as you touch each side.

Teacher Comment: **Trace the word "triangle."**

• Use a folding ruler to make a right triangle.

Teacher Comment: **Sometimes one angle can be a square corner.**

• Fold the ruler to make two sides much longer in order to form a tall, sharp isosceles triangle.

Teacher Comment: **Sometimes the triangle can be very sharp like this one.**

• Fold the ruler wider to make a wide base and two short, equal sides to form a short isosceles with an obtuse angle.

Teacher Comment: **Sometimes the triangle can be short and wide like this one.**

• Fold the ruler to make an acute triangle with three uneven sides.

Teacher Comment: **Sometimes none of the sides are the same length.**

• Fold the ruler to make an obtuse triangle with three uneven sides.

Teacher Comment: **Sometimes the triangle looks slanted and none of the sides are the same length. It doesn't matter how long the sides are or how sharp the angles are. If the shape has three sides, it is a triangle.**

• Find some examples of triangles in objects in the classroom.

Stating the Objective
Teacher Comment: **In this lesson you will find and trace triangles.**

Conducting the Lesson
Teacher Comment: **In the top box color the triangles blue. Color the other shapes yellow.**

• Check students' work.

Teacher Comment: **In the middle box find the triangle in each picture. Trace the triangles with a blue marker/crayon.**
Teacher Comment: **Name the objects that are triangles.**
  Student Response: The napkin, the musical triangle, and the sign on the road are triangles.
Teacher Comment: **In the first box on the bottom row, trace and color the triangles blue. In the next box, draw and color a blue triangle.**

• Check students' work.

Thinking About Thinking
Teacher Comment: **What did you think about to show which shapes are triangles?**
  Student Response:
  1. I checked whether the shape has three sides and three angles.
  2. I picked the colors to show whether the shape is a triangle or not.
  3. I paid attention to how it feels to trace and color a triangle.

Personal Application
Teacher Comment: **When do you need to find triangles?**
  Student Response: I need to find triangles when I draw objects such as tents, roofs, Christmas trees, or other objects that have triangles.

Page 7 - DESCRIBING TRAPEZOIDS

LESSON

Introduction
• Use a folding ruler to make a trapezoid. Hold up the trapezoid.

Teacher Comment: **This shape is a trapezoid. It looks like a triangle with its top cut off. Trace the word "trapezoid."**

• Use your finger to trace where the top of that triangle would be.
  Teacher Comment: **Notice that the trapezoid has four sides.**

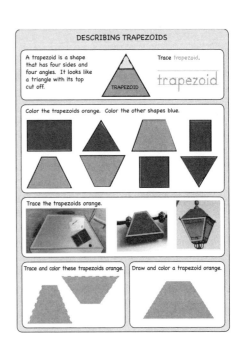

• Run your finger along all four sides, counting as you touch each side.

Teacher Comment: **Notice that the trapezoid is different from a rectangle because two of its sides are slanted.**

Stating the Objective

Teacher Comment: **In this lesson you will find and trace trapezoids.**

Conducting the Lesson

Teacher Comment: **In the top box color the trapezoids orange. Color the other shapes blue.**

• Check students' work.

Teacher Comment: **In the middle box find the trapezoid in each picture. Trace the trapezoid with an orange marker/crayon.**
Teacher Comment: **Name the objects that are trapezoids.**
Student Response: The desk, the beads, and the street light are trapezoids.

Teacher Comment: **In the first box on the bottom row, trace and color the trapezoids orange. In the next box, draw and color a trapezoid orange.**

• Check students' work.

Thinking About Thinking

Teacher Comment: **What did you think about to show which shapes are trapezoids?**
Student response:
1. I checked whether the shape has four sides.
2. I saw that two sides are slanted.
3. I picked the colors to show that the shape is a trapezoid.
4. I paid attention to how it feels to trace and color a trapezoid.

Personal Application

Teacher Comment: **When do you need to find trapezoids?**
Student Response: I need to find trapezoids when I draw objects that have them.

Page 8 - DESCRIBING HEXAGONS

LESSON

Introduction
• Use a folding ruler to make a hexagon. Hold up the hexagon.
   Teacher Comment: **This shape is a hexagon. Notice that the hexagon has six sides.**

• Run your finger along all six sides, counting as you touch each side.
   Teacher Comment: **Notice that the hexagon has six angles.**

• Point to each angle, counting as you touch it.

   Teacher Comment: **Trace the word "hexagon."
   Notice that you can make a hexagon by putting two
   trapezoids together.**

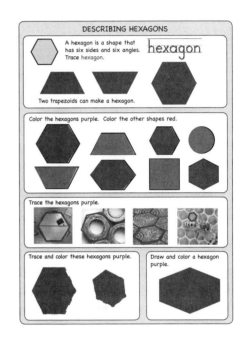

Stating the Objective
   Teacher Comment: **In this lesson you will find and
   trace hexagons.**

Conducting the Lesson
   Teacher Comment: **In the top box color the hexagons
   purple. Color the other shapes red.**

• Check students' work.

   Teacher Comment: **In the middle box find a hexagon
   in each picture. Trace the hexagon with a purple
   marker/crayon.**
   Teacher Comment: **Some of these objects may not be familiar. The hexagons are the
   table, the nut, the tiles, and a honeycomb.**

   Teacher Comment: **In the first box on the bottom row, trace and color the hexagons
   purple. In the next box, draw and color a purple hexagon.**

• Check students' work.

Thinking About Thinking
   Teacher Comment: **What did you think about to show which shapes are hexagons?**
   Student Response:
   1. I checked whether the shape had six sides.
   2. I picked the colors to show that the shape is a hexagon.
   4. I paid attention to how it feels to trace and color a hexagon.

Personal Application
   Teacher Comment: **When do you need to find hexagons?**
   Student Response: I need to find hexagons when I draw objects that have them.

Page 9 - MATCHING PICTURE, COLOR, AND NAME

LESSON

Introduction
Teacher Comment: **We have studied different shapes.**

Stating the Objective
Teacher Comment: **In this lesson you will match a shape to its color and its name.**

Conducting the Lesson
Teacher Comment: **The first color on the list is "blue." Trace the word "blue."**

Teacher Comment: **Which object is blue?**
  Student Response: The beads are blue.
Teacher Comment: **Trace the line from the word "blue" to the beads.**
Teacher Comment: **What shape is the blue bead?**
  Student Response: The blue bead is a trapezoid.
Teacher Comment: **Trace the line from the blue bead to the word "trapezoid."**

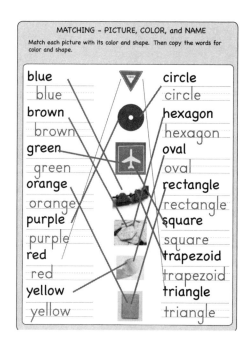

- Repeat this dialog for the word brown, instructing students to draw a line from the word "brown" to the crackers and then from the crackers to the word "hexagon." Confirm that student responses include naming the color, the object and its shape.

- Check students' work. If students correctly and confidently match the color, object, and shape, direct them to complete the rest of the exercise. If not repeat this dialog for the whole lesson.

Thinking About Thinking
Teacher Comment: **What did you think about when you matched objects to the words that describe their color and shape?**
Student Response:
1. I looked at the word for the color.
2. I found the object that has that color and drew a line to it.
3. I named the object.
4. I looked down the list to find its shape.
5. I matched the object to the word for its shape.

Personal Application
Teacher Comment: **When do you need to name both the color and the shape of objects?**
Student response: I need to name both the color and the shape of things in order to tell about them.

Page 10 - SHAPES YOU SHOULD KNOW

LESSON

Introduction
Teacher Comment: **We have matched shapes and their colors.**

Stating the Objective
Teacher Comment: **In this lesson you will match shapes to words that describe their size.**

Conducting the Lesson
Teacher Comment: **The first shape is a large square. Draw a line from the square to the word "large" and copy the word.**
Teacher Comment: **Draw a line from the square to the word "square" and copy the word.**

Teacher Comment: **The next shape is a small trapezoid. Draw a line from the small trapezoid to the word "small" and copy the word. Draw a line from the small trapezoid to the word "trapezoid" and copy the word.**

Teacher Comment: **Look at each shape and draw a line to the word for its size. Draw a line to the name for its shape and copy its name.**

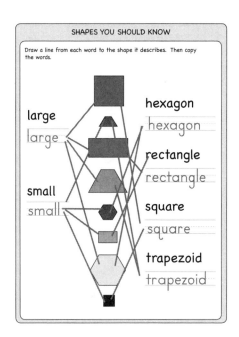

• Check students' work. Continue this dialog to discuss students' answers.

Thinking About Thinking
Teacher Comment: **What did you think about when you matched each shape to the words for its size and shape?**
Student Response:
1. I compared the size of the shape to others on the page.
2. I found the word for its size and matched it.
3. I then found the word for its shape and matched it.

Personal Application
Teacher Comment: **When do you need to name the size and shape of objects?**
Student Response: I need to tell the size and shape of objects when I write about them.

Page 11 - DESCRIBING SHAPES

Introduction
We have learned the words for size, color, and shape.

Stating the Objective
Teacher Comment: **In this lesson you will describe the size and color of shapes.**

Conducting the Lesson
Teacher Comment: **In the example we first name the shape and then write its size and color. Notice that there is a small dot at the end of the sentence. It is called a period. It tells the reader that you have finished that thought. Trace the example.**

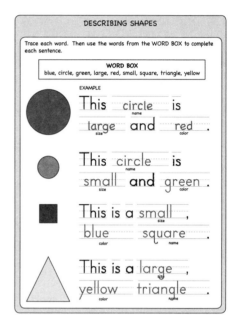

- Read aloud the directions at the top of the page.
 Teacher Comment: **Trace and complete the second sentence.**
 Teacher Comment: **Notice that in the next two sentences the word of the shape is at the end. In this sentence we named the size, the color, and then the shape. Either way of describing the shape is correct. Use the words in the word box to complete each sentence.**

- Check students' work. Continue this dialog to discuss students' answers.

- Model the sentence pattern for describing shape and color. Encourage students to speak in whole sentences using this pattern with other polygons and objects.

Thinking About Thinking
Teacher Comment: **What did you think about when you wrote a description of a shape?**
 Student Response:
 1. I named the shape, its color, and its size.
 2. I found the words for the shape and copied it. I found the words for its color and size and copied them.

Personal Application
Teacher Comment: **When do you need to write about a shape?**
 Student Response: I need to write about shapes when I write a description of what I see.

Page 12 - DESCRIBING CUBES AND SPHERES

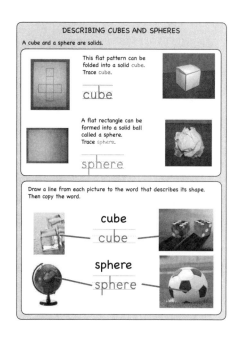

LESSON

Introduction

Teacher Comment: **In the last lessons all the shapes are drawn on a piece of paper. Those shapes are flat. If the paper is folded correctly it may form different solids. A solid is an object that you can hold in your hand.**

Stating the Objective

Teacher Comment: **In this lesson you will learn the names of two solids.**

Conducting the Lesson

• Hold up the pattern for a cube. (See the photocopy masters at the end of this book.)

Teacher Comment: **On this piece of paper all the squares are flat. When I fold the piece of paper correctly, the flat paper becomes a solid. This solid is a cube. Let's count the number of squares.**

• Point to each square as you count.

Teacher Comment: **Trace and copy the word "cube."**

• Hold up a flat piece of paper and squeeze it into a ball.

Teacher Comment: **What shape do you see?**

Student Response: I see a circle.

Teacher Comment: Rotate the ball. **What does the ball look like in all directions?**

Student Response: The ball looks like a circle from any direction.

Teacher Comment: **This ball is a solid that is called a sphere. Trace and copy the word "sphere."**

Teacher Comment: **Look at each object in the bottom box. Draw line from each picture to the word that describes its shape, then copy the word.**

Teacher Comment: **Which objects are cubes?**

Student Response: The ice cubes and the dice are cubes.

Teacher Comment: **Which objects are spheres?**

Student Response: The globe and the soccer ball are spheres.

Thinking About Thinking

Teacher Comment: **What did you think about to name a cube or a sphere?**

Student Response:

1. I looked at the picture to see what the sides look like.
2. If it looks like a square from any direction, I know that it is a cube.
3. If it looks like a circle from any direction, I know that it is a sphere.

Personal Application

Teacher Comment: **When do you need to describe a solid?**

Student Response: I describe a solid when I write about an object.

Page 13 - DESCRIBING CYLINDERS AND CONES

LESSON

Introduction

Teacher Comment: **In the last lessons we described some solids: cubes and spheres.**

Stating the Objective

Teacher Comment: **In this lesson you will learn about two other solids: cylinders and cones.**

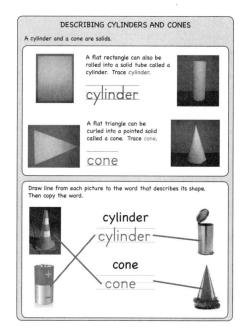

Conducting the Lesson

• Hold up a flat piece of paper.

Teacher Comment: **This piece of paper is flat.**

• Roll the paper into a cylinder. Hold the cylinder so that you and the class see through it.

Teacher Comment: **What shape do you see?**

Student Response: I see a circle.

• Hold the cylinder so that you and the class see it from its side.

Teacher Comment: **What shape do you see?**

Student Response: I see a rectangle.

Teacher Comment: **A solid that looks like a circle from one direction** (show the circle) **and a rectangle from the other** (show the rectangle) **is called a cylinder. Trace the word "cylinder."**

• Twist a piece of colored paper into a cone. Cut the base so that it is flat to create a pattern for a cone.

Teacher Comment: **This piece of paper is flat.**

• Hold up the flat pattern for the cone.

Teacher Comment: **When I roll it into a solid, it becomes a cone. When you look at it from the side, what shape do you see?**

Student Response: I see a triangle.

• Point the base toward the class.
   Teacher Comment: **When you look at the bottom, what shape so you see?**
   Student Response: The bottom is a circle.
   Teacher Comment: **A solid that looks like a triangle from the side and a circle from the bottom is called a cone. Trace and copy the word "cone."**

   Teacher Comment: **Look at each object in the bottom box. Draw line from each picture to the word that describes its shape then copy the word.**

• Check students' work.

   Teacher Comment: **Which objects are cylinders?**
   Student Response: The battery and the can are cylinders.
   Teacher Comment: **Which objects are cones?**
   Student Response: The traffic cone and the party hat are cones.

Thinking About Thinking
   Teacher Comment: **What did you think about when you matched the word for the solid to the picture?**
   Student Response:
   1. I looked at the picture to see what the sides look like.
   2. If it looks like a circle from the bottom and a rectangle from the side, I know that it is a cylinder.
   3. If it looks like a circle from the bottom and a triangle from the side, I know that it is a cone.

Personal Application
   Teacher Comment: **When do you need to know the words for different kinds of solids?**
   Student response: I need to know the words for solids in order to tell about them.

CHAPTER TWO – THINKING ABOUT POSITION (Pages 14-22)

GENERAL INTRODUCTION

CURRICULUM APPLICATIONS

Language Arts: Identify and correctly use words that describe location (above/below, inside/outside, front/behind, between, beside); describe location of objects or buildings from written directions or when discussing picture books.

Social Studies: Identify location on maps; identify locations of buildings (residences, government or recreational buildings, and stores); identify the location of various parts of buildings.

Science: Identify and correctly express the location of parts of organisms, objects, and structures; follow directions in science activities.

Art: Identify the location of parts of paintings, sculpture, and other artwork; follow directions in art activities.

Physical Education: Follow directions in physical exercises and sports activities.

LANGUAGE INTEGRATION ACTIVITIES

Drawing: Ask students to draw a picture of objects that show given locations or positions. Students may write or tell short stories in which position or location is important.

PICTURE BOOK EXTENSION

Language experiences with picture books in which location or position is important to the story.

Page 15 - DESCRIBING POSITION - FIRST TO LAST

LESSON

Introduction

You may introduce this lesson by asking three students to come to the front of the class. Identify, or ask students to identify, the individuals in first, middle, and last positions.

Stating the Objective

Teacher Comment: **In these lessons you will learn various ways to describe position - where objects are located compared to other objects. In the first lesson you will identify the shapes that show "first," "middle," and "last" position.**

Conducting the Lesson

Teacher Comment: **Look at the example at the top of the page. Find the middle shape and color it yellow. The middle shape is a square between the first and the last shapes.**

Teacher Comment: **In the next box color the first shape green.**

Teacher Comment: **Name the first shape.**

Student Response: The first shape is a rectangle.

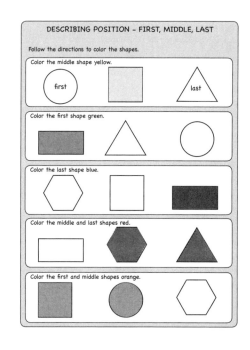

DESCRIBING POSITION – FIRST, MIDDLE, LAST

Follow the directions to color the shapes.

Color the middle shape yellow.
first   last

Color the first shape green.

Color the last shape blue.

Color the middle and last shapes red.

Color the first and middle shapes orange.

• Check students' work. Continue this dialog to discuss students' answers.

Thinking About Thinking
Teacher Comment: **What did you think about in order to decide which shapes were in first, middle, or last position.**
Student Response:
1. I looked at the first and the last ones.
2. I decided which shape was between them.
3. I found the shape that fit that position.

Personal Application
Teacher Comment: **When is it important to describe first, middle, or last position?**
Student Response: I describe position to give or follow directions or tell about the location of people, things, or events in a story.

Page 16 - DESCRIBING POSITION - FIRST TO LAST
LESSON

Introduction
Teacher Comment: **We have located first, middle, and last position.**

Stating the Objective
Teacher Comment: **In these lessons you will describe shapes in first, middle, and last position.**

Conducting the Lesson
Teacher Comment: **In the first row find the middle shape and describe its color. The middle shape is an orange circle. Trace the words that describe its color and shape.**

Teacher Comment: **Describe the first shape.**
  Student Response: The first shape is a red triangle.
Teacher Comment: **Use the WORD BOX to help you write "red triangle."**

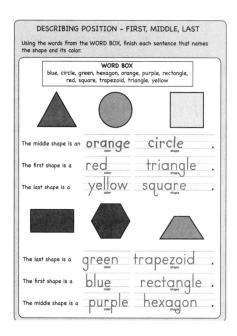

DESCRIBING POSITION - FIRST, MIDDLE, LAST

Using the words from the WORD BOX, finish each sentence that names the shape and its color.

WORD BOX
blue, circle, green, hexagon, orange, purple, rectangle, red, square, trapezoid, triangle, yellow

The middle shape is an   orange   circle   .
The first shape is a   red   triangle   .
The last shape is a   yellow   square   .

The last shape is a   green   trapezoid   .
The first shape is a   blue   rectangle   .
The middle shape is a   purple   hexagon   .

• Check students' work. Continue this dialog to discuss students' answers.

Thinking About Thinking
Teacher Comment: **What did you think about in order to describe which shapes were in first, middle, or last position?**
Student Response:
1. I looked at the first and the last ones.
2. I decided which shape was between them.
3. I found the shape that fit that position.
4. I found the word for the color and shape in that position.

Personal Application
Teacher Comment: **When is it important to describe first, middle, or last position?**
Student Response: I describe position to give or follow directions or tell about the location of people or things in a story.

Page 17 - DESCRIBING POSITION – FIRST, SECOND, THIRD, FOURTH
LESSON

Introduction
You may introduce this lesson by asking four students to come to the front of the class. Identify, or ask students to identify, the individuals in first, second, third, and fourth positions.

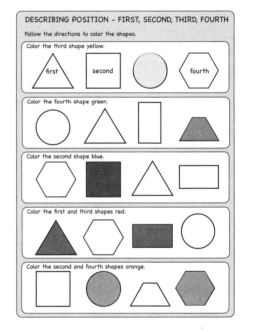

Teacher Comment: **We have described position as it appears in a line of shapes– "first," "middle," and "last" position. Another way to describe position is to count each position from left to right.**

Stating the Objective
Teacher Comment: **In this lesson you will describe position by identifying whether the shape is in first, second, third, or fourth position.**

Conducting the Lesson
Teacher Comment: **Look at the example at the top of the page. Count the shapes from left to right. What shape is in third position?**
Student Response: The circle is in the third position.
Teacher Comment: **Color the circle yellow.**

• Check students' work. Continue this dialog to discuss students' answers.

Thinking About Thinking
Teacher Comment: **What did you think about in order to decide which shapes were in first, second, third, or fourth position?**
Student Response:
1. I looked at the first shape and counted until I reached the number indicated in the directions.
2. I identified the shape in that position.

Personal Application
Teacher Comment: **When is it important to describe first, middle, or last position?**
Student Response: I describe position to give or follow directions or tell about the location of people, things, or events in a story.

Page 18 - DESCRIBING POSITION - FIRST, SECOND, THIRD, FOURTH
LESSON

Introduction
Teacher Comment: **We have located first, second, third, and fourth positions.**

Stating the Objective
Teacher Comment: **In these lessons you will describe shapes in first, second, third, and fourth positions.**

Conducting the Lesson
Teacher Comment: **In the first row find the first shape and describe its color.**
Student Response: The first shape is a purple square.
Teacher Comment: **Trace the words that describe its color and shape.**

Teacher Comment: **Describe the third shape.**
Student Response: The third shape is a green triangle.
Teacher Comment: **Use the WORD BOX to help you to write the words "green triangle."**

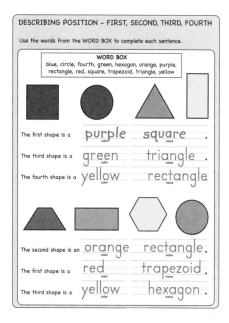

DESCRIBING POSITION - FIRST, SECOND, THIRD, FOURTH

Use the words from the WORD BOX to complete each sentence.

WORD BOX
blue, circle, fourth, green, hexagon, orange, purple, rectangle, red, square, trapezoid, triangle, yellow

The first shape is a   purple   square   .
The third shape is a   green   triangle   .
The fourth shape is a   yellow   rectangle   .

The second shape is an   orange   rectangle   .
The first shape is a   red   trapezoid   .
The third shape is a   yellow   hexagon   .

• Check students' work. Continue this dialog to discuss students' answers.

Thinking About Thinking
Teacher Comment: **What did you think about in order to write about first, second, third, and fourth positions?**
Student Response:
1. I counted the shapes from left to right.
2. I decided which shape was in the correct position.
3. I found the words for that color and shape.

Personal Application
Teacher Comment: **When is it important to describe position?**
Student Response: I describe position to give or follow directions or tell about the location of people, things, or events in a story.

Page 19 - DESCRIBING POSITION - LEFT, CENTER, AND RIGHT

LESSON

Introduction

You may introduce this lesson by asking three students to come to the front of the class and ask them to face away from the class. Ask the class to raise their left hands and to name the student who is on the same side of the group. Repeat these instructions to name the student on the right.

Teacher Comment: **We have learned to describe positions by counting from left to right.**

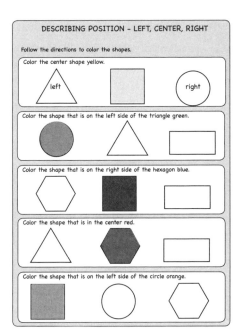

Stating the Objective

Teacher Comment: **In this lesson you will describe which shapes are to the left or the right.**

Conducting the Lesson

Teacher Comment: **Look at the example at the top of the page. Find the center shape and color it yellow. The center shape is a square between the triangle on the left and the circle on the right.**

Teacher Comment: **In the next box color the shape that is on the left side of the triangle green.**
Teacher Comment: **Name the shape that is on the left side of the triangle.**
Student Response: The shape on the left side of the triangle is a circle.

• Check students' work. Continue this dialog to discuss students' answers.

Thinking About Thinking

Teacher Comment: **What did you think about in order to decide which shapes were in the left, center, or right positions.**
Student Response:
1. I looked at the shape that is in the middle.
2. I decided which direction was left or right.
3. I found the shape that fit that position.

Personal Application

Teacher Comment: **When is it important to know which position is left, center, or right?**
Student Response: I need to know left or right positions in order to follow or to give directions or to tell about the location of people or things in a story.

Page 20 - DESCRIBING POSITION - LEFT, CENTER, AND RIGHT

LESSON

Introduction
Teacher Comment: **We have learned to find left, center, and right positions.**

Stating the Objective
Teacher Comment: **In this lesson you will describe left, center, and right positions.**

Conducting the Lesson
Teacher Comment: **Look at the example at the top of the page. The shape on the left end is a red triangle. Trace the words "red triangle."**
Teacher Comment: **For the next sentence use the WORD BOX to write the words for the color and shape of the one on the right end.**

• Check students' work. Continue this dialog to discuss students' answers.

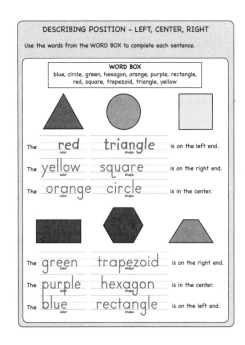

Thinking About Thinking
Teacher Comment: **What did you think about in order to decide which shapes were in the left, center, or right positions?**
Student Response:
1. I looked at the center one.
2. I decided which direction was left or right.
3. I found the shape that fit that position.

Personal Application
Teacher Comment: **When is it important to describe left, center, or right positions?**
Student Response: I describe position to give or follow directions or tell about the location of people or things in a story.

Page 21 - DESCRIBING POSITION - ABOVE, MIDDLE, BELOW

LESSON

Introduction
Teacher Comment: **We have learned to describe positions that are in a row.**

Stating the Objective
Teacher Comment: **In this lesson you describe positions that are above or below each other.**

Conducting the Lesson
Teacher Comment: **Look at the example at the top of the page. The yellow hexagon is above the middle square. The blue triangle is below the middle square. Trace the position words.**

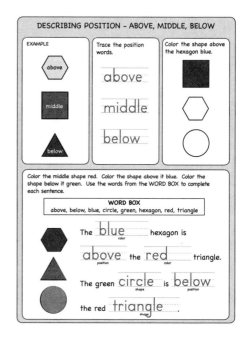

Teacher Comment: **Look at the box on the right. Color the shape above the hexagon blue.**

Teacher Comment: **In the bottom box color the middle shape red. Color the shape above it blue. Color the shape below the red shape green.**

Teacher Comment: **Use the WORD BOX to write the words that describe the shape, color and position of the polygons.**
Teacher Comment **In the first sentence write the colors of the hexagon and the triangle. Decide which is above or below the other and write the position in the blank.**

Teacher Comment: **In the second sentence write the words for the shapes that are green and red. Decide which is above or below the other and write the position in the blank.**

Thinking About Thinking
Teacher Comment: **What did you think about in order to decide which shapes were above or below the others?**
Student Response:
1. I looked at the middle one.
2. I decided which direction was above or below.
3. I decided the color and shape of the polygon in that position.

Personal Application
Teacher Comment: **When is it important to describe above or below positions?**
Student Response: I describe above or below positions to give or follow directions or tell about the location of people or things in a story.

PAGE 22 - DESCRIBING POSITION - ABOVE AND BELOW

LESSON

Introduction
Teacher Comment: **We have learned to describe above and below positions.**

Stating the Objective
Teacher Comment: **In this lesson you find shapes in photographs and describe their positions.**

Conducting the Lesson
Teacher Comment: **Look at the first picture. It shows a red triangle above a tall, narrow rectangle. Use the words in the WORD BOX to finish the sentence that describes their positions.**

• Check students' work. Continue this dialog to discuss students' answers.

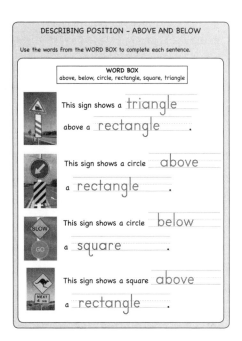

Thinking About Thinking
Teacher Comment: **What did you think about in order to tell which shape was above or below the other?**
Student Response:
1. I named the shapes of the two signs.
2. I decided which shape was above or below.
3. I looked for the clues in the sentences to tell which direction or shape I should write.

Personal Application
Teacher Comment: **When is it important to describe above or below positions?**
Student Response: I describe above or below positions to give or follow directions or tell about the location of people or things in a story.

CHAPTER THREE – SIMILARITIES AND DIFFERENCES — SHAPES (Pages 23-34)

GENERAL INTRODUCTION

TEACHING SUGGESTIONS
- Ask students to name the polygons and their properties as they explain their answers.
- Integrate these geometry concepts into your language arts program by discussing picture books.
- Model using the sentence structure of comparison (both ... and) and contrast (...but ... or ... next). Encourage students to speak and write using those terms and patterns.

CURRICULUM APPLICATIONS
Language Arts: Visual discrimination for reading readiness
Mathematics: Identify similar figures; write numerals in the correct direction (5, 7, etc.)
Science: Recognize similarly shaped leaves, insects, or shells
Social Studies: Reading maps
Enrichment Areas: Recognize shapes of road signs; discern patterns in art

Page 24 - MATCHING BY SHAPE AND COLOR

LESSON

Introduction
Teacher Comment: **In the last chapter you described positions.**

Stating the Objective
Teacher Comment: **In these lessons you will describe similarities and differences in various shapes. In the first lesson you will match shapes and colors.**

Conducting the Lesson
Teacher Comment: **The first shape in the left group is a blue hexagon. Look for the blue hexagon in the group on the right. Draw a line from the blue hexagon to its twin in the group on the right.**
Teacher Comment: **Now draw a line from each shape in the left column to the one like it in the right column.**

- Check students' work

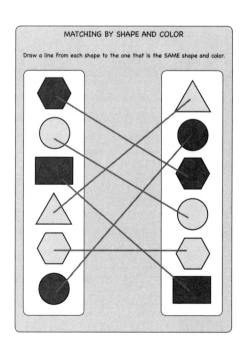

MATCHING BY SHAPE AND COLOR

Draw a line from each shape to the one that is the SAME shape and color.

Thinking About Thinking
Teacher Comment: **What did you pay attention to when you matched the shapes?**
Student Response:
1. I found the same shape.
2. I checked that it is the same color.

Personal Application
Teacher Comment: **When might you have to match shapes?**
Student Response: I have to match shapes when I put away toys or match building blocks.

Page 25 - WHICH SHAPE DOES NOT MATCH?

LESSON

Introduction
Teacher Comment: **In the last lesson we matched shapes and colors.**

Stating the Objective
Teacher Comment: **In this lesson you will find the shape that does not match the others.**

Conducting the Lesson
Teacher Comment: **Look carefully at the shapes in each box. Cross out the shape that does not match the others. Color the matching shapes blue.**

• Check students' work.

WHICH SHAPE DOES NOT MATCH

Cross out the shape that does NOT match the others. Then color the other shapes blue.

Thinking About Thinking
Teacher Comment: **What did you pay attention to when you found the shape that is different?**
Student Response:
1. I counted the number of sides.
2. I looked at the angles.

Personal Application
Teacher Comment: **When do you need to tell if shapes are alike.**
Student response: I need to tell if shapes are alike when I make requests or match blocks.

Page 26 - COMPARING SHAPES

LESSON

Introduction
Teacher Comment: **It is important to think about how shapes are alike or different.**

Stating the Objective
Teacher Comment: **In this lesson you will decide how two shapes are alike or different.**

Conducting the Lesson
Teacher Comment: **Look at the two shapes in the top box and decide how they are alike and how they are different. In this example the polygons are both purple squares. They have the same color and shape. Notice the "S" next to color and the "S" next to shape. One purple square is large and the other one is small. Notice that the "D" tells that the size is different.**
Teacher Comment: **Write "S" for "Same" and "D" for "Different" to describe each pair of shapes.**

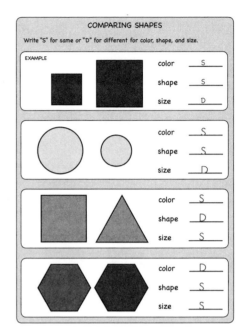

• Check students' work.

Thinking About Thinking
Teacher Comment: **What did you pay attention to when you wrote how shapes are alike and different?**
Student Response:
1. I looked to see whether the shapes were different colors.
2. I looked to see whether the polygons were a different shape or size.

Personal Application
Teacher Comment: **When do you need to tell if shapes are different?**
Student Response: I need to tell if shapes are different when I make requests or match blocks.

Page 27 - COMPARING SHAPES

Introduction
We have compared shapes for size and color.

Stating the Objective
Teacher Comment: **In this lesson you will describe similarities in the size and color of shapes.**

Conducting the Lesson
Teacher Comment: **Look at the first pair of shapes. Use the words in the WORD BOX to write a sentence to describe how they are alike.**
Teacher Comment: **Decide how the remaining pairs are alike and finish the sentences.**

• Check students' work. Continue this dialog to discuss students' answers.

• Model the sentence pattern for describing shape and color. Encourage students to speak in whole sentences using this pattern with other polygons and objects.

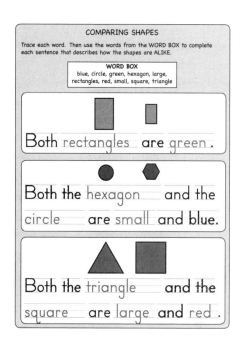

Thinking About Thinking
Teacher Comment: **What did you pay attention to when you wrote a description of shapes?**
Student Response:
1. I looked at their shapes, their size, and their color.
2. I found the words for their shapes, their size and their color and copied the words.

Personal Application
Teacher Comment: **When do you need to write about a shape?**
Student response: I need to write about shapes when I write a description of what I see.

Pages 28-29 - DESCRIBING DIFFERENCES

Introduction
Teacher Comment: **We have described how shapes are alike.**

Stating the Objective
Teacher Comment: **In this lesson you will describe how shapes are alike and different.**

Conducting the Lesson
Teacher Comment: **Look at the first pair of shapes. Write "S" for same and "D" for different to describe color, shape, and size.**

Teacher Comment: **Use the words "color," "shape," and "size" to finish the sentences.**

Teacher Comment: **Decide how the remaining pairs are alike and different and complete the sentences.**

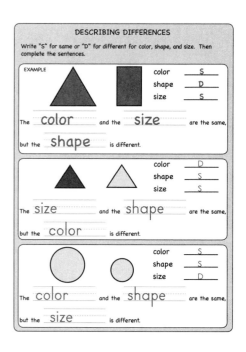

• Check students' work. Continue this dialog to discuss students' answers.

• Model the sentence pattern for describing differences. Encourage students to use this sentence pattern, showing that the word "but" signals a different characteristic. Use this pattern with other polygons and objects.

Thinking About Thinking
Teacher Comment: **What did you pay attention to when you wrote a description of shapes?**
Student Response:
1. I looked at their shapes, their size, and their color.
2. I noticed how the polygons were alike and found the word(s) to describe those similarities.
3. I named the difference after the word "but."

Personal Application
Teacher Comment: **When do you need to write about different shapes?**
Student response: I need to write about different shapes when I write a description of what I see.

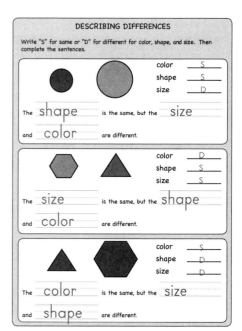

Page 30 - COLORING ONE OF TWO EQUAL PARTS

LESSON

Introduction
Teacher Comment: **We have described how shapes are alike and different. It is very important to be able to see how shapes are alike when we try to divide them into equal parts. Those equal parts are called fractions.**

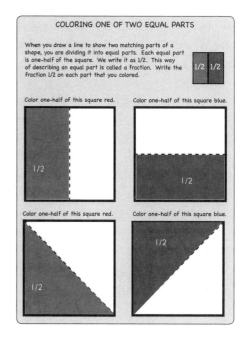

Stating the Objective
Teacher Comment: **In this lesson you will color one of two equal parts of a square.**

Conducting the Lesson
Teacher Comment: **When you draw a line to show two equal parts of a shape, you are dividing it into halves. When each part is one of two equal parts, we write it as 1/2. Write the fraction 1/2 on each part that you colored.**
Look at the example. Notice that a line divides the square into two equal parts called halves. One half of the square is colored red, and 1/2 is colored blue.
Look at the square on the top left. Color one-half of it red. Write "1/2" in the part that you colored.

• Check students' work. Continue this dialog to discuss students' answers.

Teacher Comment: **Notice that it doesn't matter which direction you draw the line. Whenever you divide a square equally, you are dividing it into halves.**

Thinking About Thinking
Teacher Comment: **What did you pay attention to when you divided a square into halves?**
Student Response:
1. I looked to see whether the two parts were exactly the same size and shape.
2. I remembered that the shape is divided into two equal parts.
3. I wrote the fraction to show that each half is one of two parts.

Personal Application
Teacher Comment: **When do you need to divide things into halves?**
Student Response: I need to divide things into halves when I must divide food equally or draw just one half of something.

Page 31 - DIVIDING SHAPES INTO HALVES

LESSON

Introduction
Teacher Comment: **We have learned to write each equal part as a fraction.**

Stating the Objective
Teacher Comment: **In this lesson you will learn many ways to divide shapes into halves.**

Conducting the Lesson
Teacher Comment: **Notice that the squares at the top of the page are divided into halves. We can divide the same shape in half in different ways. A square can be divided many ways by drawing the lines in different directions. All four drawings are correct because they divide the squares into two equal parts. Whenever you divide a shape into two equal parts, you are dividing it in half.**
Divide these shapes into halves. Draw the halves in different directions. Mark each part with the fraction 1/2.

• Check students' work. Continue this dialog to discuss students' answers.

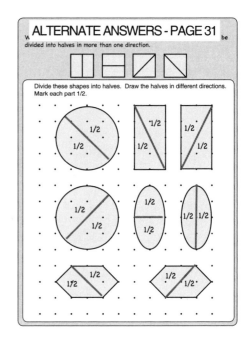

Thinking About Thinking
Teacher Comment: **What did you pay attention to when you divided a shape into halves?**
Student Response:
1. I looked to see whether the two parts were exactly the same size and shape.
2. I remembered to divide the shape into two parts.
3. I wrote the fraction to show that each half is one of two parts.

Personal Application
Teacher Comment: **When do you need to divide things into halves?**
Student response: I need to divide things into halves when I must divide food equally or draw just one half of something.

Page 32 - DIVIDING SHAPES INTO HALVES

LESSON

Introduction

Teacher Comment: **We have divided shapes into halves.**

Stating the Objective

Teacher Comment: **In this lesson you will divide shapes into halves and mark each half with the fraction 1/2.**

Conducting the Lesson

Teacher Comment: **Notice that the triangle is divided into two equal parts. Each half is marked "1/2." Divide the rectangle into halves. Mark each half with the fraction 1/2.**

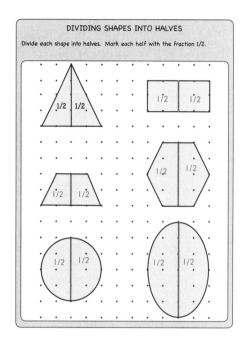

- Check students' work. Continue this dialog to discuss students' answers.

Teacher Comment: **Notice that some students divided the shapes into equal parts by drawing the lines in a different direction. Both drawings are correct. Whenever you divide a shape into two equal parts, you are dividing it in half.**

Thinking About Thinking

Teacher Comment: **What did you pay attention to when you divided a shape into halves?**

Student Response:
1. I looked to see whether the two parts were exactly the same size and shape.
2. I wrote the fraction to show that each half is one of two parts.

Personal Application

Teacher Comment: **When do you need to divide things into halves?**

Student Response: I need to divide things into halves when I must divide food equally or draw just one half of something.

Page 33 - COLORING FOURTHS

LESSON

Introduction
    Teacher Comment: **We have divided shapes into two parts to show halves.**

Stating the Objective
    Teacher Comment: **In this lesson you will color one-fourth of a shape.**

Conducting the Lesson
    Teacher Comment: **When you draw a line to show four equal parts of a shape, you are dividing it into fourths. We write each fourth as the fraction 1/4. Color one-fourth of each shape. Write 1/4 in each part that you colored.**

• Check students' work. Continue this dialog to discuss students' answers.

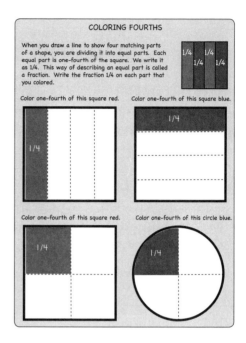

Thinking About Thinking
    Teacher Comment: **What did you pay attention to when you colored one-fourth of each shape?**
    Student Response:
    1. I looked to see whether the four parts were exactly the same size and shape.
    2. I colored one of the four parts of each shape.
    3. I wrote the fraction to show one-fourth.

Personal Application
    Teacher Comment: **When do you need to divide things into fourths?**
    Student response: I need to divide things into fourths when I must divide food equally or draw just one fourth of something.

Page 34 - DIVIDING SHAPES INTO FOURTHS

LESSON

Introduction
Teacher Comment: **We have learned to write each equal part as a fraction.**

Stating the Objective
Teacher Comment: **In this lesson you will divide shapes into four equal parts and mark each fourth with the fraction "1/4."**

Conducting the Lesson
Teacher Comment: **Notice that the first square is divided into four equal parts. Mark each fourth with the fraction "1/4." Finish dividing the square on the right into four equal parts and mark each fourth with the fraction "1/4."**

• Check students' work and discuss students' answers.

Teacher Comment: **Now divide the rest of the shapes into four equal parts and mark each fourth with the fraction "1/4."**

Thinking About Thinking
Teacher Comment: **What did you pay attention to when you divided the shapes into fourths?**
Student Response:
1. I looked to see whether the four parts were exactly the same size and shape.
2. I remembered to divide the shape into four parts.
3. I wrote the fraction to show that each fourth is one of four parts.

Personal Application
Teacher Comment: **When do you need to divide things into fourths?**
Student Response: I need to divide things into fourths when I must divide food equally.

CHAPTER FOUR – SEQUENCES OF SHAPES (Pages 36-41)

GENERAL INTRODUCTION

CURRICULUM APPLICATIONS
Language Arts: Identify letter patterns in decoding unfamiliar words
Mathematics: Identify repeating geometric patterns, simple bar graphs
Science: Identify repeating patterns in leaves, shells, and life cycles
Social Studies: Identify latitude and longitude
Enrichment Areas: Art exercises involving patterns; repeating patterns in written music

TEACHING SUGGESTION
Check that students "read" the sequence of shapes from left to right.

Page 36 - WHAT COLOR SQUARE COMES NEXT?

LESSON

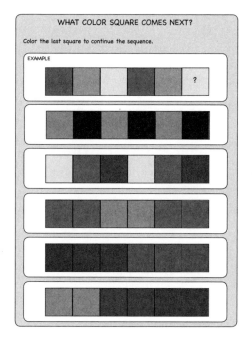

Introduction
Teacher Comment: **When the same shape or color is repeated it becomes a sequence. When sequences are repeated many times, they make a pattern. Patterns are all around us in nature and in man-made things. Where in this room can you see examples of sequences?**

Student Response: Examples may include fabric in clothing, brick or cement block walls, floor tiles, ceiling tiles, Venetian blinds, leaf arrangements on plants, etc.

Stating the Objective
Teacher Comment: **In this lesson we will identify a sequence and color the blank square to continue the sequence.**

Conducting the Lesson
Teacher Comment: **Say the color sequence that you see in the top row.**
Student Response: The sequence is red, orange, yellow, red, orange, yellow.
Teacher Comment: **Let's say the next sequence together.**
Student Response: The sequence is green, black, green, black, green.
Teacher Comment: **What color should we make the last square?**
Student Response: The last square should be black.

Teacher Comment: **Now read the colors to yourself and color the last square to finish the sequence.**

• Check students' work. Continue this dialog to discuss students' answers.

Thinking About Thinking
Teacher Comment: **What did you pay attention to when you decided what color came next?**

Student Response:
1. I looked carefully at the colors of the squares.
2. I looked for the sequence of colors.
3. I used the sequence to figure out what the next color would be.

Personal Application
Teacher Comment: **When do you need to finish a sequence?**

Student Response: I need to finish a sequence when I draw brick walls, leaves, floor or ceiling tiles, etc.

Page 37 - WHAT COLOR SQUARES COME NEXT?

LESSON

Introduction
Teacher Comment: **We have identified a sequence to determine what would come next.**

Stating the Objective
Teacher Comment: **In this lesson we will find a sequence and color two squares that continue the sequence.**

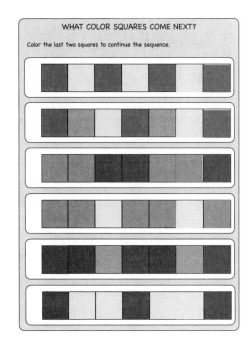

Conducting the Lesson
Teacher Comment: **Say the color sequence that you see in the top row.**

Student Response: The sequence is red, yellow, red, yellow, red.

Teacher Comment: **What should we color the next two squares?**

Student Response: The next square should be yellow and the last square should be red.

Teacher Comment: **Find the sequence and color the last two squares to finish it.**

Thinking About Thinking
Teacher Comment: **What did you pay attention to when you decided what color came next?**

Student Response:
1. I looked carefully at the colors of the squares.
2. I looked for the sequence of colors.
3. I used the sequence to figure out what the next color would be.

Personal Application
    Teacher Comment: **When do you need to finish a sequence?**
    Student Response: I need to finish a sequence when I draw brick walls, leaves, floor or ceiling tiles, etc.

Page 38 - WHICH SHAPE COMES NEXT?

LESSON

Introduction
    Teacher Comment: **In the last lesson you completed a sequence of colors that was drawn across the page.**

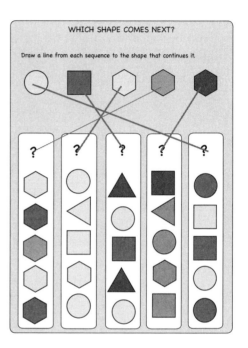

Stating the Objective
    Teacher Comment: **In this exercise the shapes are drawn up and down the page. You will find the shape that completes the sequence and draw a line to it.**

Conducting the Lesson
    Teacher Comment: **Look at the shapes in the first column. Work with a partner to identify the sequence. Which shape would complete the sequence?**
    Student Response: The orange hexagon.
    Teacher Comment: **Notice that a line is drawn from the question mark to the orange hexagon. Now that we know the sequence, let's say the whole pattern together.**
    Student Response: Orange hexagon, yellow hexagon, red hexagon, orange hexagon, yellow hexagon, red hexagon.

• Check students' work. Continue this dialog to discuss students' answers.

Thinking About Thinking
    Teacher Comment: **What did you pay attention to when you decided what shape came next?**
    Student response:
    1. I looked carefully at the colors and the shapes.
    2. I saw that the same sequence of color and shape was repeated.
    3. I figured out which polygon would complete the pattern.

Personal Application
    Teacher Comment: **When do you need to finish a sequence?**
    Student Response: I need to finish a sequence when I draw brick walls, leaves, floor or ceiling tiles, etc.

Page 39 - WHICH STACK COMES NEXT?

LESSON

Introduction
Teacher Comment: **In the last lesson you completed a sequence of colors.**

Stating the Objective
Teacher Comment: **In this lesson you will color a stack of squares to continue a sequence.**

Conducting the Lesson
Teacher Comment: **What is the sequence of the stacks of shapes in the top box.**

Student Response: One red square, then a red square and a blue square, then a red square, blue square red square, and next a red square, blue square, red square, blue square.

Teacher Comment: **Describe the sequence.**

Student Response: Each stack is one square higher and the color changes from red to blue.

Teacher Comment: **Color the last stack.**

• Check students' work. Continue this dialog to discuss students' answers.

Thinking About Thinking
Teacher Comment: **What did you pay attention to when you decided what stack came next?**

Student Response:
1. I looked at the number of squares in each stack and the color pattern.
2. I looked for a sequence of changes.
3. I figured out what the next stack would be if the sequence continued.

Personal Application
Teacher Comment: **When do you need to finish a sequence?**

Student Response: I need to finish a sequence when I draw brick walls, leaves, floor or ceiling tiles, etc.

Page 40 - DESCRIBING A SEQUENCE OF SQUARES

LESSON

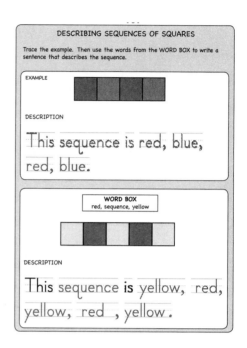

Introduction
Teacher Comment: **In the last exercises we described sequences of stacks of squares.**

Stating the Objective
Teacher Comment: **In this exercise you will write a sentence that describes a sequence of colors.**

Conducting the Lesson
Teacher Comment: **Look at the example sequence in the top box. Describe the color sequence.**

Student response: This sequence is red, blue, red, blue.

Teacher Comment: **Trace the sentence that describes this sequence.**

Teacher Comment: **Describe the color sequence in the next box.**

Student response: I see a sequence of yellow, red, yellow, red, yellow.

Teacher Comment: **Write the sentence you described.**

Thinking About Thinking
Teacher Comment: **What did you pay attention to when you wrote the description?**
Student Response:
1. I looked for a pattern of changes.
2. I wrote (or spoke) a description of what I saw.

Personal Application
Teacher Comment: **When do you need to write a sequence?**
Student Response: I need to write a sequence to write directions.

Page 41 - DESCRIBING A SEQUENCE OF SHAPES

LESSON

Introduction
Teacher Comment: **In the last exercises you described sequences of colored squares.**

Stating the Objective
Teacher Comment: **In this exercise you will write sentences that describe sequences of shapes.**

Conducting the Lesson
Teacher Comment: **Describe the sequence you see.**
Student Response: I see a sequence of yellow square, yellow circle, yellow square, and yellow circle.
Teacher Comment: **Trace the sentence that describes the sequence.**

• Check students' work. Continue this dialog to discuss students' answers.

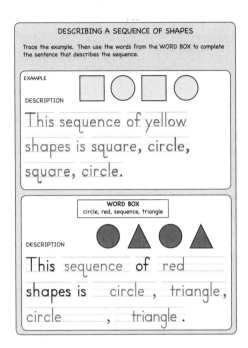

Thinking About Thinking
Teacher Comment: **What did you pay attention to when you wrote the description?**
Student Response:
1. I looked for a pattern of changes.
2. I wrote (or spoke) a description of what I saw.

Personal Application
Teacher Comment: **When do you need to write a sequence?**
Student Response: I need to write a sequence to write directions.

CHAPTER FIVE – GROUPS OF SHAPES (Pages 43-48)

GENERAL INTRODUCTION

CURRICULUM APPLICATIONS
Language Arts: Decoding in reading readiness; forming letters.
Mathematics: Recognizing properties of polygons.
Science: Classifying natural objects by shape (leaves, fish, shells, etc.).
Social Studies: Identifying road signs from their shape.

PERSONAL APPLICATION
Teacher Comment: **When do you need to classify objects by shape, color, or size?**
Student Response: I need to classify when I sort eating or cooking utensils, when I sort construction toys or tools, when I sort edge pieces from interior pieces in a picture puzzle, or when I organize objects or materials at home or in school.

Page 43 - DESCRIBING A GROUP OF SHAPES

LESSON

Introduction
Teacher Comment: **We call ourselves a "class" of students. In this class everyone is about the same age, meets in the same place, studies the same things, and has the same teacher. "Class" means more than just a school room; it also means "a group which has a common characteristic." When we describe the group by using that characteristic, we are "classifying." When we classify things, we describe how the things in the group are alike.**

DESCRIBING A GROUP OF SHAPES

Draw a line from each shape to the group in which it belongs. Then use the words from the WORD BOX to complete each sentence.

WORD BOX
blue, green, red, yellow

A group of _red_ shapes.
A group of _green_ shapes.
A group of _blue_ shapes.
A group of _yellow_ shapes.

Stating the Objective
Teacher Comment: **In this lesson you will match a shape to a group with the same color. Use words in the WORD BOX to finish the sentences.**

Conducting the Lesson
Teacher Comment: **Look at the blue triangle in the top left corner. It belongs to the group of blue shapes. Notice a line has been drawn to the group of blue shapes and the word "blue" is written in the blank to complete the sentence. Name the shape below the blue triangle.**
Student Response: The shape below the blue triangle is a red square.
Teacher Comment: **To which group does the red square belong?**
Student Response: The red square belongs to the top group of red shapes.
Teacher Comment: **Draw a line from the red square to the top group of red shapes and write the word "red" in the blank below the red shapes.**

Teacher Comment: **Match the next two shapes to their group and write their color.**

• Check students' work. Continue this dialog to discuss students' answers.

Thinking About Thinking
Teacher Comment: **What did you pay attention to in order to decide which group a shape fits?**
   Student Response:
      1. I looked at the color.
      2. I looked for the group of shapes with the same color.
      3. I wrote the color for the group.

Personal Application
Teacher Comment: **When do you need to fit something into a group?**
   Student Response: I look for color when I match socks, do puzzles, or draw flowers, animals, or objects that have the same color.

Page 44 - DESCRIBING A GROUP OF SHAPES

LESSON

Introduction
Teacher Comment: **In the first lesson we described a group of shapes by color.**

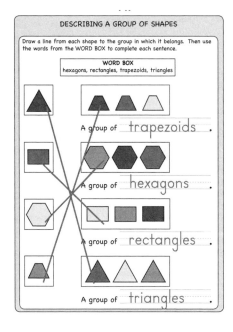

Stating the Objective
Teacher Comment: **In this lesson you will match shapes to the group that has the same shape. Again you will complete sentences that describe the group.**

Conducting the Lesson
Teacher Comment: **Name the color and shape of the shape in the top left corner.**
   Student Response: The shape is a blue triangle.
Teacher Comment: **To which group does the blue triangle belong?**
   Student Response: The blue triangle belongs with the group of triangles at the bottom of the page.
Teacher Comment: **Draw a line from the blue triangle to the group of triangles and write the word "triangles" in the sentence below them.**

Teacher Comment: **Now draw a line from each shape to the group in which it belongs. Use the words in the WORD BOX to finish the sentence.**

• Check students' work. Continue this dialog to discuss students' answers.

Thinking About Thinking
Teacher Comment: **What did you pay attention to in matching shapes to groups?**
Student Response:
1. I named the shape and color of the first shape.
2. I named the group that has the same shape.
3. I wrote the word for the shape that described the group.

Personal Application
Teacher Comment: **When do you need to pay attention to whether shape, color, or size are the same or different?**
Student Response: I look for shape, color, or size when I match socks, do puzzles, or build with blocks.

Page 45 - DESCRIBING A GROUP OF SHAPES

LESSON

Introduction
Teacher Comment: **In the first lesson we described a group of shapes by color. In the second lesson we described a group by shape.**

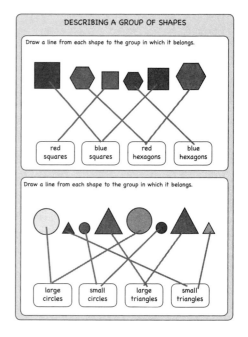

Stating the Objective
Teacher Comment: **In this lesson you will match shapes to the name of the group to which the shape belongs.**

Conducting the Lesson
Teacher Comment: **Name the four groups in which the shapes will be sorted.**
Student Response: The shape groups are red squares, blue squares, red hexagons, and blue hexagons.
Teacher Comment: **Name the first shape on the left.**
Student Response: The first shape is a blue square.
Teacher Comment: **Draw a line from the blue square to the blue square box.**
Teacher Comment: **Now draw a line from each shape to the group in which it belongs.**

• Check students' work. Continue this dialog to discuss students' answers.

Thinking About Thinking
Teacher Comment: **What did you pay attention to in matching shapes to groups?**
Student Response:
1. I named the shape and color of the first polygon.
2. I named the group that has the same color and shape.
3. I checked that it fit that group

Personal Application

Teacher Comment: **When do you need to pay attention to whether shape, color, or size are the same or different?**

Student Response: I look for shape, color, or size when I match socks, do puzzles, or build with blocks.

Pages 46-47 - WHICH SHAPE DOES NOT BELONG?

LESSON

Introduction

Teacher Comment: **We have matched shapes to their groups.**

Stating the Objective

Teacher Comment: **In this lesson you will look at a collection of shapes. You will decide how most of them are alike, and cross out the shape that does not belong to the group. Then you will use words in the WORD BOX to complete the sentences.**

Conducting the Lesson

Teacher Comment: **In the example how are most of the shapes alike?**

Student Response: In this group five of the shapes are red.

Teacher Comment: **Why is one shape crossed out?**

Student Response: The orange hexagon is not red.

Teacher Comment: **Notice that the sentence has been completed with words from the WORD BOX.**

Teacher Comment: **How are most of the next group alike?**

Student Response: In the second box five of the shapes are blue.

Teacher Comment: **Which one should be crossed out?**

Student Response: The purple rectangle is not blue and should be crossed out.

Teacher Comment: **Draw an "X" on the purple rectangle and complete the sentence.**

• Check students' work. Continue this dialog to discuss students' answers.

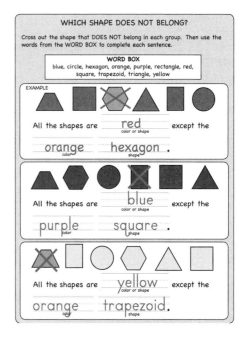

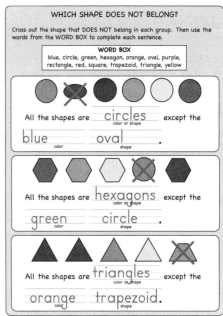

Thinking About Thinking

Teacher Comment: **What did you pay attention to in order to find the shape to cross out?**

Student Response:
1. I looked to see how five of the shapes were alike.
2. I named the characteristic of the group. (Same color, but different shape or same shape, but different color.)
3. I crossed out the polygon that didn't belong to the group.

Personal Application

Teacher Comment: **When do you need to find an object that is not like the others?**

Student Response: I need to find an object that is not like the others, when I sort eating or cooking utensils, when I sort construction toys or tools, when I sort edge pieces from interior pieces in a picture puzzle, and when I organize objects or materials at home or in school.

Pages 48 - WHICH SHAPE DOES NOT BELONG?

LESSON

Introduction

Teacher Comment: **We have matched shapes to their groups.**

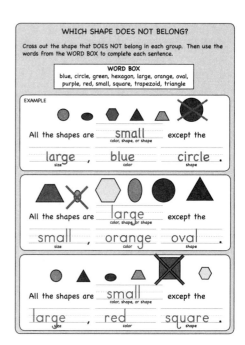

Stating the Objective

Teacher Comment: **In this lesson you will look at a collection of shapes. You will decide how most of them are alike, and cross out the shape that does not belong to the group. Then you will use four words in the WORD BOX to complete the sentences.**

Conducting the Lesson

Teacher Comment: **In the example how are most of the shapes alike?**

Student Response: All the shapes are small except the large circle.

Teacher Comment: **Notice that the shape is described by writing the shape size, then the shape color and last the shape name. Follow that pattern in the next two exercises.**

• Check students' work. Continue this dialog to discuss students' answers.

Thinking About Thinking

Teacher Comment: **What did you pay attention to in order to find the shape to cross out?**

Student Response:

1. I looked to see how five of the shapes were alike.
2. I named the characteristic of the group (color, shape or size).
3. I crossed out the shape that didn't belong to the group.

Personal Application

Teacher Comment: **When do you need to find an object that is not like the others?**

Student Response: I need to find an object that is not like the others, when I sort eating or cooking utensils, when I sort construction toys or tools, when I sort edge pieces from interior pieces in a picture puzzle, or when I organize objects or materials at home or in school.

CHAPTER SIX – THINKING ABOUT LAND FORMS AND BODIES OF WATER (Pages 49-58)

GENERAL INTRODUCTION

CURRICULUM APPLICATIONS

Language Arts: Identify the natural settings in myths and stories
Science: Identify terms for natural forms and their properties; identify plants and animals that live in various ecosystems; identify conditions that various plants and animals need to survive
Social Studies: Identify land forms and bodies of water in local communities and on common maps
Enrichment: Create student art to depict local land forms and bodies of water

TEACHING SUGGESTIONS

- In this chapter students learn the terms for various land forms and bodies of water. In each lesson that introduces these terms, identify local examples in order to relate the term and the characteristics to the students' own communities.
- Although first graders may have limited map reading skills, they begin to recognize continent and ocean, their country's map and perhaps features of maps in their vicinity. Display and discuss these maps as the land forms and bodies of water are discussed in the lesson.
- Young children may not understand that rivers and streams flow from their source to a larger body of water. Help students identify the source and flow of streams and rivers in their area.
- Students may have difficulty distinguishing the relative size of various bodies of water (streams and rivers, ponds and lakes). Identify local examples to clarify these terms.
- Students may not know which bodies of water contain fresh or salt water. Use picture books to explain the differences in the locations of familiar bodies of water and discuss the plant and animal life in them.

Page 50 - DESCRIBING LAND FORMS AND BODIES OF WATER

LESSON

Introduction
Teacher Comment: **To understand nature we need to recognize types of land and bodies of water. We need to know how high the land form is, how much water is available there for plants and animals, what plants and animals live there, and what people do there. To understand bodies of water, we need to know their size, whether or not the water is salty, what plants or animals live there, and what people do around these bodies of water.**

Stating the Objective
Teacher Comment: **In this lesson I will describe a land form or a body of water and you will select the picture that fits this description.**

Conducting the Lesson
Teacher Comment: **Look at the top row. We see a mountain, a plain, and a valley. Listen to the clues and then circle the land form that I describe. This flat land is so**

large that you cannot see where it begins and ends. There is enough rain that grass grows across its surface. Streams provide enough water that small trees grow along their sides. Small animals live in the grass and sometimes large animals move across these large spaces to eat the grass. People grow food on large farms on this flat land.

• Ask students to decide with their partners which land form has been described. Confirm the answer with the whole class. Encourage students to use as many adjectives as possible to describe the plain.

Answers will vary.
See page 20 for examples.

mountains	plain	valley
pond	river	stream
desert	hills	mountains
lake	ocean	pond

*Descriptions are available on page 20 of the free answer guide.

    Teacher Comment: **Which is the large, flat land form?**
      Student Response: The plain is the large, flat land form.
    Teacher Comment: **Circle the picture of the plain.**
    Teacher Comment: **What clues let you know that the land form in this picture is a plain?**
      Student Response: I saw large areas of grass and a row of small trees where a river may hold water.
    Teacher Comment: **Why don't the other land forms fit the description?**
      Student Response: The mountain is tall and rocky. The valley is a narrow place between mountains. It is deep and not flat.

Teacher Comment: **Look at the second row. We see a pond, a river, and a stream. Listen to the clues and then name the body of water that I describe. This body of water is so small that you can see all the way around it. It holds still, fresh water from rain, melted snow, or springs from underneath the earth. Small plants and animals live in and around it. Large animals and people use water from it.**

• Ask students to decide with their partners which land form has been described.

    Teacher Comment: **Which is the small, still body of fresh water?**
      Student Response: The pond is the small, still body of fresh water.
    Teacher Comment: **What clues let you know that the pond is the body of water that I described?**
      Student Response: It is so small that I can see its sides. I see the plants that grow around it.
    Teacher Comment: **Why don't the other bodies of water fit the description?**
      Student Response: The river is so long that I cannot see where it starts and ends. I see that the river moves in one direction. The stream is so long that I don't see its beginning or end. I see that it moves quickly over the rocks.

Teacher Comment: **Look at the third row. We see a desert, hills, and mountains. Listen to the clues and then name the land form that I describe. This land form is so large that I cannot see where it begins or ends. It is flat with a few hills or mountains. It is so dry that only a few small plants and animals can live there. It is usually very hot. Because it is so large and dry, it is difficult for people and animals to cross it.**

• Ask students to decide with their partners which land form has been described.

Teacher Comment: **Which is the large, dry, flat, land form?**
  Student Response: The desert is the large, dry, flat land form.
Teacher Comment: **What clues let you know that the desert is the land form that I described?**
  Student Response: The desert is so large that I cannot see where it begins or ends. It is so dry that I don't see plants or animals. The sun makes it hot in the daytime.
Teacher Comment: **Why don't the other land forms fit the description?**
  Student Response: The hills are not flat. They are green with plants and trees. The mountains are tall and have water (in the form of snow).

Teacher Comment: **Look at the fourth row. We see a lake, an ocean, and a pond. Listen to the clues and then name the body of water that I describe. This body of water is so large that it covers most of the earth's surface. You cannot see all the way around it. Its salty water is always moving from tides and currents. It has the deepest places on earth. It contains the largest and smallest animals on earth. People and animals get food from plants and animals that live there.**

• Ask students to decide with their partners which land form has been described.

Teacher Comment: **Which is the large body of salt water?**
  Student Response: The ocean is the large body of salt water.
Teacher Comment: **What clues let you know that the ocean is the body of water that I described?**
  Student Response: It is so large that I cannot see its sides. I see that it moves.
Teacher Comment: **Why don't the other bodies of water fit the description?**
  Student Response: The lake and the pond are small enough that I can see their sides. I remember that water in lakes and ponds is fresh and comes from rain, melted snow, and streams.

Thinking About Thinking
Teacher Comment: **What did you look for to pick out the land form or body of water that was described?**
  Student Response: I looked for its size, whether it moves, whether plants or animals live there.

Personal Application
Teacher Comment: **When is it important to understand land forms and bodies of water?**
  Student Response: I need to understand land forms and bodies of water in order to know what plants or animals can live there.

Page 51 - DESCRIBING LAND FORMS AND BODIES OF WATER

LESSON

Introduction
Teacher Comment: **We have selected a land form or a body of water from a description.**

Stating the Objective
Teacher Comment: **In this lesson you will match the photograph to the word that describes it.**

Conducting the Lesson
Teacher Comment: **Look at each picture and decide which land form or body of water is shown in the picture.**
Teacher Comment: **What does the first picture show?**
  Student Response: It shows a plain.
Teacher Comment: **Draw a line from the picture of the plain to the word "plain."**

Teacher Comment: **What does the second picture show?**
  Student Response: It shows a lake.
Teacher Comment: **Draw a line from the picture of the lake to the word "lake."**

Teacher Comment: **Draw a line from each picture to the word that describes it.**

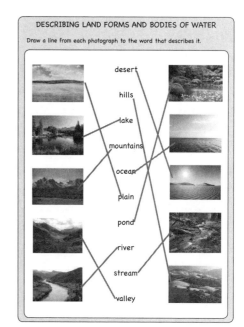

DESCRIBING LAND FORMS AND BODIES OF WATER
Draw a line from each photograph to the word that describes it.

desert
hills
lake
mountains
ocean
plain
pond
river
stream
valley

• Check students' work. Continue this dialog to discuss students' answers.

Thinking About Thinking
Teacher Comment: **What did you pay attention to in order to decide which land form or body of water is shown in the picture?**
  Student Response:
  1. I thought first about whether it was land or water.
  2. If it was land, I saw how high or flat it was and thought about whether it was wet enough for plants and animals to live there.
  3. If it was a body of water, I saw whether it was small enough to see land around it.

Personal Application
Teacher Comment: **When do you need to know different land forms or bodies of water?**
  Student Response: I need to know different land forms or bodies of water to understand what plants or animals can grow there. I need to know the right word to describe a particular place to someone else. I need to know what the land form or body of water is like to understand stories that take place there.

Page 52 - DESCRIBING LAND FORMS

LESSON

Introduction
Teacher Comment: **We have matched the words for land forms to their photographs.**

Stating the Objective
Teacher Comment: **In this lesson you will practice writing the words for different land forms. You will match the photographs to words that describe them.**

Conducting the Lesson
Teacher Comment: **Copy the word "desert" on the lines provided. Now look at the pictures. Which picture shows a desert?**
Student Response: The bottom picture shows a desert.
Teacher Comment: **Draw a line from the picture of the desert to the word "desert."**

Teacher Comment: **Look at the words on the right of the page. Which word describes a desert?**
Student Response: The word "flat" describes a desert.
Teacher Comment: **Copy the word "flat" and draw a line from the word to the picture of the desert.**

• Check students' work. Continue this dialog to discuss students' answers.

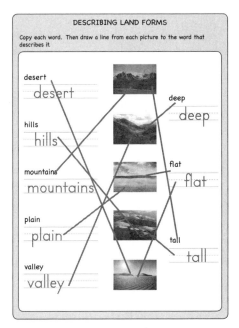

Thinking About Thinking
Teacher Comment: **What did you pay attention to in order to describe which land form is shown in the picture?**
Student Response:
1. I looked at the land form to compare it to the land around it to see how large or high it was.
2. I saw whether it was wet enough for plants and animals to live there.
3. I matched the photograph to the word for the land form.
4. I matched the photograph to the word for its height.

Personal Application
Teacher Comment: **When do you need to know different land forms?**
Student Response: I need to know different land forms to understand what plants or animals can grow there. I need to know the right word to describe a particular place to someone else. I need to know what the land form is like so that I understand stories that take place there.

Page 53 - DESCRIBING BODIES OF WATER

LESSON

Introduction

Teacher Comment: **We have matched the words for land forms to their photographs.**

Stating the Objective

Teacher Comment: **In this lesson you will practice writing the words for different bodies of water. You will match the photographs to words that describe them.**

Conducting the Lesson

Teacher Comment: **Copy the word "lake" on the lines provided. Now look at the pictures. Which picture shows a lake?**

Student Response: The second one shows a lake.

Teacher Comment: **Draw a line from the picture of the lake to the word "lake."**

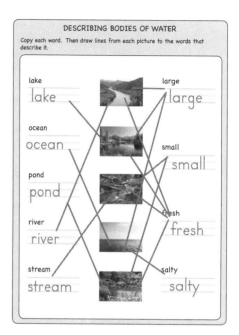

Teacher Comment: **If a body of water is surrounded by land, the water will not be salty. It will contain fresh water that comes from rain, melted snow, or springs from under the ground. Does a lake contain fresh or salty water?**

Student Response: A lake has fresh water because it is surrounded by land.

Teacher Comment: **Copy the word "fresh" and draw a line from the word to the picture of the lake. Look at the other words in the right column. Which other word can describe a lake?**

Student Response: The word "large" can describe a lake.

Teacher Comment: **Copy the word "large" and draw a line from the word to the picture of a lake.**

Teacher Comment: **Copy the name of each body of water and draw a line from the word to the picture.**

Teacher Comment: **Then draw a line from each photograph to the words that describes its size and whether it is salty. Copy those words.**

• Check students' work. Continue this dialog to discuss students' answers.

Thinking About Thinking

Teacher Comment: **What did you pay attention to in order to describe which body of water is shown in the picture?**

Student Response:

1. I looked at the body of water to compare it to the land around it in order to see how large or long it is.
2. I looked for land around it to understand whether or not it has fresh or salty water.
3. I matched the photograph to the words that name and describe that body of water.

Personal Application
Teacher Comment: **When do you need to know describe bodies of water?**
Student Response: I need to know about different bodies of water in order to understand what plants or animals can live there. I need to know the right word to describe a particular place to someone else. I need to know what a body of water is like in order to understand stories that take place there.

Page 54 - DESCRIBING LAND FORMS

LESSON

TEACHING SUGGESTION
Emphasize the key characteristics of describing a land form: size, altitude, moisture, what people or animals do there, whether plants grow there. Describe land forms by comparing size or height to other ones.

DESCRIBING LAND FORMS
Trace each word. Then use the words from the WORD BOX to complete the paragraph.

WORD BOX
flat, Hills, mountains, plain, streams, wet

A valley is the *flat* land between mountains. It is usually *wet* from water that runs in *streams* from snow and rain on the mountains. Hills are taller than a *plain* and shorter than *mountains*.

Introduction
Teacher Comment: **We have matched the words for land forms to their photographs.**

Stating the Objective
Teacher Comment: **In this lesson you will write about two land forms: a valley and hills.**

Conducting the Lesson
Teacher Comment: **The first picture shows that a valley is the low, flat land between mountains. Trace the first sentence. Use words from the WORD BOX to complete that sentence.**

Teacher Comment: **Streams, created by rain and melting snow, run down tall mountains and provide moisture to the valleys. Trace the second sentence. Use words from the WORD BOX to complete that sentence.**

Teacher Comment: **In the third picture we see the valleys between some hills. A hill is not as tall as a mountain, but taller than a plain. Trace the third sentence. Use words from the WORD BOX to complete that sentence.**

Thinking About Thinking
Teacher Comment: **What did you pay attention to in order to describe the land forms shown in the pictures?**
Student Response:
1. I compared the land form to the land around it to see how large or high it is.
2. I saw whether it was wet enough for plants and animals to live there.
3. I found the word that completed the sentence and copied it in the blank.

Personal Application
Teacher Comment: **When do you need to know different land forms?**
Student Response: I need to know different land forms to understand what plants or animals can live there. I need to know the right words to describe a particular place to someone else. I need to know what the land form is like to understand stories that take place there.

Page 55 - DESCRIBING BODIES OF WATER

LESSON

TEACHING SUGGESTION
Emphasize the key characteristics of describing a body of water: size, depth, fresh or salt water, which animals live there, or surrounding land. Compare and contrast bodies of water using these characteristics.

Introduction
Teacher Comment: **We have matched the words for land forms to their photographs.**

Stating the Objective
Teacher Comment: **In this lesson you will write about bodies of water.**

Conducting the Lesson
Teacher Comment: **The first picture shows a lake. You can see that it is a large body of water, and is surrounded by land. Trace the first sentence. Use words from the WORD BOX to complete that sentence.**

Teacher Comment: **A lake has fresh water that runs in streams from rain or snow on the mountains. Trace the second sentence. Use words from the WORD BOX to complete that sentence.**

Teacher Comment: **A lake is not as large as an ocean, but is larger than a pond. Trace the last sentence. Use words from the WORD BOX to complete that sentence.**

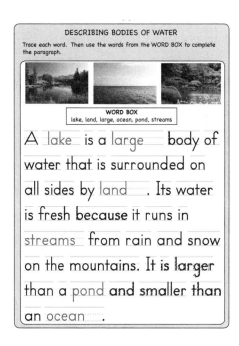

DESCRIBING BODIES OF WATER

Trace each word. Then use the words from the WORD BOX to complete the paragraph.

WORD BOX
lake, land, large, ocean, pond, streams

A lake is a large body of water that is surrounded on all sides by land. Its water is fresh because it runs in streams from rain and snow on the mountains. It is larger than a pond and smaller than an ocean.

Thinking About Thinking
Teacher Comment: **What did you pay attention to in order to describe the body of water shown in the picture?**
Student Response:
1. I compared the body of water to the land around it to see how large it was.
2. I found the word that completed the sentence and copied it in the blank.

Personal Application
    Teacher Comment: **When do you need to know different bodies of water?**
    Student Response: I need to know different bodies of water to understand what plants or animals can live there. I need to know the right word to describe a particular place to someone else. I need to know what the body of water is like to understand stories that I read.

Page 56 - KINDS OF LAND AND WATER

LESSON

Introduction
    Teacher Comment: **We have described land forms and bodies of water.**

Stating the Objective
    Teacher Comment: **In this lesson you will write examples of different kinds of land forms or bodies of water.**

Conducting the Lesson
    Teacher Comment: **The first group of pictures shows three bodies of water. Trace the words for the group on the top line. Use words from the WORD BOX to list the examples of bodies of water.**

• Check students' work

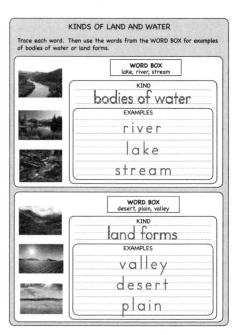

    Teacher Comment: **The second group of pictures shows three land forms. Use words from the WORD BOX to write the group on the top line. List the examples of land forms.**

• Check students' work.

Thinking About Thinking
    Teacher Comment: **What did you pay attention to in order to tell the difference between words that describe the group and words for examples?**
    Student Response:
    1. I wrote the words that described the kinds of land or water.
    2. I wrote the words that matched the examples.

Personal Application
    Teacher Comment: **When do you need to know the difference between kinds of land and water and examples of them?**
    Student Response: I need to know kinds of land and water to tell or write about them.

Page 57 - SIMILAR LAND OR WATER

LESSON

Introduction
Teacher Comment: **We have described land forms and bodies of water.**

Stating the Objective
Teacher Comment: **In this lesson you will explain how land forms or bodies of water are alike.**

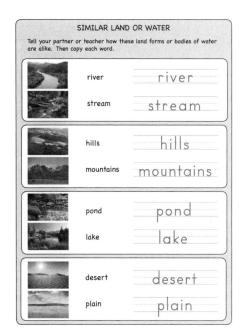

Conducting the Lesson
Teacher Comment: **The first pictures show a river and a stream. Tell your partner how a river and a stream are alike.**
Student Response: Both are bordered on two sides by land. Both are often long and narrow. Both move in one direction. Both have fresh water.
Teacher Comment: **What characteristics did you describe to explain how these bodies of water are alike?**
Student Response: I described their shape and how they are bordered by land. I described their motion and whether their water was fresh or salty.
Teacher Comment: **Copy the words "river" and "stream."**

Teacher Comment: **The next exercise shows a hill and a mountain. Tell your partner how they are alike.**
Student Response: Both are land forms that rise up from the ground and are taller than a plain.
Teacher Comment: **What characteristics did you describe to explain how these land forms are alike?**
Student Response: I described their size.
Teacher Comment: **Trace and copy the words "hills" and "mountains."**

• Check students' work. Use the same dialog to discuss students' answers.

Thinking About Thinking
Teacher Comment: **What did you think about to describe how land forms or bodies of water are alike are alike?**
Student Response:
1. For the land forms I described their size, their height, and what plants and animals live there.
2. For bodies of water I described their size, the land around them, whether they are deep or shallow, what plants and animals live in or around them and how they move.

Personal Application

Teacher Comment: **When is it important to understand how land forms or bodies of water are alike?**

Student Response: I need to understand how land forms and bodies of water are alike in order to tell or write about them.

Page 58 - COMPARING LAND FORMS OR BODIES OF WATER

LESSON

Introduction

Teacher Comment: **When we described how two things are alike, we were comparing them. One way of comparing more than two things is to arrange them in order of their size. When we arrange them in order of their size, we are ranking them.**

Stating the Objective

Teacher Comment: **In this lesson we will arrange bodies of water or land forms in order of their size or height.**

Conducting the Lesson

Teacher Comment: **Name the bodies of water in the top box.**

Student Response: They are a lake, a pond, and an ocean.

Teacher Comment: **List these bodies of water from smallest to largest. Which body of water is the smallest?**

Student Response: The pond is the smallest body of water.

Teacher Comment: **Write the word "pond" on the top line.**

Teacher Comment: **Which body of water is a little larger than a pond?**

Student Response: The lake is larger than a pond.

Teacher Comment: **Write the word "lake" on the second line.**

Teacher Comment: **Which body of water is the largest?**

Student Response: The ocean is the largest body of water.

Teacher Comment: **Write the word "ocean" on the third line.**

Teacher Comment: **Name the land forms in the bottom box.**

Student Response: They are hills, mountains, and a valley.

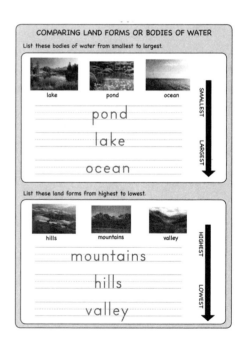

COMPARING LAND FORMS OR BODIES OF WATER

List these bodies of water from smallest to largest.

lake   pond   ocean

SMALLEST
LARGEST

pond
lake
ocean

List these land forms from highest to lowest.

hills   mountains   valley

HIGHEST
LOWEST

mountains
hills
valley

Teacher Comment: **List these land forms from highest to lowest. Which land form is the highest?**

Student Response: The mountain is the highest land form.

Teacher Comment: **Write the word "mountains" on the top line.**

Teacher Comment: **Which land form is lower than a mountain?**

Student Response: The hills are lower than the mountains.

Teacher Comment: **Write the word "hills" on the second line.**

Teacher Comment: **Which land form is the lowest land form?**

Student Response: The valley is the lowest land form.

Teacher Comment: **Write the word "valley" on the third line.**

Thinking About Thinking

Teacher Comment: **What did you think about to compare these bodies of water or land forms?**

Student Response:

1. I thought about the size or height of each example.
2. I remembered to start with the smallest size or the highest height.
3. I compared the other two examples to it.

Personal Application

Teacher Comment: **When is it important to compare bodies of water or land forms?**

Student Response: I need to compare bodies of water or land forms to tell or write about them.

CHAPTER SEVEN – THINKING ABOUT LIVING AND NON-LIVING THINGS (Pages 59-66)

GENERAL INTRODUCTION

CURRICULUM APPLICATIONS
Language Arts: Identify misconceptions in stories in which characters mistake living and non-living thing, such as *Are You My Mother?* by P.D. Eastman*;* identify stories where inanimate objects come to life, such as *The Wizard of Oz* by L. Frank Baum*,* or Disney Pixar's *Toy Story.*
Science: Identify the properties of living and non-living things and apply those properties to natural and man-made objects.
Enrichment: Create student art in which non-living things seem to have living properties.

TEACHING SUGGESTIONS
• Young children often have difficulty discriminating between organisms that are alive and objects which are not. The characteristics that commonly distinguish living from non-living things can seem unclear to young children. In this chapter students distinguish three characteristics of living things: growth, the need for food, and reproduction.

• A young child may have difficulty distinguishing between organic growth and increase in size. For example, clouds increase in size and seem to grow much like a plant does. A river can flood, appearing that it is growing. When discussing growth, clarify the difference between fluctuations in size and growth in the life cycle.

• A young child may not distinguish between food and fuel. A child may think that gasoline is "food" for an automobile or that electricity is "food" for a microwave oven. When discussing food, clarify the difference between necessary components and intake of nutrients.

• Reproduction may not be clearly understood. Clouds may seem to reproduce by appearing spontaneously or from nearby clouds. Streams may seem to be the "babies" of rivers because they are small, grow with the seasons, and can change location and the rate of flow. When discussing reproduction, clarify the difference between irregular changes and the pattern of birth and growth in the life cycle.

• These distinctions may seem obvious to adults, but they may not be so clear to young children. Students should understand these concepts correctly and realize that all three are necessary attributes of living things.

• Children may associate some characteristics of living things to inanimate objects. Because some living things move, children may believe that clouds, rivers, clocks, toys, and images on a screen are alive. Because some living things make sounds, children may believe that appliances, computers, and cell phones are alive.

• Note: Modeling clear, accurate examples of these concepts will be more helpful than illustrating potential confusion. If a student displays confusion, gently explain the difference. Otherwise, provide examples that are as clear and accurate as possible.

Page 60 - DESCRIBING LIVING AND NON-LIVING THINGS

LESSON

Introduction

Teacher Comment: **Sometimes young children believe that something is alive, when really it is not a living thing. Think of a time when you were little that you believed that something was alive until you found out that it was not. Tell your partner why you believed it was alive and how you know now that it is not.**

• After students' discussion, ask two students to explain why they thought the object was alive and how they learned that it was not.

Teacher Comment: **What clues let these students know that the object was not really alive?**

• Students' answers will vary.

Teacher Comment: **To understand the world around us, we must understand what is a living thing and what is not. Living things grow. Things that are not alive do not grow.**

Stating the Objective

Teacher Comment: **In this lesson you will decide whether certain things grow or do not grow.**

Conducting the Lesson

Teacher Comment: **Look at each picture and decide whether the object in the picture grows from being small and new to being large and mature.**
Teacher Comment: **What is the object in the first picture?**
  Student Response: It is a microwave oven.
Teacher Comment: **Does a microwave oven grow?**
  Student Response: A microwave oven does not grow.
Teacher Comment: **Draw a line from the picture of the microwave oven to the words "does not grow," then copy each word.**

Teacher Comment: **What is the animal in the second picture?**
  Student Response: The animal is a duck.
Teacher Comment: **Does a duck grow?**
  Student Response: Yes, a duck grows from a baby duckling to an adult duck.
Teacher Comment: **Draw a line from the picture of the duck to the word "grows," then copy the word.**

Teacher Comment: **Draw a line from each picture to the words that describe whether or not it grows.**

• Check students' work. Continue this dialog to discuss students' answers.

Thinking About Thinking

Teacher Comment: **What did you pay attention to in order to decide whether or not something grows?**
  Student Response:
    1. I thought about the object in the picture.
    2. I thought about what the object was like before or after the way it looks in the picture.
    3. I decided whether it got larger before or after the way it looks in the picture.

Personal Application

Teacher Comment: **When do you need to know whether or not something grows?**
  Student Response: I need to know whether or not something grows to know the space that it will need and whether I have to care for it.

Page 61 - DESCRIBING LIVING AND NON-LIVING THINGS

LESSON

TEACHING SUGGESTION

Help students to distinguish between food and fuel. A child may think that gasoline is "food" for an automobile or that electricity is "food" for a microwave oven. If an appliance, a vehicle, or machine needs energy to operate, explain where that energy comes from and differentiate that source from the concept of food.

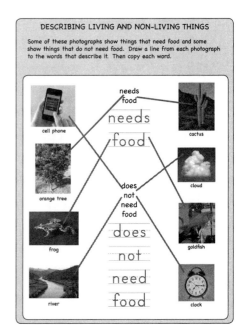

Introduction

Teacher Comment: **Things that are not alive do not need food. Living things need or make food. Animals need plants or other animals for food. Plants make their own food from soil, water, air, and sunlight.**

Stating the Objective

Teacher Comment: **In this lesson you will decide whether or not certain things need food.**

Conducting the Lesson

Teacher Comment: **Look at each picture and decide whether the object in the picture needs food or makes its own food.**
Teacher Comment: **What is the object in the first picture?**
  Student Response: It is a cell phone.
Teacher Comment: **Does a cell phone need food?**
  Student Response: A cell phone does not need food.

Teacher Comment: **Draw a line from the picture of the cell phone to the words "does not need food," then copy the words.**

Teacher Comment: **What is in the second picture?**
   Student Response: The plant is an orange tree.
Teacher Comment: **Does an orange tree need food?**
   Student Response: Yes, an orange tree makes its food from water and the soil.
Teacher Comment: **Draw a line from the picture of the orange tree to the words "needs food," then copy the words.**

Teacher Comment: **Draw a line from each picture to the words that describe whether or not it needs food.**

• Continue this dialog to discuss students' answers.

Thinking About Thinking
   Teacher Comment: **What did you pay attention to in order to decide whether or not something needs food?**
   Student Response:
      1. I thought about the object in the picture.
      2. I remembered whether or not it needs or makes its food.

Personal Application
   Teacher Comment: **When do you need to know whether or not something needs food?**
   Student Response: I need to know whether or not something needs food to know how to take care of it.

Page 62 - DESCRIBING LIVING AND NON-LIVING THINGS

LESSON

Introduction

Teacher Comment: **Living things make new forms of themselves. This is called reproduction. Animals make babies. Plants make seeds which grow into new plants. Living things are born, grow, make babies or seeds, and die. Things that are not alive do not reproduce.**

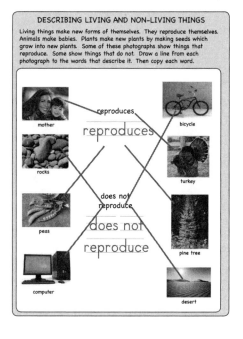

DESCRIBING LIVING AND NON-LIVING THINGS
Living things make new forms of themselves. They reproduce themselves. Animals make babies. Plants make new plants by making seeds which grow into new plants. Some of these photographs show things that reproduce. Some show things that do not. Draw a line from each photograph to the words that describe it. Then copy each word.

Stating the Objective

Teacher Comment: **In this lesson you will decide whether or not certain things reproduce.**

Conducting the Lesson

Teacher Comment: **Look at each picture and decide whether or not the object in the picture reproduces.**

Teacher Comment: **What is in the first picture?**

Student Response: It is a mother and a boy.

Teacher Comment: **Do people reproduce?**

Student Response: Yes, women have babies.

Teacher Comment: **Draw a line from the picture of the mother and the boy to the word "reproduces," then copy the word.**

Teacher Comment: **What is in the second picture?**

Student Response: The objects are rocks.

Teacher Comment: **Does a rock reproduce?**

Student Response: No, a rock does not reproduce.

Teacher Comment: **Draw a line from the picture of the rock to the words "does not reproduce," then copy the words.**

Teacher Comment: **Draw a line from each picture to the words that describe whether or not it reproduces.**

• Continue this dialog to discuss students' answers.

Thinking About Thinking

Teacher Comment: **What did you pay attention to in order to decide whether or not something reproduces?**

Student Response:
1. I thought about the object in the picture.
2. I remembered whether the object makes babies or seeds.

Personal Application

Teacher Comment: **When do you need to know whether or not something reproduces its kind?**

Student Response: I need to know whether or not something reproduces to understand whether or not there will be more of them.

Page 63 - DESCRIBING LIVING AND NON-LIVING THINGS

LESSON

Introduction

Teacher Comment: **We have learned that living things grow, need food, and reproduce.**

Stating the Objective

Teacher Comment: **In this lesson you will decide whether the object has all three characteristics.**

Conducting the Lesson

Teacher Comment: **Look at the first picture. Living things grow, need food, and reproduce. The mother grows. Write YES in the box under "grows." She needs food. Write YES in the box under "needs food." She has a child. Write YES in the box under "reproduces." We have shown that the mother has all the characteristics of a living thing.**

Look at the second picture. The desert does not grow. Write NO in the box under "grows." It does not need food. Write NO in the box under "needs food." It does not reproduce. Write NO in the box under "reproduces." We have shown that the desert is not a living thing.

Teacher Comment: **In each box write YES or NO to show whether the object in the picture has that characteristic.**

DESCRIBING LIVING AND NON-LIVING THINGS

Living things grow, need food, and reproduce. The mother grows. She needs food. She has a child. She is a living person. Tell your partner whether each picture shows a living or non-living thing. Write "YES" or "NO" in each box.

LIVING OR NON-LIVING?	Grows	Needs Food	Reproduces
mother	yes	yes	yes
desert	no	no	no
frog	yes	yes	yes
rock	no	no	no
cell phone	no	no	no
corn stalk	yes	yes	yes
clock	no	no	no
pine tree	yes	yes	yes

• Check students' work. Continue this dialog to discuss students' answers.

Teacher Comment: **We have seen that living things have all three characteristics. They grow, reproduce, and need food.**

Thinking About Thinking

Teacher Comment: **What did you pay attention to in order to decide whether or not something is alive?**

Student Response:

1. I thought about whether the object in the picture grows, needs food, and reproduces.
2. If it has these characteristics, I know that it is alive.
3. If it does not have these characteristics, then I know that it is not alive.

Personal Application

Teacher Comment: **When do you need to know whether or not something is alive?**

Student Response: I need to know whether or not something is alive to understand what it needs to survive. I need to know the difference between living things and things that are not alive when I study nature.

Page 64 - DESCRIBING LIVING AND NON-LIVING THINGS

LESSON

Introduction

Teacher Comment: **We have discussed whether or not something is alive by recognizing that it grows, needs food, and reproduces itself.**

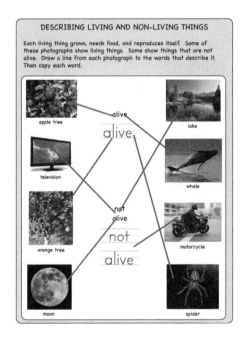

Stating the Objective

Teacher Comment: **In this lesson you will draw lines to show whether or not the objects in the pictures are alive.**

Conducting the Lesson

Teacher Comment: **Some of these photographs show living things. Some show things that are not alive.**

Teacher Comment: **What is in the first picture?**

Student Response: That is a picture of an apple tree.

Teacher Comment: **Is an apple tree alive or not alive?**

Student Response: The apple tree is alive.

Teacher Comment: **How do you know that the apple tree is alive?**

Student Response: It grows from a seed and makes its own food and fruit.

Teacher Comment: **Draw a line from the apple tree to the word "alive." Copy the word "alive."**

Teacher Comment: **What is the object in the second picture?**

Student Response: It is a television.

Teacher Comment: **Is a television alive?**

Student Response: A television is not alive.

Teacher Comment: **How do you know that a television is not alive?**
    Student Response: A television is made by people. It does not grow, need food, or reproduce.
Teacher Comment: **Draw a line from the television to the words "not alive." Copy the words "not alive."**

Teacher Comment: **Draw a line from each picture to the words that tell whether or not the object is alive.**

• Check students' work. Continue this dialog to discuss students' answers.

Thinking About Thinking

Teacher Comment: **What did you pay attention to in order to decide whether or not something alive?**
    Student Response:
    1. I thought about whether the object in the picture grows, needs food, and reproduces.
    2. If it has these characteristics, I know that it is alive.
    3. If it does not have these characteristics, then I know that it is not alive.

Personal Application

Teacher Comment: **When do you need to know whether or not something is alive?**
    Student Response: I need to know whether or not something is alive to understand what it needs to survive. I need to know the difference between living things and things that are not alive when I study nature.

Page 65 - KINDS OF LIVING THINGS

LESSON

Introduction

Teacher Comment: **We have learned how to tell the difference between living and non-living things.**

Stating the Objective

Teacher Comment: **In this lesson you will show the difference between two types of living things: plants and animals.**

Conducting the Lesson

Teacher Comment: **Plants grow in one place and make their food from sunlight and water. Large plants and trees have roots deep in the ground. Most plants make new ones from seeds. Animals move by themselves. They eat plants or other animals and make baby animals from eggs or grow them inside their bodies.**

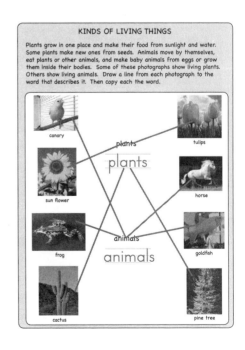

KINDS OF LIVING THINGS

Plants grow in one place and make their food from sunlight and water. Some plants make new ones from seeds. Animals move by themselves, eat plants or other animals, and make baby animals from eggs or grow them inside their bodies. Some of these photographs show living plants. Others show living animals. Draw a line from each photograph to the word that describes it. Then copy each the word.

canary   plants   tulips
sun flower   plants   horse
frog   animals   goldfish
cactus   animals   pine tree

Teacher Comment: **What is the object in the first picture?**
　Student Response: That is a picture of a canary.
Teacher Comment: **Is a canary a plant or an animal?**
　Student Response: The canary is an animal.
Teacher Comment: **How do you know that the canary is an animal?**
　Student Response: It eats seeds. It flies. It hatches from eggs.
Teacher Comment: **Draw a line from the canary to the word "animal." Copy the word "animal."**

Teacher Comment: **What is the object in the second picture?**
　Student Response: It is a sunflower.
Teacher Comment: **Is a sunflower a plant or an animal?**
　Student Response: A sunflower is a plant.
Teacher Comment: **How do you know that a sunflower is a plant?**
　Student Response: A sunflower makes its own food. Its roots to hold it in one place. It reproduces by seeds.
Teacher Comment: **Draw a line from the sunflower to the word "plant." Copy the word "plant."**

Teacher Comment: **Draw a line from each picture to the words that tell whether it is a plant or an animal.**

- Check students' work. Continue this dialog to discuss students' answers. Encourage students to use the correct verbs to describe how the animals move. You may introduce the term "locomotion" to describe animal movement.

Thinking About Thinking
Teacher Comment: **What did you pay attention to in order to decide whether a living thing is plant or an animal?**
Student Response:
1. I remembered whether it makes its own food or eats plants or other animals.
2. I thought about whether the object in the picture stays in one place or can move around by itself.
3. I remember whether it reproduces by seeds, by eggs, or in their bodies.
4. If it makes its own food, can not move itself, and reproduces by seeds, I know that it is a plant.
5. If it eats plants or other animals, can move itself, and reproduces by eggs or from inside their bodies, I know that it is an animal.

Personal Application
Teacher Comment: **When do you need to know whether or not something is a plant or an animal?**
　Student Response: I need to know whether or not something is a plant or an animal to know what it needs to survive. I need to know the difference between plants and animals to understand nature.

Page 66 - COMPARING PLANTS AND ANIMALS

LESSON

Introduction
Teacher Comment: **We have discussed the differences between plants and animals.**

Stating the Objective
Teacher Comment: **In this lesson you will compare plants and animals. You will answer questions about how the living thing gets it food and whether it can move.**

Conducting the Lesson
Teacher Comment: **Name the living thing in the first picture.**

Student Response: The first picture shows roses.

Teacher Comment: **Roses makes their own food from air, water, and sunlight. Notice that "YES" is written in the first box. Roses must stay where they are planted.**

Student Response: Yes, roses must stay where they are planted. They cannot move themselves.

Teacher Comment: **Notice that "YES" is written in the second box. Do roses need other plants or animals for food?**

Student Response: No, roses do not need other plants or animals for food.

Teacher Comment: **Notice that "NO" is written in the third box. Can roses move themselves to another place?**

Student Response: No, roses cannot move themselves to another place.

Teacher Comment: **Notice that "NO" is written in the fourth box. We have shown that roses are a plant, not an animal. Write a "P" in the last box.**

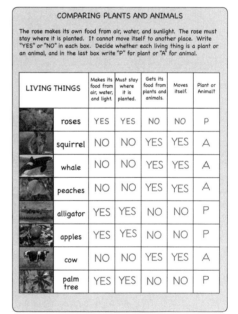

COMPARING PLANTS AND ANIMALS

The rose makes its own food from air, water, and sunlight. The rose must stay where it is planted. It cannot move itself to another place. Write "YES" or "NO" in each box. Decide whether each living thing is a plant or an animal, and in the last box write "P" for plant or "A" for animal.

LIVING THINGS		Makes its food from air, water, and light.	Must stay where it is planted.	Gets its food from plants and animals.	Moves itself.	Plant or Animal?
	roses	YES	YES	NO	NO	P
	squirrel	NO	NO	YES	YES	A
	whale	NO	NO	YES	YES	A
	peaches	NO	NO	YES	YES	A
	alligator	YES	YES	NO	NO	P
	apples	YES	YES	NO	NO	P
	cow	NO	NO	YES	YES	A
	palm tree	YES	YES	NO	NO	P

Teacher Comment: **Name the living thing in the second picture.**

Student Response: The second picture shows a squirrel.

Teacher Comment: **Can the squirrel make its own food?**

Student Response: No, the squirrel eats nuts and other plants. Its body cannot make its own food.

Teacher Comment: **Write "NO" in the first box.**

Teacher Comment: **Must the squirrel stay in one place?**

Student Response: No, the squirrel runs and climbs in trees and on the ground.

Teacher Comment: **Write "NO" in the second box.**

Teacher Comment: **Does the squirrel need other plants or animals for food?**

Student Response: Yes, a squirrel eats nuts and other plants.

Teacher Comment: **Write "YES" in the third box.**

Teacher Comment: **Can the squirrel move itself from place to place?**

Student Response: Yes, the squirrel runs and climbs in trees and on the ground.

Teacher Comment: **Write "YES" in the fourth box.**

Teacher Comment: **We have shown that the squirrel is an animal, not a plant. Write an "A" for animal in the last box.**

Teacher Comment: **Think about each of these living things. Write "YES" or "NO" to show whether it has the characteristics of a plant or an animal. Write "P" or "A" to show whether that living thing is a plant or an animal.**

• Check students' work. Continue this dialog to discuss students' answers. Encourage students to use the correct verbs to describe how the animals move. Encourage students to use as many verbs as they know to discuss the movement of animals shown in the pictures, i.e. (scamper, crawls, runs, creeps, etc.) You may introduce the term "locomotion" to describe animal movement.

Thinking About Thinking

Teacher Comment: **What did you pay attention to in order to decide how to compare plants and animals?**

Student Response:
1. I remembered whether it makes its own food or eats plants or other animals.
2. I thought about whether it stays in one place or can move around by itself.

Personal Application

Teacher Comment: **When do you need to know whether or not something is a plant or an animal?**

Student Response: I need to know whether or not something is a plant or an animal to know what it needs to survive. I need to know the difference between plants and animals to understand nature.

CHAPTER EIGHT – THINKING ABOUT FOOD (Pages 67-85)

GENERAL INTRODUCTION

CURRICULUM APPLICATIONS
Health: Recognize foods that provide good nutrition; identify a variety of foods
Science: Recognize examples of common animals (fish, birds, or mammals); recognize many kinds of plants; identify, illustrate, and describe the parts of a plant (root, stem, seed, and leaf); identify how plants are important to people; investigate the importance of seeds; identify living things as plants or animals; identify examples of various types of foods (dairy, meat, fruit, vegetables, and grains); identify the key characteristics of different types of food (source, appearance, taste, how prepared, how eaten, and special ethnic or cultural uses)

TEACHING SUGGESTIONS
• Drawing: Ask students to draw a picture of a food. Students may write or tell short descriptions or riddles about the food. Label the drawing with a description of that food. Students' drawings may be used to create a "big book."

• After classification lessons, ask students to draw a picture of any three foods from the food list and label the drawing to describe how the three foods are alike (dairy foods, meat, vegetables, fruit). Create a food bulletin board display of students' drawings.

• Storytelling: Ask students to describe to a partner a special event at which a special food was served. Ask the storyteller to relate how the food was prepared and enjoyed.

• Select a common story or fairy tale about food, such as *The Little Red Hen*. Ask students to retell the story about another food (e.g. substituting butter for bread). Discuss how the revised story is different from the original. For example the steps in making butter will be different.

• Enlarge and display the list of food on graphic master number 1 in the appendix. Refer to the word list when students discuss, write, or draw each food in order to associate the word with the food item.

• Language experiences with picture books extend this lesson and demonstrate how food is prepared across cultures. After discussing any of the picture books ask the following questions:
  Are there any new ideas about (any food) that we learned from this story?
  What ideas or details about (any food) did you get from the pictures?
  Is this information true of most (any food)?

• Read picture books about the food featured in each lesson before conducting each exercise.

• Use fresh vegetables to supplement this lesson. Whenever possible, select vegetables that are still intact with the stalks, root hairs, and leaves that are usually removed at the supermarket. For example, young children may not realize that the portion of the carrot that we eat is the root. Showing them the green tops and root hairs lets them see how the food has been changed before it gets to the customer and to understand that the root holds valuable nutrients for the plant and for the person eating it.

- If the food is a plant product, describe the type of plant that produces it (tree, vine, bush) and identify the part of the plant that we eat (seed, fruit, leaf, stem, or root). Describe the food's color, shape, and size.

- If the food is animal product, describe the kind of animal that produces it and how it is prepared.

- Encourage students to give examples of the same foods prepared differently in various ethnic backgrounds. Provide pictures of ethnic foods from magazines or cookbooks or secure samples of ethnic foods using food mentioned in the lesson. Assist students in describing and pronouncing the names of ethnic foods. Discuss how its preparation and combination with other foods affects its appearance and taste.

- "Beans" and "peas" are used interchangeably to describe legumes. Commonly "bean" means that one eats the whole pod, including the seed portion, such as green beans. Seeds are commonly called "peas," such as black-eyed peas or green peas. However the seed portion can be also be called beans, such as black beans, garbanzo beans, or lima beans. Trying to distinguish between beans and peas is probably not useful.

- Science texts offer the scientific definition of fruit which also applies to foods commonly called vegetables (tomatoes, squash, cucumbers, pumpkins, etc.). Clarify students' use of the term "fruit" in appropriate contexts: "vegetable" in cook books and grocery stores, "fruit" in scientific discussion of parts of a plant.

- While we describe a potato as the root part of the plant, it is actually a tuber, a short thickened portion of an underground stem. Since most adults believe that a potato is part of the root, the more accurate designation of a potato as tuber can be clarified in later grades.

- Many young children do not know how butter and cheese are made. Films and picture books may help them understand these processes.

- Teachers may use the graphic organizers (shown on the next page) to define terms, for bulletin board displays, student art work, or end-of-unit summary lessons.

- After classification exercises, students may create a group display. Each group of four students will use a large sheet of newsprint, pictures of foods, or index cards labeled with the names of various foods. Using a large branching diagram (see appendix) as a background, students sort the pictures or labels to create a display.

MENTAL MODEL

A mental model outlines the characteristics that one must state to describe or define a concept. After completing this chapter, each student will have applied this mental model to foods in the lessons. A mental model helps a student:

- Anticipate what he or she needs to know to understand a new food
- Remember the characteristics of a food
- State a clear definition or write an adequate description of a food
- Explain a food to someone else

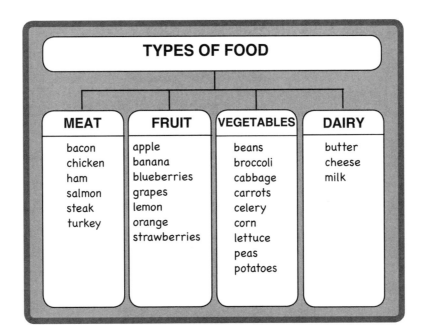

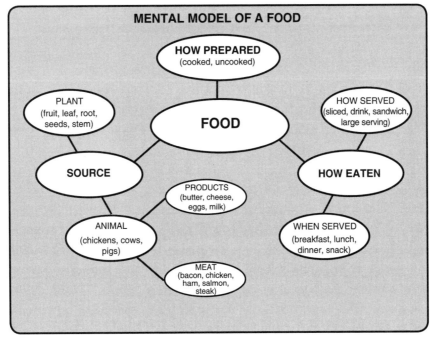

Page 68 - DESCRIBING FOOD

LESSON

Introduction
Select a food for breakfast and bring a sample or the package to class. Describe the food to the class.

Teacher Comment: **What food did I describe?**

Teacher Comment: **What clues let you know what food I was describing?**

Student Response: The kind of food (fruit, bread, meat, drink, etc.), where one gets it, or how it is prepared.

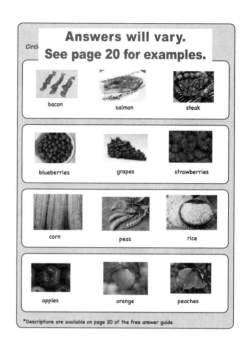

Stating the Objective
Teacher Comment: **In this lesson I will describe a food and you will select it.**

Conducting the Lesson
Teacher Comment: **Name the foods in the first row.**

Student Response: The foods are bacon, salmon, and steak.

Teacher Comment: **Select the picture that fits the following description. This food is the pink meat of a large salt-water fish. This fish is hatched in fresh water, but lives in the ocean. After a few years it returns to the fresh water place where it was hatched. There it lays its eggs. This food is often baked or grilled and served with lemon.**

Teacher Comment: **Decide with your partner which picture has been described.**

Teacher Comment: **What do we call this food?**

Student Response: This food is salmon.

Teacher Comment: **Circle the picture of a piece of salmon.**

Teacher Comment: **What clues let you know that the food in this picture is salmon?**

Student Response: I knew it was the salmon because it is the only fish in the group.

Teacher Comment: **Why don't the other foods fit the description?**

Student Response: The other foods don't fit because bacon is the meat of a pig and steak is the meat of a cow.

Teacher Comment: **Name the foods in the second row.**

Student Response: The foods are blueberries, grapes, and strawberries.

Teacher Comment: **Select the picture that fits this description: This red fruit grows on a low plant. It is used to make jelly and is a popular flavor for ice cream.**

Teacher Comment: **Decide with your partner which picture has been described.**

Teacher Comment: **What do we call this food?**
  Student Response: This food is strawberries.
Teacher Comment: **Circle the picture of strawberries.**

Teacher Comment: **What clues let you know that the food in this picture is strawberries?**
  Student Response: I knew it was strawberries because it is the only red fruit shown.
Teacher Comment: **Why don't the other foods fit the description?**
  Student Response: The other foods don't fit because they are not red.

Teacher Comment: **Name the foods in the third row.**
  Student Response: The foods are corn, peas, and rice.
Teacher Comment: **Select the picture that fits this description. This small, round, green seed grows in a case called a "pod." It is cooked and eaten as vegetable or made into a soup.**
Teacher Comment: **Decide with your partner which picture has been described.**

Teacher Comment: **What do we call this food?**
  Student Response: This food is peas.
Teacher Comment: **Circle the picture of peas.**

Teacher Comment: **What clues let you know that the food in this picture is peas?**
  Student Response: I knew it was peas because it is the only green food. The picture shows the pea pod.
Teacher Comment: **Why don't the other foods fit the description?**
  Student Response: The other foods don't fit because they are not green and they don't grow in a pod.

Teacher Comment: **Name the foods in the fourth row.**
  Student Response: The foods are apples, an orange, and peaches.
Teacher Comment: **Select the picture that fits this description: This small, round, orange fruit is eaten raw or cooked in pies or cobblers. This fruit is soft and sweet. Its skin feels fuzzy.**
Teacher Comment: **Decide with your partner which picture has been described.**

Teacher Comment: **What do we call this food?**
  Student Response: This food is a peach.
Teacher Comment: **Circle the picture of the peach.**

Teacher Comment: **What clues let you know that the food in this picture is a peach?**
  Student Response: Apples and peaches are both round and eaten raw or cooked in pies or cobblers, but the skin of the peach looks soft and fuzzy.
Teacher Comment: **Why don't the other foods fit the description?**
  Student Response: Oranges are not cooked or made into pies. The skin of an apple is shiny, not fuzzy.

Thinking About Thinking

Teacher Comment: **What did you look for when you picked out the food that was described?**

Student Response:

1. I recalled the important characteristics of the food (what it looks like, its taste, how it is prepared, where it grows, etc.).
2. I found the important characteristics in the pictures (I looked for or recalled whether it is a plant or animal product, its color, shape, flavor, size, how it is prepared.)
3. I checked that the other pictures of food do not show these important characteristics as well.

Personal Application

Teacher Comment: **When is it important to describe food accurately?**

Student Response: I need to describe food to order it in the school cafeteria or in a restaurant. I need to describe food to find it in the grocery store.

Page 69 - DESCRIBING FOOD

LESSON

Introduction

Teacher Comment: **We have picked a food that fit a description.**

Stating the Objective

Teacher Comment: **In this lesson you will draw lines to match pictures of foods with the words for them.**

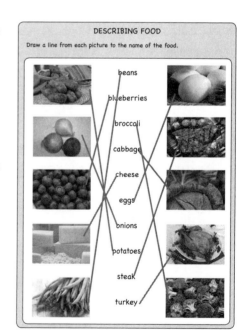

DESCRIBING FOOD

Draw a line from each picture to the name of the food.

beans
blueberries
broccoli
cabbage
cheese
eggs
onions
potatoes
steak
turkey

Conducting the Lesson

Teacher Comment: **Name the food in the first picture.**

Student Response: The first picture shows potatoes.

Teacher Comment: **Find the word "potatoes" in the list. Draw a line from the picture of the potatoes to the word "potatoes."**

Teacher Comment: **Name the food in the second picture.**

Student Response: The second picture shows onions.

Teacher Comment: **Find the word "onions" in the list. Draw a line from the picture of the onions to the word "onions."**

- Check students' work. Continue this dialog to discuss students' answers.

Thinking About Thinking

Teacher Comment: **How did you decide which word belonged with each picture?**
Student Response:
1. I looked at the details of the food in the picture.
2. I named that food.
3. I found the word for that food.

Personal Application

Teacher Comment: **When is it important to know the words for food?**
Student Response: I need to know words for food to find food in the grocery store or order it in a restaurant.

Pages 70 - DESCRIBING FOOD

LESSON

Introduction

Teacher Comment: **In the last lesson we matched pictures of food to the words for them.**

Stating the Objective

Teacher Comment: **In this lesson you will write the word for each food beside its picture.**

Conducting the Lesson

Teacher Comment: **Name the food in the first picture.**
Student Response: The first picture shows lemons.
Teacher Comment: **Describe lemons to your partner.**
Student Response: A lemon is a small, yellow fruit that grows on a tree. Its juice is sour and is mixed with sugar and water to make lemonade.
Teacher Comment: **Find the word "lemons" in the WORD BOX and write it on the lines beside picture.**

DESCRIBING FOOD
Describe each food to your partner. Then use the words from the WORD BOX to write the name of each food.

WORD BOX
bacon, butter, carrots, ham, lemons, lettuce

lemons

lettuce

ham

carrots

bacon

butter

Teacher Comment: **Name the food in the second picture.**
Student Response: The food in the second picture is lettuce.
Teacher Comment: **Describe lettuce to your partner.**
Student Response: Lettuce is a tight ball of green leaves. The bottom shows the short stem that connects to the ground. We eat lettuce in salads and sandwiches. We do not cook lettuce.
Teacher Comment: **Find the word "lettuce" in the WORD BOX and write it on the lines beside to the picture.**

Teacher Comment: **Name the food in the third picture.**

Student Response: The food in the third picture is ham.
Teacher Comment: **Describe ham to your partner.**
Student Response: Ham is a pink meat that comes from a pig. The brown covering shows that the ham has been cooked in a large, whole piece. The ham will then be cut in a thick piece to make one serving or sliced thin for sandwiches.
Teacher Comment: **Find the word "ham" in the WORD BOX and copy it beside the picture.**

• Check students' work. Continue this dialog to discuss students' answers.

Thinking About Thinking

Teacher Comment: **How did you decide which word belonged with each picture?**
Student Response:
1. I looked at the details of the food in the picture.
2. I named that food.
3. I found the word for that food and copied it.

Personal Application

Teacher Comment: **When is it important to know the words for food?**
Student Response: I need to know the words for food to find it in the grocery store or to write about it.

Page 71 - DESCRIBING FOOD

LESSON

Introduction
Teacher Comment: **We have written the words for various foods.**

Stating the Objective
Teacher Comment: **In this lesson you will decide whether a food grows on a short plant, a tall plant, a tree, or a vine. You will draw a line from each picture to the word or words that describe it.**

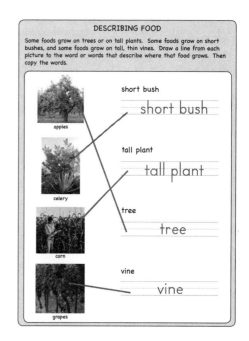

DESCRIBING FOOD

Some foods grow on trees or on tall plants. Some foods grow on short bushes, and some foods grow on tall, thin vines. Draw a line from each picture to the word or words that describe where that food grows. Then copy the words.

short bush
short bush

tall plant
tall plant

tree
tree

vine
vine

apples
celery
corn
grapes

Conducting the Lesson
Teacher Comment: **Name the first food.**
Student Response: The first food is an apple.
Teacher Comment: **On what kind of plant does an apple grow?**
Student Response: An apple grows on a tree.
Teacher Comment: **Draw a line from the picture of the apple tree to the word "tree," then copy the word.**

• Check students' work. Continue this dialog to discuss students' answers.

Thinking About Thinking

Teacher Comment: **How did you decide which plant the food grows on?**
Student Response:
1. I looked at the details of the food in the picture.
2. I decided how high above the ground the food grows.
3. I decided which kind of plant looks most like the picture.

Personal Application

Teacher Comment: **When is it important to know on what kind of plant a food grows?**
Student Response: I need to know the kind of plant food grows in order to find and pick it, or where to plant it.

Page 72 - DESCRIBING FOOD

LESSON

Introduction

Teacher Comment: **In the last lesson we learned on what kind of plant various foods grow.**

Stating the Objective

Teacher Comment: **In this lesson you will match pictures of foods to the words that describe whether a food is a plant or animal product.**

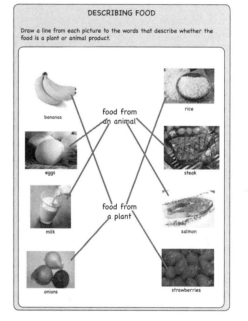

Conducting the Lesson

Teacher Comment: **Name the food in the first picture.**
Student Response: The food in the first picture is a bunch of bananas.
Teacher Comment: **Are bananas a plant or animal product?**
Student Response: Bananas grow on a tree. A banana is a plant.
Teacher Comment: **Draw a line from the picture of the bananas to the words "food from a plant."**

Teacher Comment: **Name the food in the second picture.**
Student Response: The food in the second picture is eggs.
Teacher Comment: **Are eggs a plant or animal product?**
Student Response: Eggs are laid by hens. They are an animal product.
Teacher Comment: **Draw a line from the picture of the eggs to the words "foods from an animal."**

• Check students' work. Continue this dialog to discuss students' answers.

Thinking About Thinking
 Teacher Comment: **How did you decide which word belonged with each picture?**
 Student Response:
 1. I looked at the details in the picture.
 2. I named the food in the picture and decided whether it was a plant or an animal product.

Personal Application
 Teacher Comment: **When is it important to decide whether a food comes from plants or animals?**
 Student Response: I need to know whether a food is a plant or animal product in order to find it in the grocery store.

Page 73 - DESCRIBING FOOD

LESSON

Introduction
 Teacher Comment: **In the last lesson we learned whether a food was a plant or an animal product.**

Stating the Objective
 Teacher Comment: **In this lesson you will match pictures of foods to the words that describe what part of the plant we eat.**

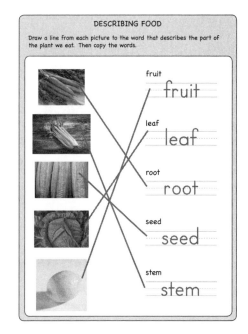

Conducting the Lesson
 Teacher Comment: **Name the food in the first picture.**
 Student Response: The food in the first picture is a bunch of carrots.
 Teacher Comment: **Carrots grow underground. What part of a plant grows underground.**
 Student Response: The root of a plant grows underground.
 Teacher Comment: **Draw a line from the picture to the word "root," then copy the word.**

 Teacher Comment: **Name the food in the second picture.**
 Student Response: The food in the second picture is celery.
 Teacher Comment: **What part of the celery plant to we eat?**
 Student Response: We eat the stem of the celery plant.
 Teacher Comment: **Draw a line from the picture to the word "stem," then copy the word.**

• Check students' work. Continue this dialog to discuss students' answers.

Thinking About Thinking
Teacher Comment: **How did you decide which word belonged with each picture?**
Student Response:
1. I looked at the details in the picture.
2. I named the food in the picture.
3. I saw or remembered where on the plant the food grows.

Personal Application
Teacher Comment: **When is it important to decide what part of the plant we eat?**
Student Response: I need to know what part of the plant we eat in order to know whether or not it has to be cooked.

Page 74 - DESCRIBING FOOD FROM AN ANIMAL

LESSON

Introduction
Teacher Comment: **In the last lesson we learned what part of a plant we eat.**

Stating the Objective
Teacher Comment: **In this lesson you will use words from a WORD BOX to finish a paragraph about an animal that we use as food. A paragraph is a group of sentences that gives us much more information about food than we can say in one sentence.**

DESCRIBING FOOD FROM AN ANIMAL

Trace the words. Then use the words from the WORD BOX to complete the paragraph. Some words will be used more than once.

WORD BOX
animal, chicken, chicks, corn, eggs, meat

A chicken is an animal that lays eggs. The baby chicks hatch from the egg and grow up. Chickens eat corn. People cook its eggs and meat.

Conducting the Lesson
Teacher Comment: **Name the animal in the picture.**
Student Response: The animal is a chicken.
Teacher Comment: **Write the word "chicken" in the first blank.**

• Give students time to write.

Teacher Comment: **Is a chicken a plant or an animal?**
Student Response: The chicken is an animal.
Teacher Comment: **Write the word "animal" in the second blank.**

Teacher Comment: **Think about what you know about chickens. Read the sample sentences to decide which words are missing. Find the words in the WORD BOX that tell about the chicken. Write the words in the blanks.**

Thinking About Thinking
    Teacher Comment: **How did you decide which word belonged in each blank?**
    Student Response:
      1. I read the words on either side of the blank.
      2. I looked in the word box to find the word that fits.
      3. I checked to be sure that the word completed the sentence.

Personal Application
    Teacher Comment: **When is it important to know which food comes from an animal?**
    Student Response: When I need to know where to find food in the grocery store.

Page 75 - DESCRIBING A FOOD FROM A PLANT

LESSON

Introduction
    Teacher Comment: **In the last lesson we described a food from an animal.**

Stating the Objective
    Teacher Comment: **In this lesson you will use words from a WORD BOX to finish a paragraph about a plant we use for food.**

Conducting the Lesson
    Teacher Comment: **Name the plant in the picture.**
      Student Response: The plant is corn.
    Teacher Comment: **Write the word "Corn" in the first blank.**

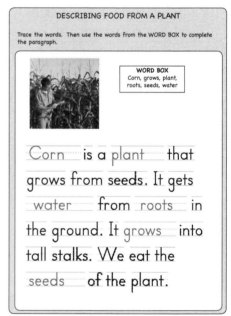

DESCRIBING FOOD FROM A PLANT

Trace the words. Then use the words from the WORD BOX to complete the paragraph.

WORD BOX
Corn, grows, plant, roots, seeds, water

Corn is a plant that grows from seeds. It gets water from roots in the ground. It grows into tall stalks. We eat the seeds of the plant.

• Give students time to write.

    Teacher Comment: **You know that corn is a plant. Write the word "plant" in the second blank.**

    Teacher Comment: **Think about what you know about corn. Read the sample sentences to decide which words are missing. Find the words in the WORD BOX that tell about the corn. Write the words in the blanks.**

Thinking About Thinking
    Teacher Comment: **How did you decide which word belonged in each blank?**
    Student Response:
      1. I read the words on either side of the blank.
      2. I looked in the word box to find the word that fits.
      3. I checked to be sure that the word completed the sentence.

Personal Application
    Teacher Comment: **When is it important to know which food comes from a plant?**
    Student Response: When I need to know where to find food in the grocery store.

Page 76 - DESCRIBING PARTS OF A GRAPE VINE

LESSON

Introduction

Teacher Comment: **In the last lesson we wrote that corn grows on tall stalks. Grapes grow on a vine. A vine is a long, thin plant. Its stem is thick, but not as thick as a tree trunk. Unless the farmer builds a frame to hold it, a vine would grow along the ground or up a tree.**

Stating the Objective

Teacher Comment: **In this lesson you will think about the parts of a grape vine, what each part does, and what would happen to the vine if that part was missing. You will use words from a WORD BOX to write about the parts of a grape vine.**

Conducting the Lesson

Teacher Comment: **What are the green parts of the grapevine that make food for the plant?**

Student Response: The small green parts are leaves.

Teacher Comment: **Write the word "leaves" in the first blank.**

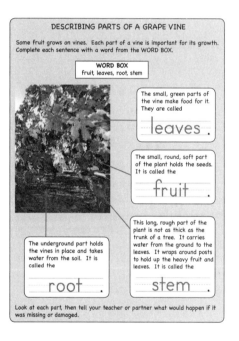

• Give students time to write.

Teacher Comment: **What would happen if the leaves were missing or damaged?**

Student Response: The grape vine could not get the food it needs to grow.

Teacher Comment: **What is the small, round, soft part of the plant that holds the seeds?**

Student Response: The small, round, soft part that holds the seeds is called the fruit.

Teacher Comment: **Write the word "fruit" in the second blank.**

• Give students time to write.

Teacher Comment: **What would happen if the fruit was missing or damaged?**

Student Response: The grape vine would not make seeds for new grapes.

• Check students' work. Continue this dialog to discuss students' answers.

Thinking About Thinking

Teacher Comment: **How did you decide which word described each part of the plant belonged in each blank?**

Student Response:
1. I read the details that tell what that part does.
2. I looked in the word box to find the word that fit the description.
3. I checked that the other words did not fit.

Personal Application
   Teacher Comment: **When is it important to know what the parts of a plant do?**
      Student Response: I need to know how each part of the plant helps the plant to grow.

Page 77 - SIMILAR FOOD

TEACHING SUGGESTIONS
• Emphasize the wording commonly used to describe similarities and differences. Repeat words that show similarity (both, and, like, similar, resemble, etc.) and encourage students to use them in their responses. Explain the term "unlike" and encourage students use words that cue differences (but, not, different, opposite, and unlike).
• In their discussions students should include identifying the part of the plant we eat, as well as words that describe the color, taste, size, and preparation of the food.

LESSON

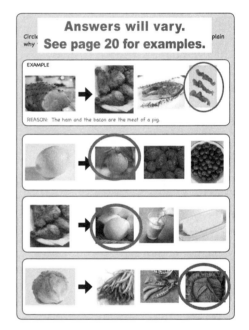

Introduction
   Teacher Comment: **We have described food that comes from plants or animals.**

Stating the Objective
   Teacher Comment: **In this lesson you will find a food that is similar to the first one in the row.**

Conducting the Lesson
   Teacher Comment: **Name the first food in the top row and describe it to your partner.**

      Student Response: This food is ham (the meat of a pig). It is usually cooked in large pieces. We usually eat ham in sandwiches, soups, or in large pieces for dinner or breakfast.
   Teacher Comment: **Trace and copy the word "ham" in the lined spaces.**
   Teacher Comment: **What characteristics did you use to explain that the food in the picture is ham?**
      Student Response: I described where the food came from, how it is prepared and when it is typically eaten.
   Teacher Comment: **Which food on the right is most like the ham?**
      Student Response: The bacon is most like a ham.
   Teacher Comment: **What clues let you know that bacon is most like ham?**
      Student Response: Both are meat from a pig. Both meats can be the main part of a meal or eaten on a sandwich.
   Teacher Comment: **How are the other foods different from ham?**
      Student Response: A potato is a vegetable, not a meat. The salmon is a fish, not the meat from a pig.

   Teacher Comment: **Name the foods in the second row.**

Student Response: The foods are lemon, orange, strawberries, and blueberries.

Teacher Comment: **Tell your partner the important things you know about a lemon.**

Student Response: A lemon is a sour fruit that grows on a tree. It is used to flavor lemonade. It is sometimes made into pies. Some people put lemon in ice tea.

Teacher Comment: **Which food is most like a lemon?**

Student Response: An orange is most like a lemon.

Teacher Comment: **What clues let you know that an orange is most like a lemon?**

Student Response: Both grow on trees. Both are covered by a peel. Both are used as drinks.

Teacher Comment: **How are the other foods different from a lemon?**

Student Response: Strawberries and blueberries are small fruit that grow on bushes. They have a thin skin, not a peel.

Teacher Comment: **Name the foods in the third row.**

Student Response: The foods are fried chicken, eggs, milk, and butter.

Teacher Comment: **Tell your partner the important things you know about fried chicken.**

Student Response: Fried chicken is the meat of a chicken that has been fried in oil.

Teacher Comment: **Which food is most like fried chicken?**

Student Response: Eggs are most like fried chicken. Both are chicken products.

Teacher Comment: **How are the other foods different from chicken?**

Student Response: Milk and butter are produced by cows.

Teacher Comment: **Name the foods in the last row.**

Student Response: The foods are lettuce, beans, peas, and cabbage.

Teacher Comment: **Tell your partner the important things you know about lettuce.**

Student Response: Lettuce is a round, green vegetable. We eat the leaves of this plant raw in salads. It grows as a ball of tightly wrapped leaves. It grows on small plants close to the ground.

Teacher Comment: **Which food is most like lettuce?**

Student Response: Cabbage is most like lettuce.

Teacher Comment: **What clues let you know that cabbage is most like the lettuce?**

Student Response: Both are round, green vegetables that grow on small plants close to the ground. Both are used in salads.

Teacher Comment: **How are the other foods different from lettuce?**

Student Response: Beans and peas are small, round seeds. They are eaten as cooked vegetables.

Thinking About Thinking

Teacher Comment: **How did you decide which foods are alike?**

Student Response:

1. I recalled the important characteristics of the first food (whether the food is a plant or animal product, how it is prepared, its taste, its appearance, etc.).
2. I looked for similar characteristics in the other foods.
3. I selected the food that has most of the same characteristics.
4. I checked to see that other foods do not fit the important characteristics better than the one I selected.

Personal Application
    Teacher Comment: **When is it important to understand how foods are alike?**
    Student Response: I need to understand how foods are similar to explain a particular food to someone who is unfamiliar with it or to find a food to substitute for another one.

Page 78 - SIMILAR FOODS

TEACHING SUGGESTION
Emphasize the wording commonly used to describe similarities. Repeat words that show similarity (both, and, like, similar, resemble, etc.) and encourage students to use them in their responses.

LESSON

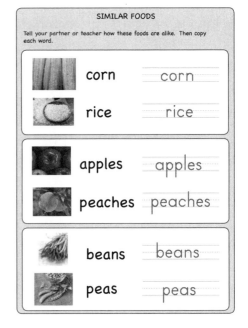

Introduction
    Teacher Comment: **In the last lesson we selected a food that was similar to another one.**

Stating the Objective
    Teacher Comment: **In this lesson you will explain how foods are alike.**

Conducting the Lesson
    Teacher Comment: **Look at the two foods in the first row. Explain how corn and rice are alike.**
    Student Response: Both are the seed part of a plant. We eat them cooked or as breakfast cereals.
    Teacher Comment: **Copy the words "corn" and "rice."**

    Teacher Comment: **Look at the two foods in the second row. Explain how an apple and a peach are alike.**
    Student Response: Both are fruit that grow on trees. Both can be eaten raw or baked in pies.
    Teacher Comment: **Copy the words "apples" and "peaches."**

    Teacher Comment: **In the last row you see beans and peas. Explain how beans and peas are alike.**
    Student Response: I remember that both are seeds that grow in pods and are eaten as vegetables in salad or soups.
    Teacher Comment: **Copy the words "beans" and "peas."**

Thinking About Thinking
Teacher Comment: **What kind of characteristics did you discuss to describe food?**
Student Response:

1. I recalled the important characteristics of the first food (whether the food is a plant or animal product, how it is prepared, its taste, its appearance, etc.).
2. I checked that both foods have these important details.
3. I checked to see that I have explained the important details of both foods.

Personal Application
Teacher Comment: **When is it important to understand how different foods are alike?**
Student Response: I need to understand how foods are alike to find them in the grocery store and to understand how they are prepared.

Page 79 - SIMILARITIES AND DIFFERENCES - FOODS

TEACHING SUGGESTIONS

• Emphasize the wording commonly used to describe similarities and differences. Repeat words that show similarity (both, and, like, similar, resemble, etc.) and encourage students to use them in their responses. Explain the term "unlike" and encourage students to use words that cue differences (but, not, different, opposite, and unlike).

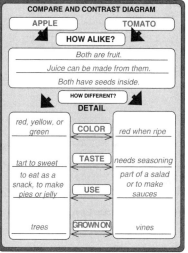

• To reinforce students' responses you may draw a compare and contrast diagram to record their answers. For a blank compare-and-contrast graphic organizer, see the appendix.

LESSON

Introduction
Teacher Comment: **We have compared foods by describing how they are alike. Sometimes we want to know how things are different in order to understand something important about them. When we describe how things are different, we contrast them.**

Stating the Objective
Teacher Comment: **In this lesson we will compare and contrast different foods.**

Conducting the Lesson
Teacher Comment: **Name the two foods in the top box.**
Student Response: They are milk and butter.
Teacher Comment: **Copy the words "milk" and "butter" on the lines provided.**
Teacher Comment: **How are milk and butter alike?**
Student Response: Both are dairy products from cows. They contain fat and must be refrigerated.

Teacher Comment: **How are these two foods different?**

Student Response: Butter is a solid substance made by churning cream. Butter is spread on bread or melted for flavor on vegetables. It is usually light yellow. Milk is a white liquid that we drink or pour on cereal.

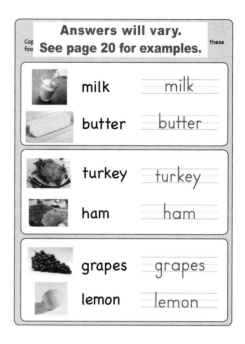

Answers will vary.
See page 20 for examples.

milk	milk
butter	butter
turkey	turkey
ham	ham
grapes	grapes
lemon	lemon

Teacher Comment: **Name the two foods in the second box.**

Student Response: They are turkey and ham.

Teacher Comment: **Copy the words "turkey" and "ham" on the lines provided.**

Teacher Comment: **How are turkey and ham alike?**

Student Response: Both are large pieces of meat that must be cooked a long time. They are served as large slices for a meal or sliced thin to make sandwiches. They are both served on special occasions such as Thanksgiving, Christmas, and special family gatherings.

Teacher Comment: **How are these two foods different?**

Student Response: Turkey is the meat of a bird. Ham is the meat of a pig, a mammal.

Teacher Comment: **Name the two foods in the third box.**

Student Response: They are grapes and a lemon.

Teacher Comment: **Copy the words "grapes" and "lemons" on the lines provided.**

Teacher Comment: **How are grapes and lemon alike?**

Student Response: They are both fruit. Both are squeezed to make juice.

Teacher Comment: **How are these two foods different?**

Student Response: Grapes are soft, sweet, fruit that are eaten as a snack just the way they grow. They are purple or green or red and grow on vines. Lemons are sour fruit that is squeezed and sweetened to make lemonade. Lemons are yellow and grow on trees.

Thinking About Thinking

Teacher Comment: **What did you think about to compare and contrast foods?**

Student Response:

1. I remembered the important characteristics of each of the foods (its appearance, whether it is a plant or animal product).
2. I thought about how the foods are alike.
3. I thought about how the foods are different.

Personal Application

Teacher Comment: **When is it important to compare and contrast foods?**

Student Response: I need to understand how foods are alike or different to find them in the grocery store and to understand how they are prepared.

Page 80 - COMPARING FOOD

TEACHING SUGGESTIONS

- This lesson teaches comparisons (smallest to largest, seldom to often). Emphasize the words for frequency (seldom, often, every day, not often, etc.)

- In this lesson bread refers to many types of bread, not just the sliced, white bread shown in the picture. Explain and/or display many types of bread (rolls, biscuits, whole wheat bread) and bread forms in different cultures (tortillas, pitas, flatbread, etc.)

- Emphasize the sentence structure that shows comparison. For example, a tomato is <u>larger than</u> a grain of rice, <u>but smaller than</u> a cabbage.

LESSON

Introduction

Display, a grape, a lemon, and an orange.

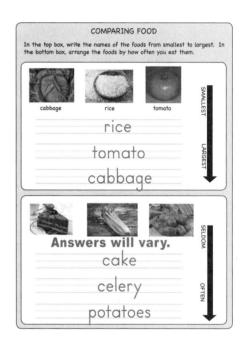

> Teacher Comment: **Here we have a grape, a lemon, and an orange. I have arranged them in order of their size. The grape is the smallest. The orange is the largest. The lemon is larger than the grape, but smaller than the orange.**

> Teacher Comment: **I can also arrange them by how often we drink their juice. We seldom drink grape juice. We often drink orange juice. We drink lemonade more often than grape juice and less often than orange juice.**

Stating the Objective

> Teacher Comment: **In this lesson you will arrange foods in order.**

Conducting the Lesson

> Teacher Comment: **Name the three foods in the top box.**
> Student Response: They are cabbage, rice, and tomato.

> Teacher Comment: **Put cabbage, rice, and tomatoes in order by their size. List them in order from smallest to largest. Which food is the smallest?**
> Student Response: Rice is the smallest food.

> Teacher Comment: **Write the word "rice"on the top line.**

> Teacher Comment: **Which food is the largest?**
> Student Response: The cabbage is the largest.

> Teacher Comment: **Write the word "cabbage" on the bottom line.**

Teacher Comment: **Which food is larger than rice, but smaller than cabbage?**
Student Response: The tomato is larger than rice, but smaller than cabbage.
Teacher Comment: **Write the word "tomato" on the middle line.**

Teacher Comment: **In the bottom box you see cake, celery, and potatoes. List these foods in the order of how often you eat them.**

• Teaching Suggestion: Student responses may vary; discuss student answers to check for understanding.

Thinking About Thinking

Teacher Comment: **What do you think about to put foods in order of size or how often we eat them.**
Student Response:
1. I thought about which food is smallest or eaten less often.
2. I thought about which food is the largest or eaten most often.
3. I thought about which food is not as large or eaten as often as others.

Personal Application

Teacher Comment: **When is it important to arrange foods in order?**
Student Response: I need to arrange foods in order to understand how often our families need these foods, how frequently we buy them, and to find them in the grocery store.

Page 81 - KINDS OF FOOD

TEACHING SUGGESTION
Use the terms "groups," "types," "kind of," and "classes" to help students conceptualize classification. Encourage students to use these words in their discussions.

LESSON

Introduction

Teacher Comment: **When we discuss kinds of food we are classifying them. We have classified some foods such as dairy foods and grains. What are dairy foods?**

Student Response: Dairy foods are milk and food made from milk.

Teacher Comment: **What are some different dairy foods?**

Student Response: Butter, cheese, ice cream, and yogurt are dairy foods.

Teacher Comment: **What are grains?**

Student Response: Grains are the seeds of plants that we eat or grind up to make other products (bread, cereal).

Teacher Comment: **What are some different grains?**

Student Response: Wheat and rice are grains.

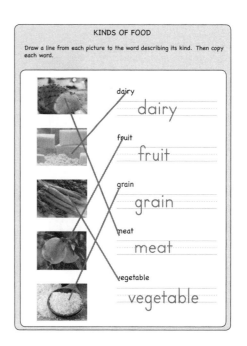

Stating the Objective

Teacher Comment: In this lesson you will match foods to the group in which they belong.

Conducting the Lesson.

Teacher Comment: **What is the food in the first picture?**

Student Response: That food is ham.

Teacher Comment: **What kind of food is ham?**

Student Response: Ham is a meat.

Teacher Comment: **Draw a line from the picture of the ham to the word "meat." Copy the word "meat."**

Teacher Comment: **What kind of food is cheese?**

Student Response: Cheese is a dairy food.

Teacher Comment: **Draw an arrow from the picture to the word "dairy." Copy the word "dairy."**

• Check students' work. Continue this dialog to discuss students' answers.

Thinking About Thinking

Teacher Comment: **What did you think about to match each food to its kind?**

Student Response:
1. I looked at the food and thought about whether it came from a plant or an animal.
2. If it was a food from a plant, I decided whether it was a vegetable, a fruit, or a grain.
3. I looked for the word for that kind of food.
4. If it is a food from an animal, I decided whether it was the meat of an animal or something else produced by the animal, and where I find it in the supermarket.
5. I looked for the word for that kind of food.

Personal Application

Teacher Comment: **When is it important to know kinds of foods?**

Student Response: It is important to understand the advertisements and signs in grocery stores, to select foods from menus, to explain a particular food to someone that is unfamiliar with it, and to identify food that you like.

Page 82 - KINDS OF FOOD

TEACHING SUGGESTION

Use a class and members diagram like the one at the right to record students' answers. A blank class and members diagram can be found in the appendix.

FRUIT	
MEMBER	MEMBER
apple	orange
MEMBER	MEMBER
peach	grapes

LESSON

Introduction

Teacher Comment: **We have described various kinds of foods.**

Stating the Objective

Teacher Comment: **In this lesson you will write the word that describes a kind of food and list examples of that kind of food.**

Conducting the Lesson

Teacher Comment: **Name the foods in the top box.**
Student Response: The foods are apples, peaches, and an orange.

Teacher Comment: **How are these three foods alike?**
Student Response: They are sweet foods that grown on trees.

Teacher Comment: **What do we call these sweet foods?**
Student Response: They are fruit.

Teacher Comment: **Write the word "fruit" on the line labeled "CLASS." Write the foods of that kind on the lines labeled "EXAMPLES."**

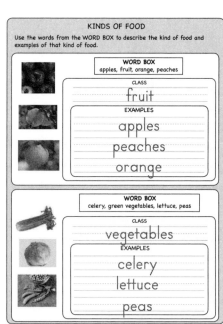

KINDS OF FOOD

Use the words from the WORD BOX to describe the kind of food and examples of that kind of food.

WORD BOX
apples, fruit, orange, peaches

CLASS
fruit

EXAMPLES
apples
peaches
orange

WORD BOX
celery, green vegetables, lettuce, peas

CLASS
vegetables

EXAMPLES
celery
lettuce
peas

• Check students' work. Continue this dialog to discuss students' answers.

Thinking About Thinking
Teacher Comment: **What did you think about to decide which word describes a kind of food?**
Student Response:
1. I decided how the three foods are alike.
2. I found the word that describes that kind of food.

Personal Application
Teacher Comment: **When is it important to know kinds of foods?**
Student Response: I need to know kinds of foods to find them in a grocery store.

Page 83 - A DIFFERENT KIND OF FOOD

LESSON

Introduction
Teacher Comment: **We have named types of foods. The name for that kind of food is called the class in which the food fits.**

Stating the Objective
Teacher Comment: **In this lesson you will identify a food that is not like the others, and draw a circle around it.**

Conducting the Lesson
Teacher Comment: **Name the foods shown in the pictures in the first row.**
Student Response: These foods are fried chicken, ham, milk, and turkey.

Teacher Comment: **Ham, turkey, and fried chicken are the meat of an animal. Milk is a different kind of food. It is a dairy food made from the milk of an animal. Notice that milk is circled.**

Teacher Comment: **Look at the foods in the second row. How are these three foods alike?**
Student Response: The beans, celery, and peas are green vegetables that grow above the ground.
Teacher Comment: **Which food is not a green vegetable that grows above the ground?**
Student Response: Potatoes are brown and grow below the ground.

• Check students' work. Continue this dialog to discuss students' answers.

Thinking About Thinking

Teacher Comment: **What do you think about to decide which was a different kind of food?**

Student Response:

1. I remembered the important characteristics of the food (whether it is a plant or animal product, how it is prepared, what part of the plant we eat).
2. I remembered the word for that kind of food.
3. I explained why one food is not the same kind as the others.

Personal Application

Teacher Comment: **When is it important to understand how a food may be different from others?**

Student Response: I need to understand whether a food is different from others to find it in the grocery store.

Pages 84-85 - KINDS OF FOOD

TEACHING SUGGESTIONS

• Use the terms "groups," "types," or "kind" to help students conceptualize classification. Encourage students to use these words in their discussions.

• It may be helpful to draw the sorting diagram to record students' answers.

LESSON

Introduction

Teacher Comment: **We have named types of food.**

Stating the Objective

Teacher Comment: **In this lesson we will sort foods by the classes: meat, fruit, or vegetable.**

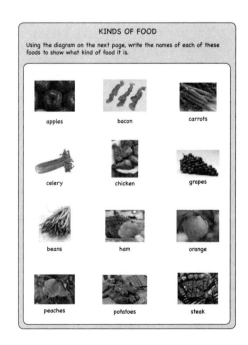

Conducting the Lesson

Teacher Comment: **Name the food in the first picture.**
Student Response: That food is apples.

Teacher Comment: **What kind of food is an apple?**
Student Response: An apple is a fruit.

Teacher Comment: **On the next page trace the word "apple" under the word "fruit."**

Teacher Comment: **Name the food in the second picture.**
Student Response: That food is bacon.

Teacher Comment: **What kind of food is bacon?**

Student Response: Bacon is a meat.

Teacher Comment: **On the next page trace the word "bacon" under the word "meat."**

Teacher Comment: **Name the food in the third picture.**

Student Response: That food is carrots.

Teacher Comment: **What kind of food are carrots?**

Student Response: Carrots are vegetables.

Teacher Comment: **On the next page trace the word "carrots" under the word "vegetable."**

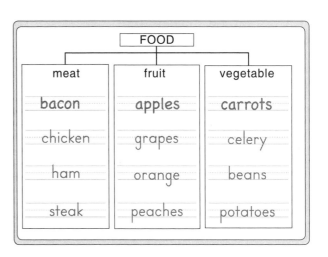

• If students can complete this exercise independently, allow them time to finish.

• If not, continue this dialog to discuss students' answers.

Thinking About Thinking

Teacher Comment: **What did you think about to decide which word describes a kind of food?**

Student Response:
1. I looked at each picture and thought about the important details of the food (whether it is a plant or animal product, what part of the plant we eat, how it is prepared.)
2. I found the word that describes that kind of food.

Personal Application

Teacher Comment: **When is it important to know kinds of foods?**

Student Response: I need to know kinds of foods to find them in a grocery store.

CHAPTER NINE – THINKING ABOUT ANIMALS (Pages 86-104)
GENERAL INTRODUCTION

CURRICULUM APPLICATIONS
Language Arts: Identify the properties of various animals as they appear in myths and stories
Science: Identify living things as plants or animals; state what animals need to live and grow; recognize examples of common animals (insects, fish, birds, amphibians, reptiles, mammals); identify key characteristics of common types of animals (appearance, habitat, food, reproduction and locomotion)
Enrichment: Create student art that shows the properties of various animals

TEACHING SUGGESTIONS
• Drawing: Ask students to draw a picture of an animal. Students may write or tell short descriptions of the animal.

• After classification lessons, ask students to draw a picture of any three animals from the animal list and label the drawing to describe how the three animals are alike (insects, birds, fish, mammals, reptiles, and amphibians). Students may classify animals by other characteristics, such as habitat, location on the globe, or locomotion. Create an animal bulletin board display of students' drawings.

• Read *What Animal Am I? An Animal Guessing Game,* by Iza Trapani. This book models animal riddles with pictures. Select a picture of an animal or allow students to find or draw a picture of an animal. Ask students to create a riddle that they will tell or write for a partner.

• Drama: Ask students to use animal puppets to act out *Brown Bear, Brown Bear, What Do You See?* by Eric Carle and Bill Martin, Jr. for various animals discussed in the lesson.

• Storytelling: Select a common story or fairy tale about an animal, such as *Are You My Mother?* by P.D. Eastman. Ask students to retell the story about another type of animal (e.g. substituting a duck and a duckling for bird and a mother bird). Discuss how the revised story is different from the original. For example, since the duckling's home is in the water, he would meet different animals and must get home another way.

• Enlarge and display the list of animals on graphic master number 2 in the appendix. Refer to the word list when students discuss, write, or draw each animal in order to associate the word with the animal.

• After classification exercises, students may create a group display. Each group of four students will use a large sheet of newsprint, pictures of animals, or index cards labeled with the names of various animals. Using a large branching diagram as a background students sort the pictures or labels to create a display.

• Create a chart or bulletin board display of different kinds of animals. Discuss how each animal reproduces, whether it warm- or cold-blooded, and other special characteristics:
  1. Birds: egg-laying with feathers and wings
  2. Fish: egg-laying animals that swim and have scales and gills
  3. Reptiles: egg-laying animals that crawl and have scales
  4. Amphibians: egg-laying animals that crawl and have moist skin
  5. Mammals: animals whose babies grow inside mother's body, run and have hair

• Teachers may use the graphic organizer at the right for bulletin board displays, student art work, or an end-of-unit summary lesson.

MENTAL MODEL

A mental model is a framework for understanding a concept. It outlines the characteristics that one must state to describe or define a concept. After completing this chapter, each student will have applied this mental model to animals in the lessons. A mental model helps a student:
  • Anticipate what he or she needs to know to understand a new animal
  • Remember the characteristics of an animal
  • State a clear definition or write an adequate description of an animal
  • Explain an animal to someone else

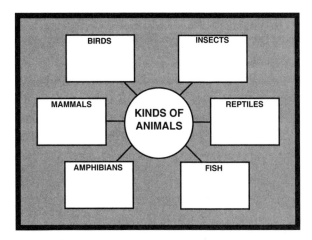

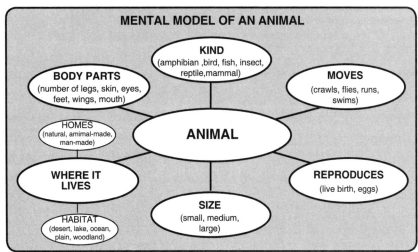

Page 87 - DESCRIBING ANIMALS

LESSON

Introduction
• Ask a student to describe to the class in three to five sentences an animal that they have studied or seen recently.

• Ask the class to name the animal that has been described.
  Teacher Comment: **What details let you know which animal was described?**
    Student Response: I remembered its size and what its body looks like. I remembered where it lives and what it eats.

Stating the Objective
  Teacher Comment: **In this lesson I will describe an animal and you will circle its picture.**

Conducting the Lesson
  Teacher Comment: **Look at the top row. Name these animals.**
    Student Response: The animals are an eagle, an ostrich, and a turkey.
  Teacher Comment: **Listen to the clues and name the animal that I describe. This bird has a very large body and long legs. Its body is so large that the bird cannot fly. Its long legs allow it to run fast. Its long neck lets it eat leaves from short trees and bushes. Its babies hatch from eggs. It lives on the grassy plains of Africa.**

• Ask students to decide with their partners which picture has been described. Confirm the answer with the whole class. Encourage students to use as many verbs as possible to describe how the ostrich moves.

  Teacher Comment: **What do we call this animal?**
    Student Response: This animal is an ostrich.
  Teacher Comment: **Circle the picture of the ostrich.**

  Teacher Comment: **What clues let you know that the animal in this picture is an ostrich?**
    Student Response: I saw its large body and long legs. It seems to be running, not flying. I see its long neck that allows it to reach the leaves of trees.
  Teacher Comment: **Why don't the other animals fit the description?**
    Student Response: The eagle can fly, but it does not run. The turkey does not have long legs and does not run fast.

  Teacher Comment: **Look at the second row. Name these animals.**
    Student Response: The animals are a bat, a butterfly, and a blue jay.
  Teacher Comment: **Listen to the clues and name the animal that I describe. This is the only mammal that can fly. What appear to be wings are actually arms. At the end of the arms are long fingers with skin growing between them. This large, flat hand works like a wing. This animal eats insects and flies from tree to tree. When flying at night, it "sees" by screeching and listening for the echo.**

- Ask students to decide with their partners which picture has been described. Confirm the answer with the whole class.

Answers will vary.
See page 21 for examples.

eagle · ostrich · turkey

bat · butterfly · blue jay

ant · spider · grasshopper

goldfish · shark · salmon

*Descriptions are available on page 21 of the free answer guide.

   Teacher Comment: **What do we call this animal?**
      Student Response: This animal is a bat.
   Teacher Comment: **Circle the picture of the bat.**

   Teacher Comment: **What clues let you know that the animal in this picture is a bat?**
      Student Response: I saw its long arms that look like wings. I saw that it flies at night.
   Teacher Comment: **Why don't the other animals fit the description?**
      Student Response: The butterfly is an insect. The blue jay is a bird.

   Teacher Comment: **Look at the third row. Name these animals.**
      Student Response: The animals are an ant, a spider, and a grasshopper.
   Teacher Comment: **Listen to the clues and name the animal that I describe. This animal has eight legs. Most are larger than insects, but smaller than birds. Its babies hatch from tiny eggs. This animal makes webs out of a thin thread that they make from their bodies. The webs become their home and a trap for flies and other insects that they eat.**

- Ask students to decide with their partners which picture has been described. Confirm the answer with the whole class.

   Teacher Comment: **What do we call this animal?**
      Student Response: This animal is a spider
   Teacher Comment: **Circle the picture of the spider.**

   Teacher Comment: **What clues let you know that the animal in this picture is the spider?**
      Student Response: I saw that it has eight legs and lives in a web that traps its food.
   Teacher Comment: **Why don't the other animals fit the description?**
      Student Response: Neither ants nor grasshoppers have eight legs or spin webs.

   Teacher Comment: **Look at the fourth row. Name these animals.**
      Student Response: The animals are a goldfish, a shark, and salmon.
   Teacher Comment: **Listen to the clues and then name the animal I describe. This large fish is hatched in fresh water (rivers) and travels to the ocean. It eats insects and small fish. When it grows up, it returns to the fresh water where it was hatched to lay its eggs. Sometimes this fish has to jump waterfalls on its way back to the fresh water where it was hatched.**

- Ask students to decide with their partners which picture has been described.

Teacher Comment: **What do we call this animal?**
  Student Response: This animal is a salmon.
Teacher Comment: **Circle the picture of the salmon.**

Teacher Comment: **What clues let you know that the animal in this picture is a salmon?**
  Student Response: In the picture it is jumping a waterfall.
Teacher Comment: **Why don't the other animals fit the description?**
  Student Response: The goldfish is small. The shark lives in the ocean.

• Check students' work.

Thinking About Thinking

Teacher Comment: **What did you look for to pick out the animal that was described?**
  Student Response:
  1. I recalled the important characteristics of the animal.
  2. I found the important characteristics in the picture.
  3. I checked that the other pictures of animals do not show these important characteristics as well.

Personal Application

Teacher Comment: **When is it important to describe animals well?**
  Student Response: I need to know how to describe animals to tell about trips to the zoo, television shows, books, and pictures.

Page 88 - DESCRIBING ANIMALS

TEACHING SUGGESTION
The last lesson we established the pattern of describing animals by their size, body structure, what it eats, how it reproduces, and where it lives. Repeat this pattern when describing animals in other contexts, particularly when discussing non-fiction picture books about animals. Later in this chapter students learn additional key concepts for describing animals. These characteristics include locomotion and body covering.

LESSON

Introduction
Teacher Comment: **In the last lesson we picked an animal that fit a particular description.**

Stating the Objective
Teacher Comment: **In this lesson you will match pictures of a animals with the words for them.**

Conducting the Lesson
Teacher Comment: **Name the animal in the first picture.**
  Student Response: That animal is a bee.
Teacher Comment: **What details show that the animal in the picture is a bee?**

Student Response: I can see its stinger and wings.
Teacher Comment: **Find the word "bee" in the list of words and draw an arrow from the picture of the bee to the word "bee."**
Teacher Comment: **Name the second animal.**
Student Response: That animal is a canary.
Teacher Comment: **What details show that the animal in the picture is a canary?**
Student Response: It is a small yellow bird.
Teacher Comment: **Find the word "canary" in the list of words and draw a line from the picture of the canary to the word "canary."**

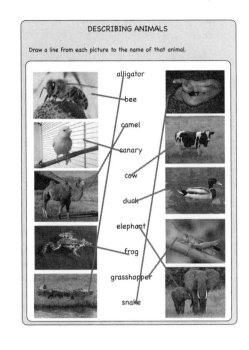

• Check students' work. Continue this dialog to discuss students' answers.

Thinking About Thinking

Teacher Comment: **How did you decide which word matched each picture?**
Student Response:
1. I looked at the details of the animal in the picture.
2. I named that animal.
3. I found the word for that animal.

Personal Application

Teacher Comment: **When is it important to know the names of animals?**
Student Response: I need to know the names of animals to describe trips to the zoo, television shows, books, or pictures.

Pages 89 - DESCRIBING ANIMALS

LESSON

Introduction

• Ask a student to describe to the class in three to five sentences an animal that they have studied or seen recently.

• Ask the class to name the animal that has been described.
Teacher Comment: **What details let you know which animal was described?**
Student Response: I listened for appearance, coloring, behavior, how it moves, where it lives, what it eats or what animals eat it.

Stating the Objective

Teacher Comment: **In this lesson you will write the word for each animal beside its picture.**

Conducting the Lesson

Teacher Comment: **Name the animal in the first picture.**

Student Response: The animal in the first picture is a whale.

Teacher Comment: **Describe the whale to your partner.**

Student Response: The whale is a large animal that eats small fish. Its body is shaped like a fish, but it is really a mammal that breathes air through a hole in the top of its head. It lives in the ocean and travels long distances to give birth to its young.

Teacher Comment: **Find the word "whale" in the WORD BOX and write it on the lines beside the picture.**

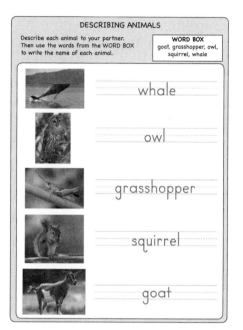

DESCRIBING ANIMALS

Describe each animal to your partner. Then use the words from the WORD BOX to write the name of each animal.

WORD BOX
goat, grasshopper, owl, squirrel, whale

whale

owl

grasshopper

squirrel

goat

Teacher Comment: **Look at the second picture. Name this animal.**

Student Response: The animal in the second picture is an owl.

Teacher Comment: **Describe the owl to your partner.**

Student Response: The owl is a large bird that eats small animals. It has large, round eyes that see well in the dark.

Teacher Comment: **Find the word "owl" in the WORD BOX and write it on the lines beside the picture.**

Teacher Comment: **Look at the third picture.   Name this animal.**

Student Response: This animal is a grasshopper.

Teacher Comment: **Describe the grasshopper to your partner.**

Student Response: A grasshopper is a large insect. It is usually green or brown. It has six legs and long wings.

Teacher Comment: **Find the word "grasshopper" in the WORD BOX and write it on the lines beside the picture.**

• Check students' work. Continue this dialog to discuss students' answers.

Thinking About Thinking

Teacher Comment: **How did you decide which word fit each picture?**

Student Response:
1. I looked at the details of the animal in the picture.
2. I remembered whether it hatches or gives live birth, where it lives, and what it eats.
3. I named that animal.
4. I found the word for that animal and copied it.

Personal Application
    Teacher Comment: **When is it important to know the words for animals?**
    Student Response: I need to know the words for animals to tell about trips to the zoo, television shows or books about animals, and pictures of them.

Page 90 - DESCRIBING ANIMALS – HOW THEY MOVE

LESSON

Introduction
    Teacher Comment: **In the last lesson you described animals to your partner and wrote the word for the animal. In this lesson you describe how animals move. When we describe how an animal moves, we are describing its locomotion.**

Stating the Objective
    Teacher Comment: **In this lesson you will write about each animal's locomotion.**

Conducting the Lesson
    Teacher Comment: **The first sentence tells about an eagle. Look for the eagle in the pictures. How does the eagle move?**
    Student Response: The eagle flies.
    Teacher Comment: **Find the word "flies" in the WORD BOX and write it in the blank.**

• Check students' work. Continue this dialog to discuss students' answers.

Thinking About Thinking
    Teacher Comment: **How did you decide which word describes the animal's locomotion?**
    Student Response:
    1. I looked at the details of the animal in the picture.
    2. I thought about how that animal moves.
    3. I found the word that describes how that animal moves and wrote it in the blank.

Personal Application
    Teacher Comment: **When is it important to know how an animal moves?**
    Student Response: I need to know how an animal moves to tell about trips to the zoo, television shows or books about animals.

Page 91 - DESCRIBING ANIMALS – THEIR BODY COVERING

LESSON

Introduction

Teacher Comment: **Body coverings help an animal keep warm and protect its body from injury. Some animals' bodies are covered with soft feathers that open and close to keep their bodies warm and protect them from scratches. Some animals have hair to keep in their body heat and protect the skin underneath. Some animals have scales that pick up heat from the ground or water around them. Scales are small hard pieces that protect the animal from harm.**

Stating the Objective

Teacher Comment: **In this lesson you will match each animal to the word that describes its body covering.**

Conducting the Lesson

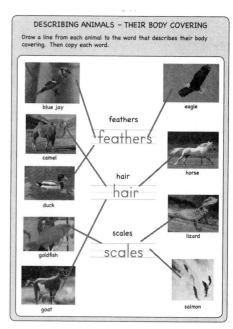

DESCRIBING ANIMALS – THEIR BODY COVERING
Draw a line from each animal to the word that describes their body covering. Then copy each word.

Teacher Comment: **Name the animal in the first picture.**
Student Response: That animal is a blue jay.
Teacher Comment: **What covers a blue jay's body?**
Student Response: The blue jay is covered with feathers.
Teacher Comment: **Draw a line from the blue jay to the word "feathers," then copy the word "feathers."**

Teacher Comment: **Name the animal in the second picture.**
Student Response: That animal is a camel.
Teacher Comment: **What covers a camel's body?**
Student Response: The camel is covered with hair.
Teacher Comment: **Draw a line from the camel to the word "hair," then copy the word "hair."**

• Check students' work. Continue this dialog to discuss students' answers.

Thinking About Thinking

Teacher Comment: **How did you decide the body covering of each animal?**
Student Response:
1. I looked at the body covering of the animal in the picture.
2. I matched what I know about the body covering of birds, mammals, and fish to what I saw in the pictures.
3. I found the word for the body covering for that animal.
4. I copied the word for each type of body covering.

Personal Application

Teacher Comment: **When is it important to know the body covering of an animal?**
Student Response: I need to know the body covering of an animal to know how it keeps warm and protects itself from danger or injury.

Page 92 - DESCRIBING ANIMALS – THEIR HOMES

LESSON

Introduction
Teacher Comment: **We have described how animals move.**

Stating the Objective
Teacher Comment: **In this lesson you will match animals to their homes. Some farm animals sleep in barns that farmers build. Some animals use a hole in a tree or a hole in the ground as their home. Some animals build their own homes. Draw a line from each animal to its home.**

Conducting the Lesson
Teacher Comment: **Name the animal shown in the first picture.**
    Student Response: That animal is an owl.

Teacher Comment: **Which picture shows the home of an owl?**
    Student Response: The owl lives in a hole in a tree.

Teacher Comment: **How does a hole in the tree protect the owl from weather or danger?**
    Student Response: The thick wood of the tree makes a warm place for the owl to live and protects the owl and its babies from other animals.

Teacher Comment: **Draw a line from the owl to the hole in the tree.**

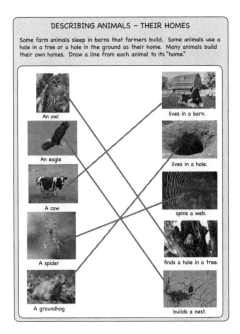

DESCRIBING ANIMALS – THEIR HOMES

Some farm animals sleep in barns that farmers build. Some animals use a hole in a tree or a hole in the ground as their home. Many animals build their own homes. Draw a line from each animal to its "home."

An owl — lives in a barn.
An eagle — lives in a hole.
A cow — spins a web.
A spider — finds a hole in a tree.
A groundhog — builds a nest.

• Check students' work. Continue this dialog to discuss students' answers.

Thinking About Thinking
Teacher Comment: **What did you think about to match an animal to its home?**
    Student Response:
    1. I named the animal.
    2. I looked at the land or air around it.
    3. I remembered what I know about the animal's needs.
    4. I found the home that fits the animal's needs and the place where it lives.

Personal Application
Teacher Comment. **When is it important to know where animals live?**
    Student Response: I need to learn about animal homes to understand how their home fits their needs for shelter and protection.

Page 93 - DESCRIBING ANIMALS – THEIR HABITATS

LESSON

Introduction

Teacher Comment: **We have matched animals to their homes. Another way to tell where an animal lives is to describe its habitat. Its habitat is the land form or body of water where an animal lives. Some animals live on the land. Some animals live in or near a body of water.**

Stating the Objective

Teacher Comment: **In this lesson you will match animals to their habitats. Draw a line from each animal to its habitat.**

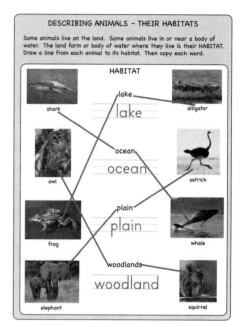

Conducting the Lesson

Teacher Comment: **Name the animal shown in the first picture.**
  Student Response: That animal is a shark.
Teacher Comment: **Where does a shark live?**
  Student Response: A shark lives in the ocean.
Teacher Comment: **Draw a line from the picture of the shark to the word "ocean," then copy the word on the lines provided.**

• Check students' work. Continue this dialog to discuss students answers

Thinking About Thinking

Teacher Comment: **What did you think about to match an animal to its habitat?**
  Student Response:
  1. I named the animal.
  2. I looked at the land or water around it.
  3. I remembered whether the place where it lives is wet or dry, small or open.

Personal Application

Teacher Comment. **When is it important to understand where an animal lives?**
  Student Response. I need to know where an animal lives to understand what it needs to survive.

Page 94 - DESCRIBING AN ANIMAL

LESSON

Introduction
Teacher Comment: **In the last lesson we learned about animal habitats.**

Stating the Objective
Teacher Comment: **In this lesson you will complete a paragraph that describes a turtle. A paragraph is a group of sentences that tell more about an animal than we can say in one sentence.**

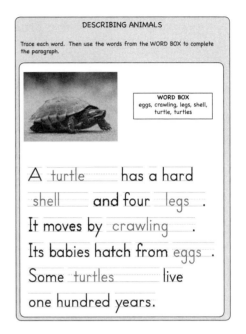

DESCRIBING ANIMALS

Trace each word. Then use the words from the WORD BOX to complete the paragraph.

WORD BOX
eggs, crawling, legs, shell,
turtle, turtles

A turtle has a hard shell and four legs. It moves by crawling. Its babies hatch from eggs. Some turtles live one hundred years.

Conducting the Lesson
Teacher Comment: **Name the animal in the picture.**
Student Response: The animal is a turtle.
Teacher Comment: **Write the word "turtle" in the first blank.**

• Give students time to write.

Teacher Comment: **What is the hard part that the turtle has on its back?**
Student Response: The turtle has a shell on its back.
Teacher Comment: **Write the word "shell" in the second blank.**

Teacher Comment: **Think about what you know about a turtle. Read the sample sentences to decide which words are missing. Find the words in the WORD BOX that tell about the turtle. Write the words in the blanks.**

• Check students' work.

Thinking About Thinking
Teacher Comment: **What did you pay attention to when you described a turtle?**
Student Response:
1. I remembered details about a turtle.
2. I looked for the words that tell about a turtle.
3. I wrote the words that complete a whole paragraph about the turtle.

Personal Application
Teacher Comment: **When is it important to describe an animal?**
Student Response: I need to know how to describe an animal to tell or write about them.

Page 95 - DESCRIBING PARTS OF A BEE

LESSON

Introduction
Teacher Comment: **To describe animals we sometimes need to know the parts of the animal and to explain how each part is important for the animal to be healthy and to survive.**

Stating the Objective
Teacher Comment: **In this lesson we will think about the parts of a bee, what each part does, and what would happen to the bee if that part was missing or damaged.**

PARTS OF A BEE

Look at the picture of the bee. Then complete each sentence with one of the words from the WORD BOX.

WORD BOX
antenna, eye, mouth, stinger, wing

This part is very large. It helps the bee find the flowers. It is called the ___eye___.

This part lets the bee fly from flower to flower. It is called the ___wing___.

This part looks like a long hair. It helps the bee find food by feeling the flower. It is called the ___antenna___.

Through this part the bee collects juice from flowers which it makes into honey. It is called the ___mouth___.

This part protects the bee from other animals. It is called the ___stinger___.

Tell your teacher or partner why each part is important. What would happen if that part was missing or damaged?

Conducting the Lesson
Teacher Comment: **What part of the bee is needed for it to find the flowers?**
Student Response: The bee needs eyes to see the part of the flower where it gets its food.
Teacher Comment: **Write the word "eye" on the first top blank.**
Teacher Comment: **What would happen if the eyes were missing or damaged?**
Student Response: The bee could not find food.

Teacher Comment: **What part of the bee is needed for it to fly?**
Student Response: The bee needs wings to fly and to find food and to get away from danger.
Teacher Comment: **Write the word "wings" on the second top blank.**
Teacher Comment: **What would happen if the wings were missing or damaged?**
Student Response: The bee could not fly. It could not find food or escape from animals that could harm it.

Teacher Comment: **This part is long and thin. It helps the bee to feel the flower and to find food inside it. What is it?**
Student Response: This part is the antenna.
Teacher Comment: **Write the word "antenna" on the third blank.**
Teacher Comment: **What would happen if the antenna was missing?**
Student Response: The bee could not feel the flower to get food.

Teacher Comment: **What part of the bee collects nectar from the flower?**
Student Response: The mouth of the bee collects nectar from the flower.
Teacher Comment: **Write the word "mouth" on the fourth blank.**

Teacher Comment: **What would happen if the mouth was missing?**
Student Response: The bee could not collect its food.

Teacher Comment: **What part of the bee protects it from other animals?**
 Student Response: The stinger protects the bee.
Teacher Comment: **Write the word "stinger" on the last blank.**
Teacher Comment: **What would happen if the stinger was missing or damaged?**
 Student Response: The bee could not protect itself.

Thinking About Thinking
Teacher Comment: **What did you think about to describe the parts of an animal?**
 Student Response:
 1. I looked at each part and named it correctly.
 2. I remembered what each part does.
 3. I thought about what each part did to help the animal be healthy and safe.

Personal Application
Teacher Comment: **When is it important to describe the parts of an animal?**
 Student Response: I need know how to describe the parts of an animal correctly to tell a story about it.

Page 96 - KINDS OF ANIMALS
TEACHING SUGGESTIONS
• Use the terms "groups," "types," "kinds," and "classes" to help students conceptualize classification. Encourage students to use these words in their discussions.

• Have students prepare a bulletin board display with pictures of animals that belong to the various classes. See the appendix for a central idea graphic.

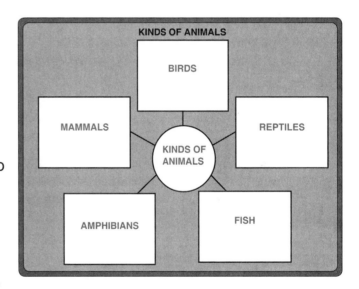

LESSON

Introduction
Teacher Comment: **Amphibians are egg-laying animals that can live on land or in water and usually have smooth skin. Fish are egg-laying animals that live in water and have scaly skin. Reptiles are egg-laying animals that have scaly skin and move on land by crawling.**

Stating the Objective
Teacher Comment: **In this lesson you will classify three kinds of animals; amphibians, fish, and reptiles.**

Conducting the Lesson
Teacher Comment: **Name the animal in the first picture.**
 Student Response: That animal is a frog.
Teacher Comment: **The picture shows a frog in the water. A frog can live on land or in water. What kind of animal is a frog?**

Student Response: A frog is an amphibian.
Teacher Comment: **How do know that the frog is an amphibian?**
Student Response: I know that the frog is an amphibian because its skin is smooth and because it can live on land or in water.
Teacher Comment: **Write the word "amphibian" in the blank beside the frog.**

Teacher Comment: **Name the animal in the second picture.**
Student Response: That animal is a lizard.
Teacher Comment: **What kind of skin does the lizard have?**
Student Response: The lizard has scaly skin.
Teacher Comment: **What kind of animal is the lizard?**
Student Response: The lizard is a reptile.
Teacher Comment: **How do you know that the lizard is reptile?**
Student Response: The lizard lives on land and has scaly skin.
Teacher Comment: **Write the word "reptile" in the blank beside the lizard.**

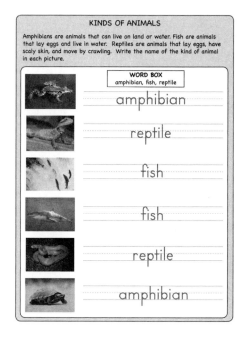

KINDS OF ANIMALS

Amphibians are animals that can live on land or water. Fish are animals that lay eggs and live in water. Reptiles are animals that lay eggs, have scaly skin, and move by crawling. Write the name of the kind of animal in each picture.

WORD BOX
amphibian, fish, reptile

amphibian
reptile
fish
fish
reptile
amphibian

Teacher Comment: **Name the animal in the third picture.**
Student Response: That animal is a salmon.
Teacher Comment: **What kind of animal is a salmon?**
Student Response: The salmon is a fish.
Teacher Comment: **How do you know that the salmon is a fish?**
Student Response: I know that the salmon is a fish because it has scaly skin and lives in water.
Teacher Comment: **Write the word "fish" in the blank beside the salmon.**

• Check students' work. Continue this dialog to discuss students' answers.

Thinking About Thinking

Teacher Comment: **What did you think about to classify an animal?**
Student Response:
1. I named the animal.
2. I looked at its skin and surroundings.
3. I remembered whether its habitat is wet or dry.
4. I found the word that describes that kind of animal.

Personal Application

Teacher Comment. **When is it important to classify an animal?**
Student Response. I need to classify an animal to describe it and understand what it needs to survive.

Page 97 - KINDS OF ANIMALS

LESSON

TEACHING SUGGESTION
When observing the picture of the ant students may confuse the antennas for another pair legs. As you start the lesson, count the number of legs and emphasize that the small threads of the antennae grow out of the ant's head, not its body.

Introduction
Teacher Comment: **We have learned to classify animals as amphibians, fish, or reptiles.**

Stating the Objective
Teacher Comment: **In this lesson you will classify three more kinds of animals: insects, birds, and mammals. Insects are small animals with six legs and antennae. Birds lay eggs and have feathers and wings. Mammals have hair. Mammal mothers carry their babies inside their bodies and make milk to feed their babies after they are born. You will write the word for the kind of animal in the picture.**

Conducting the Lesson
Teacher Comment: **Name the animal in the first picture.**
  Student Response: That animal is an ant.
Teacher Comment: **What kind of animal is an ant?**
  Student Response: The ant is an insect.
Teacher Comment: **How do you know that an ant is an insect?**
  Student Response: An ant is a small animal with six legs and two antennae.
Teacher Comment: **Write the word "insect" in the blank beside the ant.**

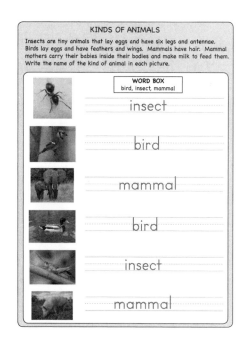

KINDS OF ANIMALS

Insects are tiny animals that lay eggs and have six legs and antennae. Birds lay eggs and have feathers and wings. Mammals have hair. Mammal mothers carry their babies inside their bodies and make milk to feed them. Write the name of the kind of animal in each picture.

WORD BOX
bird, insect, mammal

insect
bird
mammal
bird
insect
mammal

Teacher Comment: **Name the animal in the second picture.**
  Student Response: That animal is a blue jay.
Teacher Comment: **What kind of animal is a blue jay?**
  Student Response: The blue jay is a bird.
Teacher Comment: **How do you know that a blue jay is a bird?**
  Student Response: The blue jay has feathers and wings.
Teacher Comment: **Write the word "bird" in the blank beside the blue jay.**

Teacher Comment: **Name the animal in the third picture.**
  Student Response: That animal is an elephant.
Teacher Comment: **What kind of animal is an elephant?**

Student Response: The elephant is a mammal.

Teacher Comment: **How do you know that an elephant is a mammal?**

Student Response: This elephant gave live birth to the young elephant by its side. It has hair on its skin, not feathers or scales.

Teacher Comment: **Write the word "mammal" in the blank beside the elephant.**

• Check students' work. Continue this dialog to discuss students' answers.

Thinking About Thinking

Teacher Comment: **What did you think about to classify an animal?**

Student Response:

1. I named the animal.
2. I looked at its skin, its body parts, and its surroundings.
3. I remembered whether its habitat is wet or dry.
4. I found the word for that kind of animal.

Personal Application

Teacher Comment. **When is it important to classify an animal?**

Student Response. I need to know the class of an animal to describe it and to understand what it needs to survive.

Pages 98 - SIMILAR ANIMALS

LESSON

Introduction

Teacher Comment: **We have described animals different ways.**

Stating the Objective

Teacher Comment: **In this lesson you will find an animal that is most like another one.**

Conducting the Lesson

Teacher Comment: **Name the animals in the example.**

Student Response: The animals are a zebra, a pig, a giraffe, and a horse.

Teacher Comment: **You are going to select the animal that is most like the zebra. Tell your partner all the important things that you know about a zebra.**

Student Response: A zebra is a wild animal with stripes. It has four legs, hooves, a short mane, and a tail.

Teacher Comment: **Which animal on the right is most like a zebra?**

Student Response: The horse is most like a zebra.

Teacher Comment: **What clues let you know that horse is most like a zebra?**

Answers will vary.
See page 21 for examples.

EXAMPLE

REASON: The zebra and horse are large mammals with four legs, hooves, a mane, and a tail. They eat grass or hay. The zebra and horse are not short and fat like the pig, nor do they have long necks like the giraffe.

Student Response: Both have four legs, hooves, hair, a mane, and a tail
Teacher Comment: **How are the other animals different from the horse and zebra?**
Student Response: The pig does not have stripes and does not have a mane. The giraffe is much taller than a zebra and has spots, not stripes.

Teacher Comment: **Name the animals shown in the second row.**
Student Response: The animals are a chicken, an ostrich, a turkey, and an owl.
Teacher Comment: **Tell your partner the important things you know about a chicken.**
Student Response: A chicken is a medium-sized bird with short legs. It has a short neck and it lives on a farm. People eat chicken prepared many ways.
Teacher Comment: **Which animal is most like a chicken?**
Student Response: A turkey is most like a chicken.
Teacher Comment: **What clues let you know that a turkey is most like an chicken?**
Student Response: Both are medium-sized birds with short legs and are commonly eaten.
Teacher Comment: **How are the other birds different from a chicken?**
Student Response: The ostrich is a large bird with very long legs and a very long, thin neck. The owl's neck and legs are almost too short to see.
Teacher Comment: **Circle the picture of the turkey.**

Teacher Comment: **Name the animals shown in the third row.**
Student Response: The animals are a lizard, a frog, a spider, and an alligator.
Teacher Comment: **Tell your partner the important things you know about a lizard.**
Student Response: A lizard is a reptile that lives in dry areas. The scales on its skin protect it. It eats small animals. It has a long tail and four legs with claws on the ends.
Teacher Comment: **Which animal is most like a lizard?**
Student Response: An alligator is most like a lizard because it is a reptile. It has a very long body, a long tail, and four legs with claws on the end.
Teacher Comment: **How are the other animals different from a lizard?**
Student Response: Neither the frog nor the spider are reptiles. Neither has a tail. A spider has eight legs. The frog is an amphibian with smooth skin.
Teacher Comment: **Circle the picture of the alligator.**

Teacher Comment: **Name the animals in the last row.**
Student Response: The animals are a cow, an elephant, a camel, and a goat.
Teacher Comment: **Tell your partner the important things you know about a cow.**
Student Response: A cow is a large mammal that lives on a farm and produces milk that we drink and make into cheese and butter.
Teacher Comment: **Which animal is most like a cow?**
Student Response: A goat is most like a cow because it is a mammal that produces milk that people drink and make into cheese. Both animals live on farms.
Teacher Comment: **How are the other animals different from a cow?**
Student Response: An elephant and a camel are not used to produce dairy products. They do not live on farms.

Thinking About Thinking
Teacher Comment: **What kind of characteristics did you discuss to describe the animals?**
Student Response:
1. I named the animals.
2. I thought about the type of animal (mammal, reptile, bird, etc.).
3. I thought about where the animals live and what they eat.
4. I compared the animals to determine which one was most like the given animal.

Page 99 - SIMILARITIES AND DIFFERENCES – ANIMALS

TEACHING SUGGESTIONS

• Emphasize the wording commonly used to describe similarities and differences. Repeat words that show similarity (both, and, like, similar, resemble, etc.) and encourage students to use them in their responses. Explain the term "unlike" and encourage students use words that cue differences (but, not, different, opposite, and unlike).

• To reinforce students' responses you may draw a compare and contrast diagram to record their answers. For a blank compare-and-contrast graphic organizer, see the appendix.

• Students may need reminders that a bat is the only mammal that can fly. What appear to be wings are actually arms. At the end of the arms are hands with long fingers that have skin growing between them. When the bat opens its fingers, the stretched skin acts like wings. A bat eats insects and flies from tree to tree. When flying at night a bat "sees" by screeching and listening for the echo like an airplane that uses radar.

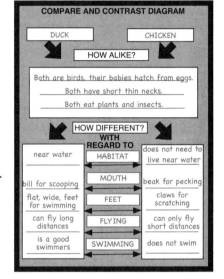

LESSON

Introduction

Teacher Comment: **We have compared animals by describing how they are alike. Sometimes we want to know how they are different in order to understand something important about them. When we describe how animals are different, we contrast them.**

Stating the Objective

Teacher Comment: **In this lesson we will compare and contrast different animals.**

Conducting the Lesson

Teacher Comment: **Name the two animals in the top box.**
Student Response: They are an owl and a bat.
Teacher Comment: **Find the words in the WORD BOX to name these animals. Write the words in the blanks.**

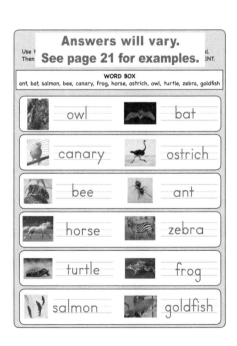

Teacher Comment: **How are an owl and a bat alike?**
Student Response: Both animals fly and are active at night.
Teacher Comment: **How are these two animals different?**
Student Response: An owl is a bird; a bat is a mammal.

Teacher Comment: **Name the two animals in the second box.**
Student Response: They are a canary and an ostrich.
Teacher Comment: **Find the words in the WORD BOX that name these animals. Write the words in the blanks.**

Teacher Comment: **How are a canary and an ostrich alike?**
Student Response: Both a canary and an ostrich are birds.

Teacher Comment: **How are these two animals different?**
Student Response: The canary is a small bird that flies fast. An ostrich is a large bird that can run fast but cannot fly.

Teacher Comment: **Name the two animals in the third box.**
Student Response: They are a bee and an ant.
Teacher Comment: **Find the words in the WORD BOX that name these animals. Write the words in the blanks.**
Teacher Comment: **How are a bee an ant alike?**
Student Response: A bee and an ant are insects that live in large groups.
Teacher Comment: **How are these two animals different?**
Student Response: The bee produces honey from nectar it gathers from flowers. Bees live in hives above ground. Ants live in colonies below ground.

Teacher Comment: **Name the two animals in the fourth box.**
Student Response: They are a horse and a zebra.
Teacher Comment: **Find the words in the WORD BOX that name these animals. Write the words in the blanks.**
Teacher Comment: **How are a horse and zebra alike?**
Student Response: They both are large mammals with four legs, hooves, a mane, and a tail.
Teacher Comment: **How are these two animals different?**
Student Response: Horses are found on farms. Zebras are wild animals that can be seen at the zoo. Zebras are striped. Horses are not striped.

Teacher Comment: **Name the two animals in the fifth box.**
Student Response: They are a turtle and a frog.
Teacher Comment: **Find the words in the WORD BOX that name these animals. Write the words in the blanks.**
Teacher Comment: **How are a turtle and a frog alike?**
Student Response: They both lay eggs and live near the water.

Teacher Comment: **How are these two animals different?**
Student Response: The turtle is a reptile. It has a hard shell. The frog is an amphibian and has thin, soft skin.

Teacher Comment: **Name the two animals in the last box.**

Student Response: They are a salmon and a goldfish.

Teacher Comment: **Find the words in the WORD BOX that name these animals. Write the words in the blanks.**

Teacher Comment: **How are salmon and goldfish alike?**

Student Response: The salmon and goldfish are fish.

Teacher Comment: **How are these two animals different?**

Student Response: The salmon is a large fish that lives in the ocean. A goldfish is a small fish that lives in fresh water.

Thinking About Thinking

Teacher Comment: **What did you think about to compare and contrast animals?**

Student Response:

1. I remembered the important characteristics of each of the animals (appearance, body structure, how it gives birth).
2. I thought about how the animals are alike.
3. I thought about how the animals are different.

Personal Application

Teacher Comment: **When is it important to understand how different animals are alike or different?**

Student Response: I need to understand how animals are alike or different to tell or write about them.

Page 100 - COMPARING ANIMALS

TEACHING SUGGESTION

Emphasize sentence structure that shows comparison. For example, a duck is <u>larger than</u> a canary, <u>but smaller than</u> a turkey.

LESSON

Introduction

Teacher Comment: **We have described animals by their size.**

Stating the Objective

Teacher Comment: **In this lesson you will arrange animals in order of their size from smallest to largest.**

Conducting the Lesson

Teacher Comment: **Name the three mammals in the top box.**

Student Response: They are a squirrel, a giraffe, and a pig.

Teacher Comment: **Which animal is the smallest?**

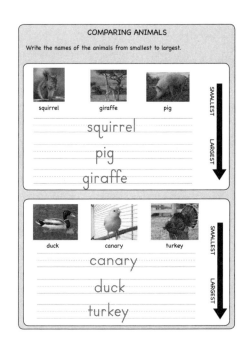

Student Response: The squirrel is the smallest animal.
Teacher Comment: **Write the word "squirrel"on the top line**.
Teacher Comment: **Which animal is the largest?**
Student Response: The giraffe is the largest.
Teacher Comment: **Write the word "giraffe" on the bottom line.**

Teacher Comment: **Which animal is larger than a squirrel, but smaller than a giraffe?**
Student Response: The pig is larger than a squirrel, but smaller than giraffe.
Teacher Comment: **Write the word "pig" on the middle line.**

Teacher Comment: **Name the three birds in the bottom box.**
Student Response: They are a duck, a canary, and a turkey.

Teacher Comment: **Which bird is the smallest?**
Student Response: The canary is the smallest.
Teacher Comment: **Write the word "canary"on the top line**.

Teacher Comment: **Which bird is the largest?**
Student Response: The turkey is the largest.
Teacher Comment: **Write the word "turkey" on the bottom line.**

Teacher Comment: **Which bird is larger than a canary, but smaller than a turkey?**
Student Response: A duck is larger than a canary, but smaller than a turkey.
Teacher Comment: **Write the word "duck" on the middle line.**

Thinking About Thinking
Teacher Comment: **What did you think about to put animals in a particular order?**
Student Response:
1. I decided which animal was the smallest.
2. I decided which animal was the largest.
3. I decided which animal was in-between the smallest and the largest.

Personal Application
Teacher Comment: **When is it important to understand the size of animals?**
Student Response: I need to understand the size of animals to know how much food or space they need.

Page 101 - KINDS OF ANIMALS

TEACHING SUGGESTIONS

- Use the terms "groups," "types," "kind of," and "classes" to help students conceptualize classification. Encourage students to use these words in their discussions.
- Remind students of the characteristics of amphibians, birds, fish, mammals, and reptiles. The glossary at the end of the student book has a definition of terms. Enlist students in preparing a bulletin board display with pictures of animals that belong to the various classes.

LESSON

Introduction

Teacher Comment: **When we discussed kinds of animals such as amphibians, birds, fish, insects, mammals, and reptiles, we were classifying them.**

Stating the Objective

Teacher Comment: **In this lesson you will match each animal to its kind (class).**

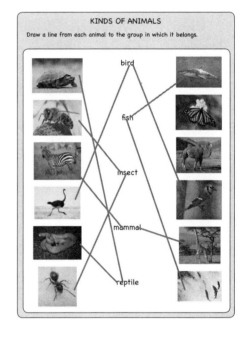

Conducting the Lesson

Teacher Comment: **What is the animal in the first picture?**

Student Response: That animal is a turtle.

Teacher Comment: **What do you know about a turtle?**

Student Response: A turtle lays eggs and has scaly skin. It crawls slowly. Some turtles live on land; some live in the water. Turtles breathe air.

Teacher Comment: **What kind of animal is a turtle?**

Student Response: A turtle is a reptile.

Teacher Comment: **Draw a line from the turtle to the word "reptile."**

Teacher Comment: **Name the second animal.**

Student Response: That animal is a bee.

Teacher Comment: **What do you know about a bee?**

Student Response: A bee is a tiny animal that lives in large groups. It hatches from eggs. It flies fast and has a stinger for protection. Its antennas helps it find food. It collects nectar from flowers to make honey to feed the group.

Teacher Comment: **What kind of animal is a bee?**

Student Response: A bee is an insect.

Teacher Comment: **Draw a line from the picture of the bee to the word "insect."**

Teacher Comment: **Name the third animal.**

Student Response: That animal is a zebra.

Teacher Comment: **What do you know about a zebra?**

Student Response: A zebra is a large animal with four hoofed feet. It looks like a horse, but it has a short mane and black and white stripes. Its babies are born, not hatched. They drink milk from the mother. A zebra is a wild animal that lives in open grasslands of Africa. We see zebras in zoos.

Teacher Comment: **What kind of animal is a zebra?**

Student Response: A zebra is a mammal.

Teacher Comment: **Draw a line from the zebra to the word "mammal."**

Teacher Comment: **Name the animal in the fourth picture.**

Student Response: That animal is an ostrich.

Teacher Comment: **What do you know about an ostrich?**

Student Response: An ostrich is the largest bird. It has small wings, but cannot fly. It runs very fast. Its long neck and long legs allow it to eat the leaves of small trees. It lays large eggs. It is a wild animal that lives in the grasslands of Africa. We see ostriches in zoos.

Teacher Comment: **What kind of animal is an ostrich?**

Student Response: An ostrich is a bird.

Teacher Comment: **Draw a line from the ostrich to the word "bird."**

Teacher Comment: **Name the fifth animal.**

Student Response: That animal is a snake.

Teacher Comment: **What do you know about a snake?**

Student Response: A snake is a cold-blooded animal that lays eggs. It has scaly skin.

Teacher Comment: **What kind of animal is a snake?**

Student Response: A snake is a reptile.

Teacher Comment: **Draw a line from the snake to the word "reptile."**

• Check students work. Continue this dialog to discuss students' answers.

Thinking About Thinking

Teacher Comment: **What did you think about to match each animal to its kind?**

Student Response:

1. I looked at the animal and thought about its body and its habitat.
2. I remembered whether its babies hatch or are born from the mother.
3. I remembered how it moves and gets food.
4. I fit these characteristics to the definition of that kind of animal.
5. I looked for the word for that kind of animal.

Personal Application

Teacher Comment: **When is it important to know kinds of animals.**

Student Response: I need to know kinds of animals to describe them correctly and to read or write about them.

Page 102 - A DIFFERENT KIND OF ANIMAL

LESSON

TEACHING SUGGESTION

Students may need reminders that a bat is the only mammal that can fly. What appear to be wings are actually arms. At the end of the arms are hands with long fingers that have skin growing between them. When the bat opens its fingers, the stretched skin acts like wings. A bat eats insects and flies from tree to tree. When flying at night a bat "sees" by screeching and listening for the echo like an airplane that uses radar.

A DIFFERENT KIND OF ANIMAL

Three of these animals are the same kind. Circle the animal that is different. Then explain your answer to your partner or teacher.

EXAMPLE

REASON: A grasshopper, the ant, and the bee are insects. The canary is a bird.

Introduction
Teacher Comment: **We have named different kinds of animals.**

Stating the Objective
Teacher Comment: **In this lesson you will identify an animal that is not like the others of that kind.**

Conducting the Lesson
Teacher Comment: **Name the animals in the first row.**
Student Response: These animals are a grasshopper, an ant, a bee, and a canary.

Teacher Comment: **How are three of these animals alike?**
Student Response: The grasshopper, ant and bee are insects. They have six legs and antennae.

Teacher Comment: **Notice that the canary has been circled. The canary is a bird, not an insect.**

Teacher Comment: **Name the animals in the second row.**
Student Response: These animals are a bat, an eagle, an owl, and a blue jay.

Teacher Comment: **How are three of these animals alike?**
Student Response: The eagle, owl, and blue jay are birds. They have feathers and wings. Their babies hatch from eggs.
Teacher Comment: **Which animal is not a bird?**
Student Response: A bat is not a bird, it is a mammal. It does not have feathers or lay eggs.
Teacher Comment: **Circle the bat.**

• Continue this dialog for the last three rows of animals.

Thinking About Thinking

Teacher Comment: **What did you think about when you decided which animal was not like the others?**

Student Response:

1. I looked at the picture of each animal and identified whether it was a bird, insect, mammal, or reptile.
2. I found three animals that were the same kind.
3. I identified the animal that does not fit that group and explained why.

Personal Application

Teacher Comment. **When is it important to understand how an animal may be different from others?**

Student Response. I need to know how an animal may be different from others in order to understand how its body and needs are different.

Page 103 - CLASSIFYING ANIMALS

LESSON

Introduction

Teacher Comment: **When we describe kinds of animals, we are putting them in the same class. We call ourselves a "class." All the students in this class are about the same age, are in the same grade, and have the same teacher. When we describe animals by the same important characteristics, we are classifying them.**

Stating the Objective

Teacher Comment: **In this lesson you will look at pictures of three animals and decide to which class they belong.**

Conducting the Lesson

Teacher Comment: **The first class of animals are mammals. This group of mammals have hooves. A hoof is a hard covering on the foot of the animal that protects the animal from injury when it runs. Find the word "mammals" in the WORD BOX and write it on the lines below the word "class." Discuss with your partner how these hoofed mammals are alike.**

Student Response: They have four long, thin legs. They can run really fast. Their heads, necks, bodies, and legs are in about the same positions. They eat grass or leaves.

Teacher Comment: **Use words in the WORD BOX to write the examples of mammals in the box marked "EXAMPLES."**

Teacher Comment: **Name the animals in the bottom box.**
Student Response: These animals are a blue jay, a canary, and a turkey.

Teacher Comment: **With your partner discuss how these animals are alike.**
Student Response: They lay eggs. Most of them live on land. They eat insects or grain. They move by flying or walking.

Teacher Comment: **What word can we use to describe all these animals**?
Student Response: All these animals are birds.

Teacher Comment: **Write the word "birds" on the line marked CLASS.**

Teacher Comment: **Use words in the WORD BOX to write the examples of birds in the box marked "EXAMPLES."**

Thinking About Thinking

Teacher Comment: **What characteristics did you think about to classify these animals?**
Student Response: I thought about body structure, size, whether it hatches or gives live birth, where it lives, how it moves, what it eats.

Personal Application

Teacher Comment: **When is it important to classify animals?**
Student Response: I need to classify animals to understand their needs and to tell them apart from other kinds of animals that we find at the zoo or the pet store.

Page 104 - CLASSIFYING ANIMALS - SORTING

LESSON

Introduction
Teacher Comment: **We have named classes of animals.**

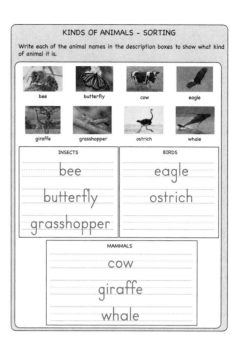

Stating the Objective
Teacher Comment: **In this lesson you will sort animals into three classes: birds, insects, and mammals.**

Conducting the Lesson
Teacher Comment: **Name the first animal shown in the pictures in the first row.**
Student Response: That animal is a bee.

Teacher Comment: **Is a bee a bird, an insect, or a mammal?**
Student Response: The bee is an insect.
Teacher Comment: **Write the word "bee" in the insect box.**

• Check students work. Continue this dialog to discuss students' answers.

Thinking About Thinking
Teacher Comment: **What did you think about to classify an animal?**
Student Response:
1. I named the animal.
2. I looked at its skin, its body parts, and its surroundings.
3. I remembered whether its habitat is wet or dry.
4. I wrote the word for it in its class.

Personal Application
Teacher Comment. **When is it important to classify an animal?**
Student Response. I need to classify an animal to describe them and to remember what they need to survive.

CHAPTER TEN – THINKING ABOUT FAMILY MEMBERS
(Pages 105-118)

GENERAL INTRODUCTION

CURRICULUM APPLICATIONS
Social Studies: Examine roles of family members and cite examples of interdependence; examine the roles of various family members in celebrating holidays and traditions across cultures
Social Studies: Identify similarities and differences among people

MENTAL MODEL
A mental model outlines the characteristics that one must state to describe or define a concept. After completing this chapter, each student will have applied this mental model to family members in the lessons. A mental model helps a student:
- Anticipate what he or she needs to know to understand a family member
- Remember the characteristics of a family members
- State a clear definition or write an adequate description of a family members
- Explain a family member to someone else

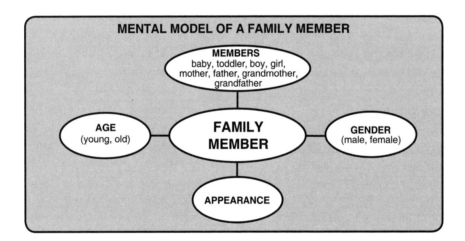

Page 106-107 - NAMING FAMILY MEMBERS

LESSON

Introduction

Teacher Comment: **We know that members of a family need each other. We will study how they are related and why each person is important to the family.**

Stating the Objective

Teacher Comment: **In this lesson you will name family members by matching a picture to the word for that family member.**

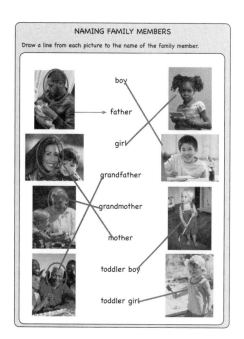

Conducting the Lesson

Teacher Comment: **Name the family member shown in the first picture.**

Student Response: That family member is a father.

Teacher Comment: **What clues let you know that he is a father?**

Student Response: He is a man and he's holding a baby.

Teacher Comment: **Draw a line from the picture of the father to the word "father."**

Teacher Comment: **Look at each picture. Find the word for that family member. Draw a line to connect them.**

• Check students' work.

Teacher Comment: **Look at each picture. Find the word for each family member In the WORD BOX. Write it on the blank below its picture.**

Thinking About Thinking

Teacher Comment: **How did you decide which word belonged with each picture?**

Student Response:

1. I looked at the details in the picture and named the family member.
2. I looked for the word in the WORD BOX that describes the family member.
3. I wrote the word for the family member on the blank.

Personal Application

Teacher Comment: **When is it important to write the words for family members?**

Student Response: I need to know the words for family member names to tell or write about them.

Page 108 - DESCRIBING FAMILY MEMBERS

LESSON

Introduction

Teacher Comment: **In the last lesson we wrote the words for family members.**

Stating the Objective

Teacher Comment: **In this lesson you will complete a paragraph that describes a family member. A paragraph is a group of sentences about a subject. A paragraph gives us much more information about a family member than we can say in one sentence.**

Conducting the Lesson

Teacher Comment: **Think about what a baby can do. Trace the words on the lines, then find the words in the WORD BOX that complete the sentences. Write the words in the blanks.**

• Check students' work.

Teacher Comment: **Think about what a toddler can do. Trace the words on the lines, then find the words in the WORD BOX that complete the sentences. Write the words in the blanks.**

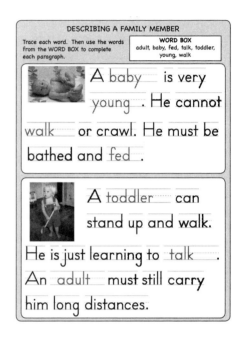

DESCRIBING A FAMILY MEMBER

Trace each word. Then use the words from the WORD BOX to complete each paragraph.

WORD BOX
adult, baby, fed, talk, toddler, young, walk

A baby is very young. He cannot walk or crawl. He must be bathed and fed.

A toddler can stand up and walk. He is just learning to talk. An adult must still carry him long distances.

Thinking About Thinking

Teacher Comment: **What did you pay attention to when you described a child?**
Student Response:
1. I remembered what a child can and cannot do.
2. I looked for the words that tell about a young child.
3. I wrote the words that complete a whole paragraph about the child.

Personal Application

Teacher Comment: **When is it important to describe a family member?**
Student Response: I need to describe a family member to tell or write about them.

Page 109 - DESCRIBING FAMILY MEMBERS

LESSON

Introduction
Teacher Comment: **We have been writing about family members.**

Stating the Objective
Teacher Comment: **In this lesson you will decide whether these family members are grown-up or children. Someone who has grown up is called an adult. Adults can take care of themselves and other people.**

Conducting the Lesson
Teacher Comment: **Name the family member in the first picture.**

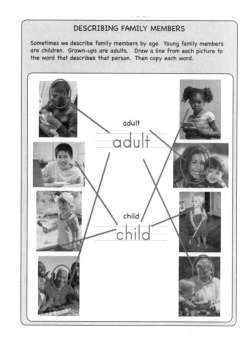

DESCRIBING FAMILY MEMBERS

Sometimes we describe family members by age. Young family members are children. Grown-ups are adults. Draw a line from each picture to the word that describes that person. Then copy each word.

Student Response: That family member is a father.

Teacher Comment: **Is the father an adult or a child?**

Student Response: The father is a grown-up. He is an adult.

Teacher Comment: **Draw a line from the picture of the father to the word "adult." Copy the word "adult."**

Teacher Comment: **Name the family member shown below the father.**

Student Response: That family member is a boy.

Teacher Comment: **Is a boy an adult or a child?**

Student Response: The boy is a child.

Teacher Comment: **Draw a line from the picture of the boy to the word "child." Copy the word "child."**

• Check students' work. Repeat this dialog to discuss students' answers.

Thinking About Thinking
Teacher Comment: **What did you pay attention to in order to decide whether a family member was an adult or a child?**

Student Response:
1. I looked to see whether the family member is young or old.
2. I remembered that grown-up family members are adults and that young family members are children.

Personal Application
Teacher Comment: **When do you need to tell whether a person is an adult or a child?**

Student Response: I need to tell whether a person is an adult or a child to tell or write about them. I need to explain what they can and cannot do and what kind of help they need or can give.

Page 110 - DESCRIBING FAMILY MEMBERS

LESSON

Introduction

Teacher Comment: **We have studied whether family members are adults or children.**

Stating the Objective

Teacher Comment: **In this lesson you will describe whether a family member is male or female.**

Conducting the Lesson

Teacher Comment: **We use the word "gender" to describe whether a person is a man or a woman. Men and boys are males. Women and girls are females.**

Teacher Comment: **The first picture shows a girl. Is the girl a male or a female?**

Student Response: The girl is a female.

Teacher Comment: **Draw a line from the picture of the girl to the word "female." Copy the word "female."**

Teacher Comment: **Name the family member shown below the picture of the girl.**

Student Response: That family member is a mother

Teacher Comment: **What is the gender of the mother?**

Student Response: The mother is a female.

Teacher Comment: **Draw a line from the picture of the mother to the word "female."**

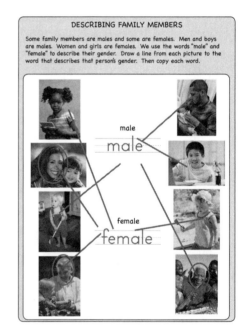

• Check students' work. Repeat this dialog to discuss students' answers.

Thinking About Thinking

Teacher Comment: **What did you pay attention to in order to decide whether a family member was a male or a female?**

Student Response: I looked at their hair and clothing to decide whether the person was male or female.

Personal Application

Teacher Comment: **When do you need to tell whether a person is a male or a female?**

Student Response: I need to describe whether someone is male or female when I tell or write about them.

Page 111 - DESCRIBING FAMILY MEMBERS

LESSON

Introduction

Teacher Comment: **We have studied whether family members are male or female.**

Stating the Objective

Teacher Comment: **In this lesson you will describe family members by their age and gender.**

Conducting the Lesson

Teacher Comment: **In the first sentence we read about the boy and the father. We know that the boy and the father are the same gender. Find the word in the WORD BOX that tells how the boy and the father are alike.**

   Student Response: The boy and the father are males.

Teacher Comment: **Write the word "males" in the first blank.**

Teacher Comment: **In the second sentence we read about the girl and the mother. We know that the girl and the mother are the same gender. Find the word in the WORD BOX that tells how the girl and the mother are alike.**

   Student Response: The girl and the mother are females.

Teacher Comment: **Write the word "females" in the second blank.**

DESCRIBING FAMILY MEMBERS

Use the words from the WORD BOX to complete each sentence.

WORD BOX
adults, children, female, females, male, males, older

The boy and the father are   males   . _gender_

The girl and the mother are   females   . _gender_

The father and mother are   adults   . _adults or children_

The boy and the girl are   children   . _adults or children_

The grandfather is an   older   male   . _age   gender_

The grandmother is an   older   female   . _age   gender_

• Check students' work. Repeat this dialog to discuss students' answers.

Thinking About Thinking

Teacher Comment: **What did you pay attention to in order to tell the age and gender of a person?**

   Student Response: I looked at the hair and clothing to decide the age and gender of a person.

Personal Application

Teacher Comment: **When is it important to compare family members well?**

   Student Response: I need to compare family members to relate incidents that happen at home, to explain how each family member helps the family meet its needs, to introduce family members to friends, or to tell or write stories about family members.

Page 112 - SIMILAR FAMILY MEMBERS

TEACHING SUGGESTION
Emphasize words that show similarity (both, and, like, similar, resemble, etc.) and encourage students to use them in their responses. Explain the term "unlike" and encourage students use words that describe differences (but, not, different, opposite, and unlike).

LESSON

Introduction
Teacher Comment: **One way that we describe family members is to explain how they are like other family members.**

Stating the Objective
Teacher Comment: **In this lesson we will identify family members that are most like others in the family.**

Conducting the Lesson
Teacher Comment: **The first picture shows a toddler. Let's think about what we know about a toddler. Toddlers are two years old or younger. They can still be lifted and carried, but are heavier than infants. They are learning to talk. When they walk by themselves, they are not steady. That's how they get the name "toddler." A toddler has some teeth and can eat many foods by themselves if it is cut into small pieces. Toddlers can recognize their family and know where to find things in their home.**

Teacher Comment: **What family member is most like a toddler?**

Student Response: A baby is most like a toddler.

Teacher Comment: **How is a baby most like a toddler?**

Student Response: Babies and toddlers are very young children, and must be cared for by an adult. A baby needs diapers. Sometimes a toddler needs diapers, too. Both like to play, smile, and talk, and often take naps during the day.

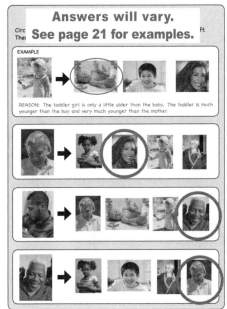

Teacher Comment: **What clues let you know that a baby is most like a toddler?**

Student Response: The small size of the baby and the toddler tells me that both are very young children. Both the toddler and the baby are just learning to do things that other members of the family already know how to do.

Teacher Comment: **How are the boy and mother not like the toddler and the baby?**

Student Response: The boy and mother are older. They take care, or help take care of the baby and the toddler. They already know how to do the things that people need to know in order to take care of themselves.

Teacher Comment: **In the second row you see a picture of a grandmother. Tell your partner all the important things that you know about a grandmother.**

Teacher Comment: **What do you know about a grandmother?**

Student Response: A grandmother is an older woman whose son or daughter is a father or mother. Sometimes grandmothers take care of their grandchildren. Grandmothers remember events and places that younger members of the family may not know.

Teacher Comment: **Which family member is most like a grandmother?**

Student Response: A mother is most like a grandmother.

Teacher Comment: **How is a mother most like a grandmother?**

Student Response: Both a mother and a grandmother are women who have a son or daughter. Both a mother and a grandmother take care of children. Both a mother and a grandmother help children get food, keep them clean and safe, and teach children how to take care of themselves. Like grandmothers, mothers show a child that he or she is loved and special.

Teacher Comment: **What clues let you know that a mother is most like a grandmother?**

Student Response: Both a mother and a grandmother are female. Both have sons or daughters and take care of children.

Teacher Comment: **Circle the picture of the mother.**

• Check students' work. Continue this dialog to discuss students' answers.

Thinking About Thinking

Teacher Comment: **What did you think about to tell how family members are alike?**

Student Response:

1. I recalled the important characteristics of the family members. (Age, gender, relationships to other members of the family, roles, feelings about them, interests or experiences that make them special.)
2. I looked for similar characteristics in the other family members.
3. I selected the family member that has most of the same characteristics.
4. I checked to see that other family members do not fit the important characteristics better than the one I selected.

Personal Application

Teacher Comment: **When is it important to tell how family members are alike?**

Student Response: I need to compare family members to relate incidents that happen at home, to explain how each family members helps the family meet its needs, to introduce family members to friends, or to tell or write stories about family members.

Page 113 - SIMILARITIES AND DIFFERENCES - FAMILY MEMBERS

TEACHING SUGGESTIONS
- To reinforce students' responses you may draw a compare and contrast diagram to record their answers. An example is shown. For a blank graphic see the appendix.
- This lesson involves comparative forms of adjectives. Repeat the adjectives that show age (young, younger, youngest, or old, older, oldest).

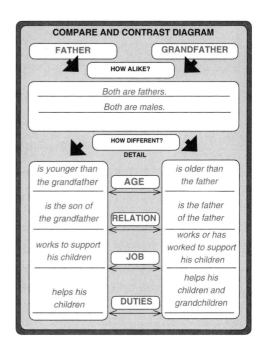

LESSON

Introduction
Teacher Comment: **We have described how family members are alike.**

Stating the Objective
Teacher Comment: **In this lesson you will tell how family members are different in age.**

Conducting the Lesson
Teacher Comment: **The first sentence tells about a father and a grandfather. Is the grandfather older or younger than the father?**
Student Response: The grandfather is the father's father. The grandfather is older.
Teacher Comment: **Write the word "older" to complete the sentence.**

Teacher Comment: **In the second sentence which family member is younger than the grandfather, but older than the boy?**
Student Response: The father is younger than the grandfather and older than the boy.
Teacher Comment: **Write the word "father" to complete the sentence.**

- Check students' work. Continue this dialog to discuss students' answers.

Thinking About Thinking
Teacher Comment: **What did you think about to compare family members?**
Student Response:
1. I thought about the oldest person and remembered their gender.
2. I thought about the youngest person and remembered their gender.
3. I used words to compare their age and gender.

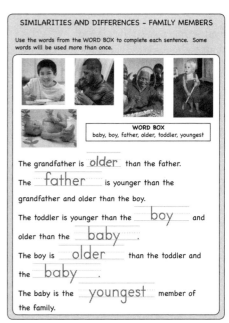

Personal Application
Teacher Comment: **When is it important to compare family members?**

Student Response: I need to compare family members to relate incidents that happen at home, to explain how each family member helps the family meet its needs, to introduce family members to friends, or to tell or write stories about family members.

Page 114 - SIMILARITIES AND DIFFERENCES - FAMILY MEMBERS

LESSON

Introduction
Teacher Comment: **We have described how family members are alike and different.**

Stating the Objective
Teacher Comment: **In this lesson you will compare a mother and son by age and gender.**

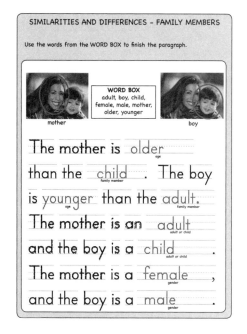

Conducting the Lesson
Teacher Comment: **What does gender tell about a person?**

Student Response: The gender of a person tells if the person is a male or female. Men and boys are male, Women and girls are females.

Teacher Comment: **The first picture shows the mother. What is the mother's gender?**

Student Response: The mother is female.

Teacher Comment: **Which of these family members is older?**

Student Response: The mother is older than the boy.

Teacher Comment: **Use words from the WORD BOX to complete the paragraph.**

Thinking About Thinking
Teacher Comment: **What did you think about to compare family members?**

Student Response:
1. I thought about the oldest person and remembered her gender.
2. I thought about the youngest person and remembered his gender.
3. I used words to compare their ages and genders.

Personal Application
Teacher Comment: **When is it important to compare family members?**

Student Response: I need to compare family members to relate incidents that happen at home, to explain how each family member helps the family meet its needs, to introduce family members to friends, or to tell or write stories about family members.

Page 115 - COMPARING FAMILY MEMBERS

LESSON

TEACHING SUGGESTION
This lesson practices comparative forms of adjectives. Encourage students to repeat the adjectives that show age (old, older, oldest).

Introduction
Teacher Comment: **When we described family members by their age, we were comparing them to each other. We explained their ages from young, younger, youngest. We named them in the order that they were born.**

Draw a large arrow on a long piece of paper or cardboard.

- Ask four students to come to the front of the classroom. Write the birthday of each student on piece of paper. Ask the four students to face the class holding their birthday sign so that the class can see them.
 Teacher Comment: **Which student was born first?**

- Move that student to the far left, facing the class.
 Teacher Comment: **Which student was born next?**

- Move that student to the second position, facing the class.
 Teacher Comment: **Which student was born next?**

- Move that student to the third position, facing the class.
 Teacher Comment: **We have now arranged the students in order of age from the youngest to the oldest. Name the students in order of their ages from the youngest to the oldest.**

- Hold the large arrow over the heads of the students to show the order of their ages.
 Teacher Comment: **Name the students in order of their ages from the oldest to the youngest.**

- Reverse the large arrow over the heads of the students to show the difference in the order of their ages.

- This lesson practices comparative forms of adjectives. Encourage students to repeat the adjectives that show age (old, older, oldest).

Stating the Objective
Teacher Comment: **In this lesson you will arrange family members from youngest to oldest.**

Conducting the Lesson
Teacher Comment: **Which of the family members is the youngest?**
 Student Response: The baby is the youngest.

Teacher Comment: **Write the word "baby" in the first blank.**

Teacher Comment: **Which family member is just a little older than the baby?**
  Student Response: The toddler girl is just a little older than the baby.
Teacher Comment: **Write "toddler girl" in the second blank.**

• Continue this dialog to discuss students' answers.

Thinking About Thinking

Teacher Comment: **What did you think about to write the family members in order of their age?**
Student Response:
1. I named the youngest family member first.
2. I named the family member that is slightly older.
3. I continued to name the family member that is slightly older.
4. I named the family member that is oldest.

Personal Application

Teacher Comment: **When is it important to name family members in order of age?**
Student Response: I need to name family members in order of age when I describe my brothers, sister, or cousins.

Page 116 - GROUPS OF FAMILY MEMBERS

LESSON

Introduction

Teacher Comment: **You call yourselves a "class" of students. You are about the same age. You meet in the same classroom. You study the same things and have the same teacher. "Class" means more than just a school room; it also means "a group of people that have some important characteristics in common." When we describe a group by important characteristics, we are "classifying them."**

Stating the Objective

Teacher Comment: **In this lesson you will group family members two ways. Each family member is either an adult or a child. Each family member is either a male or a female.**

Conducting the Lesson

Teacher Comment: **The first picture shows a boy. To which two groups does the boy belong?**
  Student Response: The boy is a male child.

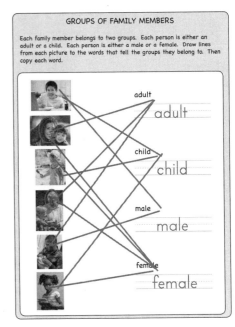

GROUPS OF FAMILY MEMBERS

Each family member belongs to two groups. Each person is either an adult or a child. Each person is either a male or a female. Draw lines from each picture to the words that tell the groups they belong to. Then copy each word.

adult
adult
child
child
male
male
female
female

Teacher Comment: **Draw one line from the picture of the boy to the word "child" and another line to the word "male." Copy the words "male" and "child."**

Teacher Comment: **The second picture shows a mother. To which two groups does the mother belong?**
   Student Response: The mother is an adult female.
Teacher Comment: **Draw one line from the picture of the mother to the word "adult" and another line to the word "female." Copy the words "adult" and "female."**

• Check students' work. Continue this dialog to discuss students' answers.

Thinking About Thinking
   Teacher Comment: **How did you classify family members in this exercise?**
   Student Response: I classified these family members by age and gender.

Personal Application
   Teacher Comment: **When is it important to know how to explain the characteristics of family members?**
   Student Response: I need to explain a person's characteristics to tell or write about them.

Page 117 - A DIFFERENT FAMILY MEMBER

TEACHING SUGGESTION
"Exception" is an abstract concept for most young children. Since they usually think in terms of their concrete observations, identifying a property that is <u>not</u> true of a person, animal, or thing may be puzzling. Students become comfortable with identifying exceptions if they have frequent practice doing so. Use the term "exception" often and encourage students to do so. Acknowledge instances when students use the term independently.

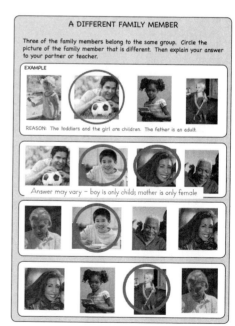

LESSON

Introduction
   Teacher Comment: **We have named groups of family members.**

Stating the Objective
   Teacher Comment: **In this lesson we will identify a family member who is not in same group as the others. That family member is called the "exception."**

Conducting the Lesson
   Teacher Comment: **Look at the family members in the example. How are three of the family members alike?**

© 2015 The Critical Thinking Co.™ • www.CriticalThinking.com • 800-458-4849

Student Response. The boy, toddler girl, and girl are children.
Teacher Comment: **Which family member is not a child?**
Student Response: The father is not a child. He is an adult.
Teacher Comment: **The father is the exception to the group "children." Circle the picture of the father.**

Teacher Comment: **Look at the family members in the second row. How are three of the family members alike?**
Student Response. The father, boy, and grandfather are all males. (Alternately, the father, mother, and grandfather are all adults.)
Teacher Comment: **Which family member is the exception?**
Student Response: The mother is the exception. (Alternately, the boy is the exception.)
Teacher Comment: **Draw a circle around the picture of the mother. (Alternately, draw a circle around the boy.)**
Teacher Comment: **Discuss with your partner why the mother (or the boy) is the exception.**

• Check students' work. Continue this dialog to discuss students' answers.

Thinking About Thinking
Teacher Comment: **What did you think about to decide which family member is the exception?**
Student Response:
1. I decided how three of the family members are alike.
2. I thought about how the other family member is different by age or gender.
3. I explained why that family member is the exception because of age or gender.

Personal Application
Teacher Comment: **When is it important to explain which family member is different from others?**
Student Response: When I need to explain how a family member is different from the others to tell or write about them or to describe events that happen in the family.

Page 118 - CLASSIFYING FAMILY MEMBERS

LESSON

Introduction
Teacher Comment: **We have grouped family members by age and gender.**

Stating the Objective
Teacher Comment: **In this lesson you will group three family members by a common characteristic.**

Conducting the Lesson

Teacher Comment: **Name the family members in the pictures in the top box.**

Student Response: The family members are a toddler girl, a baby, and a toddler boy.

Teacher Comment: **To which group do these three family members belong.**

Student Response: These family members are all children.

Teacher Comment: **Find the word "children" in the WORD BOX and write it on the top line. This identifies the group to which these family members belong.**

Teacher Comment: **Write the members of the group in the next three blanks.**

Teacher Comment: **Name the three family members shown in the bottom box.**

Student Response: The family members are a girl, a mother, and a grandmother.

Teacher Comment: **To which group do these three family members belong.**

Student Response: The family members are all females.

Teacher Comment: **Write "females" on the top line and write the names of the group members on the bottom three lines.**

Thinking About Thinking
Teacher Comment: **What did you think about to classify family members in this exercise?**

Student Response: I classified these family members by age and gender.

Personal Application
Teacher Comment: **When is it important to know how to classify family members?**

Student Response: I need to classify family members to describe or write about them.

CHAPTER ELEVEN – THINKING ABOUT JOBS (Pages 119-130)

GENERAL INTRODUCTION

CURRICULUM APPLICATIONS
Health: Identify people who produce and distribute food. Identify health and emergency workers

Social Studies: Define a consumer as a user of goods and services; identify how a family depends upon products and services to meet its needs; identify some job roles in the home, school, and community; cite examples of community needs and services; recognize the differences between producing and selling goods; understand how community helpers are an example of interdependence

TEACHING SUGGESTIONS
• Drawing: Each student may illustrate a person's job. Label the drawing with a description of that job. Students' drawings may be used to create a "big book."

• Enlarge and display the list of jobs on graphic master number 3 in the appendix. Refer to the word list when students discuss, write, or draw each worker in order to associate the word with the job.

• Telling: Select a common story or fairy tale about a job, such as *The Elves and the Shoemaker* by Jacob Grimm. Ask students to retell the story about another job (e.g. substituting a construction worker for a shoemaker). Discuss how the revised story is different from the original. For example, how might the elves help the construction worker and what might the construction worker make for the elves in return?

• Drama: Collect or construct hats from different professions and articles used in the job. Ask students to enact the worker and the customer seeking goods or services from these workers.

• Encourage students to identify individuals in their local community that provide the goods and services described in this chapter.

• Students may not commonly use the term "occupation." Discuss with students the common synonyms for jobs - livelihood, career, work, etc.

MENTAL MODEL
A mental model outlines the characteristics that one must state to describe or define a concept. After completing this chapter, each student will have applied this mental model to jobs in the lessons. A mental model helps a student:

• Anticipate what he or she needs to know to understand a new job
• Remember the characteristics of a job
• State a clear definition or write an adequate description of a job
• Explain a job to someone else

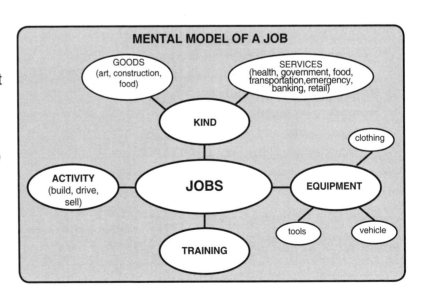

Page 120 - DESCRIBING JOBS

LESSON

Introduction
Teacher Comment: **A community is made up of families, businesses, and buildings, jobs that people in the community need. Family members have jobs that the community needs. Families need what other people in the community make or do for them. Tell your partner about a job that one of your family members has and why people need someone to do that job.**

• After students have discussed a family member's job, ask two or three students to describe their family member's job to the class and why other people need the goods or services that the job provides.

Stating the Objective
Teacher Comment: **I will describe a job and you will select it.**

Conducting the Lesson
Teacher Comment: **Look at pictures in the first box. I will describe one of the jobs. You will select the picture that fits the description. This person works in a school or public library. She helps readers find books and makes a record of the books that readers borrow.**

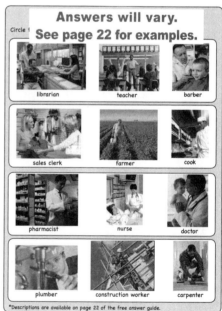

• Ask students to decide with their partners which job has been described.

Teacher Comment: **What do we call this job?**
Student Response: This person is a librarian.
Teacher Comment: **Circle the picture of the librarian.**

Teacher Comment: **What clues let you know that the person in this picture is a librarian?**
Student Response: The picture shows the librarian checking out books.
Teacher Comment: **Why don't the other jobs fit this description?**
Student Response: The teacher works in a classroom and teaches many students at one time. The barber cuts hair and does not work with books.

Teacher Comment: **Look at the second group of pictures. Select the picture that fits this description. This person helps shoppers find the things that they want. She also takes the customer's money or credit card to pay for the things she sells. With your partner decide which job I described.**

Teacher Comment: **What do we call this job?**

Student Response: This person is a sales clerk.

Teacher Comment: **Circle the picture of the sales clerk.**

Teacher Comment: **What clues let you know that the person in this picture is a sales clerk?**

Student Response: She works in a clothing store and is showing clothing to a shopper.

Teacher Comment: **Why don't the other jobs fit this description?**

Student Response: The cook prepares food in a restaurant. The farmer grows food in open fields. He does not work in stores.

Teacher Comment: **Look at the third group of pictures. Select the picture that fits the description. This person works in a pharmacy (a store or part of a store where medicines are sold). He fills prescriptions which are notes from a doctor that tells which medicine a person needs. He has studied how our bodies work to understand how each medicine helps our bodies heal. He often wears a white coat to show that the medicines are kept in clean surroundings. With your partner decide which job I described.**

Teacher Comment: **What do we call this job?**

Student Response: This person is a pharmacist.

Teacher Comment: **Circle the picture of the pharmacist.**

Teacher Comment: **What clues let you know that the person in this picture is a pharmacist?**

Student Response: I see the shelves of medicines behind him. He wears a white coat.

Teacher Comment: **Why don't the other jobs fit this description?**

Student Response: The doctor tells the pharmacist what medicine to sell. The nurse gives medicine to patients in a doctor's office or in a hospital, but does not sell medicines.

Teacher Comment: **Look at the fourth group of pictures. Select the picture that fits the description. This person builds and repairs houses or buildings. He works with hammers, nails, saws, rulers for measuring, and power tools. He cuts, measures, and fastens pieces of wood that become walls, floors, and ceilings. He may lay tiles in bathrooms or nail large coverings for walls and ceilings. With your partner decide which job I described.**

Teacher Comment: **What do we call this job?**

Student Response: This person is a carpenter.

Teacher Comment: **Why don't the other jobs fit this description?**

Student Response: The plumber works with the water systems of the house. He fixes metal or plastic pipes. The construction worker builds large buildings, bridges, tunnels, and other large structures. He may drive large vehicles to move metal and sand.

Thinking About Thinking

Teacher Comment: **What did you look for when you picked out the job that was described?**

Student Response:

1. I listened for the important characteristics of the job.
2. I found the important characteristics in the pictures (activities, goods or services, training, equipment, etc.).
3. I named the jobs.
4. I checked that the other photographs of jobs don't show those important characteristics as well.

Personal Application

Teacher Comment: **When is it important to describe what workers do in their jobs?**

Student Response: I describe jobs to explain what friends or family members do for a living, to describe commercials, or to describe businesses to a newcomer.

Page 121 - DESCRIBING JOBS

LESSON

Introduction

Teacher Comment: **We have selected a job from its description.**

Stating the Objective.

Teacher Comment: **In this lesson you are going to match the pictures of the jobs to the words for them.**

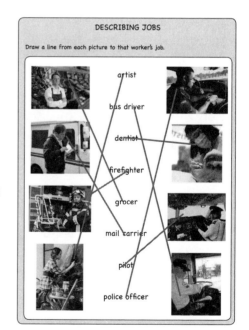

Conducting the Lesson

Teacher Comment: **Name the job in the first picture.**

Student Response: The first picture shows a grocer.

Teacher Comment: **What details show that the person is a grocer?**

Student Response: He is standing in the fruit and vegetable section of a grocery store. He wears an apron to protect his clothes from stains when he cuts and stacks the vegetables.

Teacher Comment: **Draw a line is drawn from the picture of the grocer to the word "grocer."**

Teacher Comment: **Name the job shown in the second picture.**

Student Response: The second picture shows a mail carrier.

Teacher Comment: **What details show that the person is a mail carrier?**

Student Response: He is standing beside a mail truck. He wears a postal service uniform. He is checking the addresses of letters to be sure they are delivered to the correct person.

Teacher Comment: **Draw a line from the picture to the word "mail carrier."**

• Check students' work. Continue this dialog to discuss students' answers.

Thinking About Thinking
Teacher Comment: **How did you decide which word belonged with each picture?**
Student Response:
1. I saw what the person was doing.
2. I looked at the clothes, equipment, and surroundings.
3. I named the job.
4. I looked for its name.

Personal Application
Teacher Comment: **When is it important to know the word for a job?**
Student Response: I need to know the words for jobs in order to write about them.

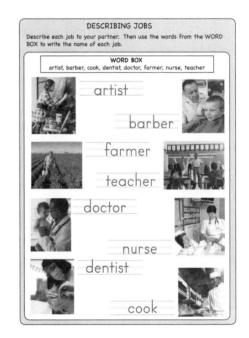

Page 122 - DESCRIBING JOBS

LESSON

Introduction
Teacher Comment: **We have found the word for some jobs.**

Stating the Objective
Teacher Comment: **In this lesson you will look at a photograph and describe the job that the person is doing.**

Conducting the Lesson
Teacher Comment: **Look at the first picture. Name this job and describe it to your partner.**
Student Response: The first picture shows an artist. An artist is a person who uses paints, colored pencils, ink, or charcoal to draw pictures.
Teacher Comment: **What details show that the person is an artist?**
Student Response: The person is painting a picture. We see the paint and the brushes that she is using.
Teacher Comment: **Find the word "artist" in the WORD BOX and write it on the first blank.**

Teacher Comment: **Look at the second picture. Name this job and describe it to your partner.**
Student Response: The second picture shows a barber. A barber cuts people's hair. He sometimes wears a white coat to show that the barber shop is clean. He uses scissors or clippers to cut hair.

Teacher Comment: **What details show that the person is a barber?**
Student Response: He is cutting a boy's hair with scissors or clippers.
Teacher Comment: **Find the word "barber" in the WORD BOX and write it on the lines next to the picture of the barber.**

Teacher Comment: **Look at the third picture. Name this job and describe it to your partner.**
Student Response: This picture shows a farmer. A farmer grows crops to provide food. He uses machines to farm large fields. Some farmers raise animals in addition to growing plants.
Teacher Comment: **What details show that the person is a farmer?**
Student Response: The farmer is working in a field of crops.

Teacher Comment: **Find the word "farmer" in the WORD BOX and write it on the lines next to the picture of the farmer.**

• Check students' work. Continue this dialog to discuss students' answers.

Thinking About Thinking
Teacher Comment: **How did you decide which word belonged with each picture?**
Student Response:
1. I looked at the details in the picture and named the job.
2. I looked for the word in the WORD BOX that describes the job.
3. I wrote the word for the job on the blank.

Personal Application
Teacher Comment: **When is it important to write job names?**
Student Response: I need to know job names to tell or write about them.

Page 123 - DESCRIBING JOBS

LESSON

Introduction
Teacher Comment: **We have written words for different jobs.**

Stating the Objective
Teacher Comment: **In this lesson you will match a picture of a job to the word that describes what the worker does.**

Conducting the Lesson
Teacher Comment: **Name the job in the first picture.**
Student Response: That job is a construction worker.
Teacher Comment: **What details show that the job in the picture is a construction worker?**
Student Response: He is working with large metal bars to build a large building. He works high in the air and wears a hard hat to protect his head.

Teacher Comment: **What does the construction worker do.**

Student Response: A construction worker builds.

Teacher Comment: **Draw a line from the picture of the construction worker to the word "builds." Copy the word "builds."**

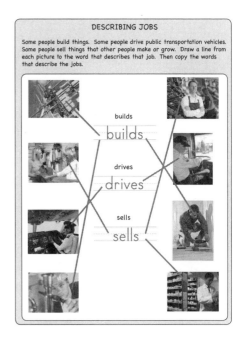

Teacher Comment: **Name the second job.**

Student Response: That job is a sales clerk.

Teacher Comment: **What details show that the job in the picture is a sales clerk?**

Student Response: She is showing clothing to a shopper. The clothing hanging on racks show that this is a store. She stands behind a counter where the shopper pays for the purchases.

Teacher Comment: **What does the sales clerk do?**

Student Response: The sales clerk sells.

Teacher Comment: **Draw a line from the picture of the sales clerk to the word "sells." Copy the word "sells."**

Teacher Comment: **Name the third job.**

Student Response: That job is a pilot.

Teacher Comment: **What details show that the job in the picture is a pilot?**

Student Response: She sits in the front section of an airplane. She looks out of a windshield like the one in cars. She reads the dials and lights that show that the plane is safe and operating correctly. She turns a steering wheel that changes the direction of an airplane. She wears a special uniform that shows the passengers that she is the pilot of the plane.

Teacher Comment: **What does the pilot do?**

Student Response: The pilot drives.

Teacher Comment: **Draw a line from the picture of the pilot to the word "drives." Copy the word "drives."**

• Check students' work. Continue this dialog to discuss students' answers.

Thinking About Thinking

Teacher Comment: **How did you decide which word matched what each worker does?**

Student Response:

1. I looked at the details of the job in the picture.
2. I named that job.
3. I found the word that describes what that worker does.

Personal Application

Teacher Comment: **When is it important to know what a worker does?**

Student Response: I need to know what each worker does to understand how they can help customers and to write or tell about them.

Pages 124 - DESCRIBING JOBS

LESSON

Introduction

Teacher Comment: **In the last lesson you matched jobs with what they do.**

Stating the Objective

Teacher Comment: **In this lesson you will complete a paragraph that describes a bank teller. A paragraph is a group of sentences that tell more information about a job than we can say in one sentence.**

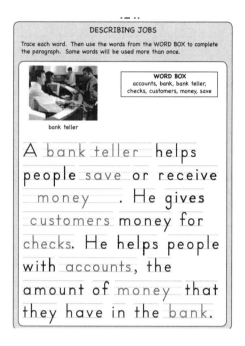

Conducting the Lesson

Teacher Comment: **You already know that a bank teller helps people with money. The bank teller gives the customer money for checks. A check is a note that tells the bank that the person who signs the check wants the bank to give the customer money from the signer's account. An account is the amount of money that a person has put in the bank for saving or for writing checks. Find the words in the WORD BOX that tell about the bank teller. Write the words in the blanks.**

• Check students' work.

Thinking About Thinking

Teacher Comment: **What did you pay attention to when you described a bank teller?**
Student Response:
1. I remembered what a bank teller does.
2. I looked for the words that tell about a bank teller.
3. I wrote the words that completed a whole paragraph about the bank teller.

Personal Application

Teacher Comment: **When is it important to describe an job?**
Student Response: I need to describe a job to tell or write about it.

Page 125 - SIMILAR JOBS

LESSON

Introduction
Teacher Comment: **In the last lesson you completed a paragraph about a job.**

Stating the Objective
Teacher Comment: **In this lesson you will find a job that is similar to another one.**

Conducting the Lesson
Teacher Comment: **Name the jobs in the example.**

   Student Response: The jobs are a bus driver, a mail carrier, a firefighter, a pilot, and a police officer.

Teacher Comment: **In the example, you will select the job that is most like the bus driver. Tell your partner all the important things that you know about a bus driver.**

   Student Response: A bus driver drives a large bus that holds many passengers. He drives on the same roads and lets passengers get on and off the bus at the same time every day. He sits in the front of the bus and looks out a large windshield. He turns a wheel to steer the bus carefully. He wears a uniform that shows the passengers that he is the person who is qualified to drive the bus safely.

Teacher Comment: **Which job on the right is most like a bus driver?**

   Student Response: The pilot is most like a bus driver.

Teacher Comment: **What clues let you know that the pilot is most like a bus driver?**

   Student Response: Both drive large passenger vehicles. They look out of large windows that let them see where they are going. They both change the direction of the vehicle by turning a wheel. They both wear a uniform to show the passengers that they are qualified to drive the vehicle.

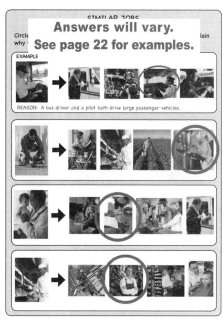

Teacher Comment: **How are the other jobs different from the bus driver and the pilot?**

   Student Response: The mail carrier delivers mail and does not drive passengers. The police officer drives passengers only in emergencies.

Teacher Comment: **Name the jobs shown in the second row.**

   Student Response: The jobs are a carpenter, an artist, a cook, a farmer, and a plumber.

Teacher Comment: **Tell your partner the important things you know about a carpenter.**

   Student Response: A carpenter builds or repairs homes and small buildings. He usually works on the wood that builds or repairs homes.

Teacher Comment: **Which job is most like a carpenter?**

   Student Response: A plumber is most like a carpenter.

Teacher Comment: **What clues let you know that a plumber is most like an carpenter?**

   Student Response: Both are shown working with tools. Both are building or repairing something.

Teacher Comment: **How are the other jobs different from a carpenter?**
Student Response: The other jobs produce something. The artist is producing a painting. The cook is producing a meal, the farmer is producing a crop.

Teacher Comment: **Name the jobs shown in the third row.**
Student Response: The jobs are a doctor, a bank teller, a dentist, a sales clerk, and a mail carrier.
Teacher Comment: **Tell your partner the important things you know about a doctor.**
Student Response: A doctor takes care of sick people and tells the pharmacist what medicine to sell and tells the nurses how to care for patients.
Teacher Comment: **Which job is most like a doctor?**
Student Response: A dentist is most like a doctor because they are health care workers.
Teacher Comment: **How are the other jobs different from a doctor?**
Student Response: The other jobs provide the services of giving out money, selling things, or delivering things.

Teacher Comment: **Name the jobs in the last row.**
Student Response: The jobs are a cook, a construction worker, a grocer, a pharmacist, and a barber.
Teacher Comment: **Tell your partner the important things you know about a cook.**
Student Response: A cook works in a restaurant and prepares meals.
Teacher Comment: **Which job is most like a cook?**
Student Response: A grocer is most like a cook because they are both food workers.
Teacher Comment: **How are the other jobs different from a cook?**
Student Response: The others are not food workers. The construction worker builds things. The pharmacists prepares medicines, the barber provides a service.

Thinking About Thinking
Teacher Comment: **What kind of characteristics did you discuss to describe the jobs?**
Student Response:
1. I recalled the important characteristics of the first job (whether the job provides a service or produces a product, whether the worker builds things, or sells things).
2. I looked for similar characteristics in the other jobs.
3. I selected the job that has most of the same characteristics.
4. I checked to see that other jobs do not fit the important characteristics better than the one I selected.

Personal Application
Teacher Comment: **When is it important to understand how different jobs are alike?**
Student Response: I need to understand how jobs are similar to write or tell about them.

Page 126 - SIMILARITIES AND DIFFERENCES – JOBS

TEACHING SUGGESTION
To reinforce students' responses you may draw a compare and contrast diagram to record their answers. For an example see right. For a blank compare and contrast graphic see the appendix.

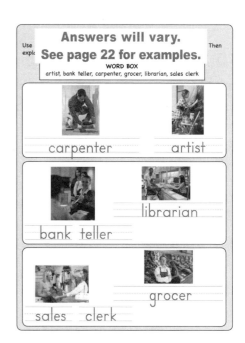

LESSON

Introduction
Teacher Comment: **We have described how two jobs are alike; we compared them. Sometimes we want to know how jobs are different in order to understand something important about them. When we describe how jobs are different, we contrast them.**

Stating the Objective
Teacher Comment: **In this lesson you will look at pictures of two jobs and compare and contrast them.**

Conducting the Lesson
Teacher Comment: **The first row shows a carpenter and an artist. Write the words "carpenter" and "artist" on the blank lines. How are these jobs alike?**

Student Response: Both workers use tools to produce a product.

Teacher Comment: **How are these jobs different?**

Student Response: The carpenter uses a hammer and saw to build or improve a room. The artists uses brushes and paint to make a picture.

Teacher Comment: **Look at the second row. It shows a bank teller and a librarian. Write the words "bank teller" and "librarian" on the blank lines. How are these jobs alike?**

Student Response: Both jobs provide a service to customers.

Teacher Comment: **How are these jobs different?**

Student Response: The bank teller helps people with money. The librarian helps people with books.

Teacher Comment: **Look at the third row, It shows a sales clerk and a grocer. Write the words "sales clerk" and "grocer" on the blank lines. How are these jobs alike?**

Student Response: Both sell things to customers.

Teacher Comment: **How are these jobs different?**

Student Response: The sales clerk is selling clothing. The grocer is selling fruits and vegetables.

Thinking About Thinking

Teacher Comment: **What did you think about to compare and contrast jobs?**
Student Response:
1. I remembered the important characteristics of each of the jobs (the worker's appearance, special equipment).
2. I thought about how the jobs are alike.
3. I thought about how the jobs are different.

Personal Application

Teacher Comment: **When is it important to compare and contrast jobs?**
Student Response: I need to compare and contrast jobs to tell or write about them.

Page 127 - COMPARING JOBS

TEACHING SUGGESTION

Emphasize the sentence structure that shows comparison. For example, a student needs the services of dentist <u>more</u> <u>often</u> <u>than</u> the services of a firefighter, <u>but less often</u> <u>than</u> the services of a teacher.

LESSON

Introduction

Teacher Comment: **One way that we can describe jobs is to compare them to other jobs. Sometimes we compare jobs by describing the order in which workers produce something that we need. Sometimes we compare how often we need the goods or services that the worker provides.**

Stating the Objective

Teacher Comment: **In this lesson we will arrange jobs in order.**

Conducting the Lesson

Teacher Comment: **Name the three jobs in the top box.**
Student Response: They are a cook, a farmer, and a grocer.

Teacher Comment: **We will put these jobs in the order in which they help us get food. Which job provides food first?**
Student Response: The farmer grows the food.
Teacher Comment: **Write the word "farmer" on the top line.**

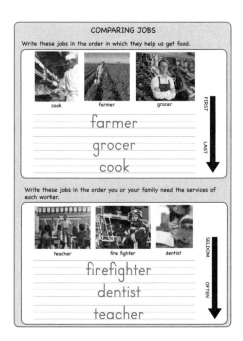

Teacher Comment: **Which of the jobs is next in helping your family get food?**
  Student Response: The farmer sells food to the grocer.
Teacher Comment: **Who is the last person to provide your food?**
  Student Response: The cook prepares food that the grocer sells.
Teacher Comment: **Write the word "grocer"on the second line and the word "cook" on the last line.**
Teacher Comment: **What clues let you know how to arrange these jobs?**
  Student Response: I think about what the job does and how it fits in with the other jobs.

Teacher Comment: **In the bottom box you see a teacher, a firefighter, and a dentist. Write these jobs in the order that you or your family needs their services. Which of these workers do you see most often?**
  Student Response: I see my teacher five days a week.
Teacher Comment: **Write the word "teacher" on the bottom line.**

Teacher Comment: **Which of these workers do you need least often?**
  Student Response: I may not ever need the service of the firefighter.
Teacher Comment: **Write the word "firefighter" on the top line**

Teacher Comment: **Which of these workers do you see more often than the firefighter, but less often than the teacher?**
  Student Response: I see the dentist more often than the firefighter, but less often than my teacher.
Teacher Comment: **Write the word "dentist" on the middle line.**

Thinking About Thinking
Teacher Comment: **What do you think about to put jobs in a particular order?**
  Student Response: I think about what the workers do, and how often our families need them.

Personal Application
Teacher Comment: **When is it important to understand how to arrange jobs in order?**
  Student Response: I need to understand how often we need other people's work in order to understand how much we depend on the goods or services that people offer our families.

Page 128 - KINDS OF JOBS

LESSON

Introduction
Teacher Comment: **In earlier lessons we have discussed what workers do: those that build, those that drive, and those that sell.**

Stating the Objective
Teacher Comment: **In this lesson you will match jobs to the group to which it belongs.**

Conducting the Lesson
Teacher Comment: **Name the job in the first picture.**
  Student Response: That picture shows a cook.
Teacher Comment: **What kind of worker is a cook?**
  Student Response: A cook is a food worker.
Teacher Comment: **Draw a line from the picture of the cook to the words "food worker."**

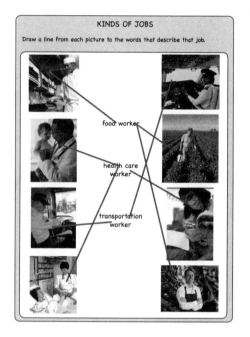

Teacher Comment: **Name the job of the second person.**
  Student Response: That person is a doctor.
Teacher Comment: **What kind of worker is a doctor?**
  Student Response: A doctor is a health care worker.
Teacher Comment: **Draw a line from the photograph of the doctor to the words "health care worker."**

Teacher Comment: **Name the job in the third picture.**
  Student Response: That picture shows a bus driver.
Teacher Comment: **What kind of job is a bus driver?**
  Student Response: A bus driver is a transportation worker.
Teacher Comment: **Draw a line from the photograph of the bus driver to the words "transportation worker."**

• Check students' work. Continue this dialog to discuss students' answers.

Thinking About Thinking
Teacher Comment: **How did you decide what kind of job the worker does?**
  Student Response:
  1. I looked at the details of the worker in the picture.
  2. I named that kind of job.
  3. I found the word that describes what kind of job the worker does.

Personal Application
Teacher Comment: **When is it important to know what kind of job a worker does?**
  Student Response: I need to know what kind of job a worker does to understand how they can help customers and to write or tell about them.

Page 129 - A DIFFERENT KIND OF JOB

LESSON

Introduction
Teacher Comment: **We have named types of jobs.**

Stating the Objective
Teacher Comment: **In this lesson you will identify a job that is not like the others.**

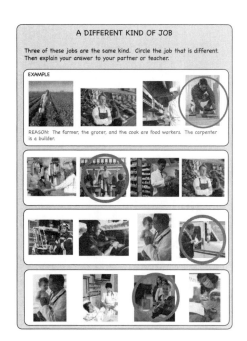

Conducting the Lesson
Teacher Comment: **Name the jobs shown in the pictures in the first row.**
  Student Response: These jobs are a farmer, a grocer, a cook, and a carpenter.
Teacher Comment: **Discuss with your partner how three of the four jobs are alike.**

Teacher Comment: **How are three of these jobs alike?**
  Student Response: The farmer, cook, and grocer are food workers.

Teacher Comment: **Which job is not a food worker?**
  Student Response: The carpenter is a builder, not a food worker.
Teacher Comment: **Notice that a circle is drawn around the carpenter.**

• Check students' work. Continue this dialog to discuss students' answers.

Thinking About Thinking
Teacher Comment: **What do you think about when you decide which job is not like the others?**
  Student Response:
  1. I looked at the picture of each worker and identified what kind of job it is.
  2. I found three jobs that were the same kind.
  3. I identified the job that does not fit that group and explained why.

Personal Application
Teacher Comment. **When is it important to understand how a job may be different from others?**
  Student Response. I need to know how a job may be different from others in order to understand what the worker does for the customer and what kind of training, equipment, or clothing that the job requires.

Page 130 - CLASSIFYING JOBS

LESSON

Introduction

Teacher Comment: **We have learned about food workers, health care workers, and transportation workers. When we name kinds of jobs, we are classifying them.**

Stating the Objective

Teacher Comment: **In this lesson you will look at pictures of three jobs and name the class to which they belong.**

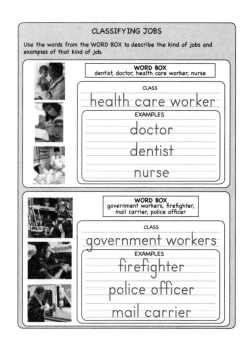

Conducting the Lesson

Teacher Comment: **Name the jobs in the top box.**

Student Response: The jobs are a doctor, a dentist, and a nurse.

Teacher Comment: **How are these jobs alike**

Student Response: These three workers help people stay healthy and help them heal if they have an illness or accident.

Teacher Comment: **Find the words "health care worker" in the WORD BOX and write them on the lines labeled "CLASS." Use words in the WORD BOX to write the names of the jobs on the lines labeled "EXAMPLES."**

Teacher Comment: **Name the jobs in the bottom box.**

Student Response: These workers are firefighter, police officer, and mail carrier.

Teacher Comment: **With your partner discuss how these jobs are alike.**

Student Response: All these workers work for the government. The firefighter and police officer work for a city or county. The mail carrier works for the United States Postal Service, part of our national government.

Teacher Comment: **Write the words "government worker" on the line labeled "CLASS." Use words in the WORD BOX to write the names of the jobs on the lines labeled "EXAMPLES."**

Thinking About Thinking

Teacher Comment: **What kind of characteristics did you discuss to decide the class of these three jobs?**

Student Response:
1. I looked at the picture of each worker and identified what kind of job it is.
2. I found the word for that class of jobs.

Personal Application

Teacher Comment: **When is it important to understand how jobs are alike?**

Student Response: I need to know kinds of jobs in order to understand what the worker does for the customer and what kind of training, equipment, or clothing that the job requires.

PAGE 131 - CLASSIFYING JOBS

LESSON

Introduction
Teacher Comment: **We have classified jobs.**

Stating the Objective
Teacher Comment: **In this lesson you will sort jobs into two classes: food workers and builders**

Conducting the Lesson
Teacher Comment: **Name the job in the first picture.**
   Student Response: That job is a cook.
Teacher Comment: **What kind of job is a cook?**
   Student Response: A cook is a food worker.
Teacher Comment: **Write the word "cook" on the first line in the box marked "FOOD WORKERS."**

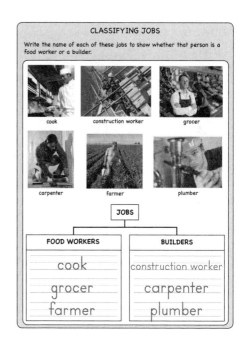

Teacher Comment: **Name the job in the second picture.**
   Student Response: That job is a construction worker.
Teacher Comment: **Write the words "construction worker" on the first line in the box marked "BUILDERS."**

• Check students' work. Continue this dialog to discuss students' answers.

Thinking About Thinking
Teacher Comment: **What do you think about to classify jobs?**
   Student Response:
   1. I looked at the picture and identified whether the worker is a food worker or a builder.
   2. I found the word for that class of jobs.
   3. I wrote the word for each job under the word for its class.

Personal Application
Teacher Comment. **When is it important to understand how to classify jobs?**
   Student Response: I need to know kinds of jobs in order to understand what the worker does for the customer and what kind of training, equipment, or clothing that the job requires.

CHAPTER TWELVE – THINKING ABOUT VEHICLES (Pages 132-146)

GENERAL INTRODUCTION

TEACHING SUGGESTION

Enlarge and display the list of vehicles on graphic master number 4 in the appendix. Refer to the word list when students discuss, write, or draw, each vehicle in order to associate the word with the vehicle.

MENTAL MODEL

A mental model is a framework for understanding a concept. It outlines the characteristics that one must state to describe or define a concept. After completing this chapter, each student will have applied this mental model to vehicles in the lessons. A mental model helps a student:

- Anticipate what he or she needs to know to understand a new vehicle
- Remember the characteristics of a vehicle
- State a clear definition or write an adequate description of a vehicle
- Explain a vehicle to someone else

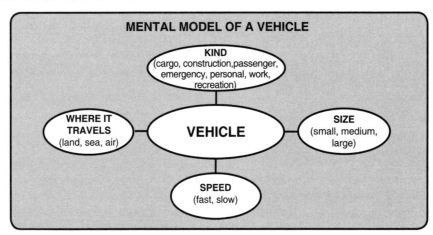

Pages 133 - DESCRIBING VEHICLES

LESSON

Introduction

Without naming it, in three to five sentences describe a vehicle not in the example. Ask the class to identify the vehicle that was described.

> Teacher Comment: **What clues let you know what vehicle was described?**
>
> Student Response: Students cite number of wheels, how many people or what kind of cargo it carries, where it goes, whether one has to pay to ride it, etc.

Stating the Objective

> Teacher Comment: **In this lesson I will describe a vehicle and you will select it.**

Conducting the Lesson

> Teacher Comment: **Select the picture that fits the description. This vehicle is a special tractor that crawls on movable treads. Treads are oval wheels with groves to grip the ground so that the vehicle can move heavy loads. In front there is a blade that is used to push dirt and other materials.**

Student Response: That vehicle is a bulldozer.
Teacher Comment: **Circle the picture of the bulldozer.**

Teacher Comment: **What clues let you know that the vehicle that was described was a bulldozer?**
Student Response: It has treads, not wheels. Its blade pushes dirt.
Teacher Comment: **Why don't the other vehicles fit the description?**
Student Response: The tractor and the truck move on wheels, do not have a blade, and do not push dirt in front of it.

Teacher Comment: **Look at the second row of vehicles and select the vehicle I describe. This vehicle has a long arm and wire ropes that are used for lifting heavy materials. It is often used to load and unload freight.**
Student Response: That vehicle is a crane.
Teacher Comment: **Circle the picture of the crane.**
Teacher Comment: **What clues let you know that the vehicle that was described was a crane?**
Student Response: The long arm and wire ropes to lift heavy things.
Teacher Comment: **Why don't the other vehicles fit the description?**
Student Response: The dump truck carries things, it does not lift them. The fire truck has a long ladder, but it is not used to lift freight.

Teacher Comment: **Look at the third row of vehicles. I will describe one of the vehicles. Select the picture that fits the description. This large, wide, vehicle moves many cars across rivers or lakes. Cars drive onto and off of its wide deck. Because it is so large and carries so much weight, it moves slowly. Passengers can sit upstairs in a wide room or in their cars.**
Student Response: That vehicle is a ferry.
Teacher Comment: **Circle the picture of the ferry.**

Teacher Comment: **What clues let you know that the vehicle that was described was a ferry?**
Student Response: It carries many passengers and their automobiles. It has a wide deck to hold many cars.
Teacher Comment: **Why don't the other vehicles fit the description?**
Student Response: The speed boat goes fast and carries a few people. The cargo ship carries goods, not passengers across oceans.

Teacher Comment: **Look at the fourth row of vehicles. I will describe one of the vehicles. Select the picture that fits the description. This vehicles is a small vehicle that only holds a few people. It has no motor, the passengers must paddle to make it move slowly in the water. People use it for recreation.**
Student Response: That vehicle is a canoe.

Teacher Comment: **Circle the picture of the canoe.**
Teacher Comment: **What clues let you know that the vehicle that was described was a canoe?**
　Student Response: It is a small boat that people paddle.
Teacher Comment: **Why don't the other vehicles fit the description?**
　Student Response: The bicycle and the motorcycle travel on land and have wheels.

Thinking About Thinking

Teacher Comment: **What details did you look for when you picked out the vehicle that was described?**
Student Response:
1. I listened for and remembered the important characteristics of the vehicle.
2. I found the important characteristics in the pictures.
3. I checked which picture shows those important characteristics.
4. I checked that the other pictures of vehicles don't show those important characteristics as well.

Personal Application

Teacher Comment: **When is it important to describe vehicles accurately?**
　Student Response: I must describe vehicles to tell or write about deliveries, traffic, or directions.

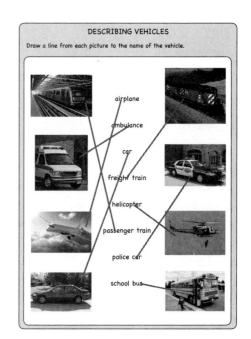

Pages 134 - DESCRIBING VEHICLES

LESSON

Introduction
Teacher Comment: **We have been learning about vehicles.**

Stating the Objective
Teacher Comment: **In this lesson you will match vehicles to their names**

Conducting the lesson
Teacher Comment: **Name the vehicle shown in the first picture**
　Student Response: The first picture shows a passenger train.
Teacher Comment: **Draw a line from the picture of the passenger train to the words "passenger train."**

Teacher Comment: **Name the vehicle shown in the second picture.**
　Student Response: The second picture shows an ambulance.
Teacher Comment: **Draw a line from the picture of the ambulance to the word "ambulance."**

• Check students' work. Continue this dialog to discuss students' answers.

Thinking About Thinking
Teacher Comment: **How did you decide which word belonged with each picture?**
Student Response:
1. I looked at the details of the vehicle in the picture.
2. I named that vehicle.
3. I found the word for that vehicle.

Personal Application
Teacher Comment: **When is it important to understand how to name vehicles?**
Student Response: I need to know vehicle names to write stories about them.

Page 135 - DESCRIBING VEHICLES

LESSON

Introduction
• Ask a student to describe to the class in three to five sentences a vehicle that they have studied or seen recently.
• Ask the class to name the vehicle that has been described.

Teacher Comment: **What details let you know which vehicle was described?**
Student Response: I listened for its appearance, its size, whether it travels in the air, on land, or on water, how it moves, and how fast it goes.

Stating the Objective
Teacher Comment: **In this lesson you will describe vehicles.**

Conducting the Lesson
Teacher Comment: **Name the first vehicle and describe it to your partner.**
Student Response: This vehicle is an ambulance. It carries sick or injured people to the hospital. Emergency workers use medicine and equipment to help sick or injured people on the trip to the hospital. It can go fast in traffic because flashing lights and sirens warn people to get out of the way.
Teacher Comment: **What details do you describe to explain that the vehicle in the picture is an ambulance?**
Student Response: I described what it is used for, its speed, and what it carries.
Teacher Comment: **Find the word "ambulance" in the WORD BOX and write it in the lined spaces.**

Teacher Comment: **Look at the second picture.   Name this vehicle and describe it to your partner.**

    Student Response: This very large vehicle is an airplane. It has very large engines that make it fly fast. It carries many passengers long distances.

Teacher Comment: **What details do you describe to explain that the vehicle in the picture is an airplane?**

    Student Response: I described its size, how it moves, and its passengers.

Teacher Comment: **Write the word "airplane" in the lined spaces.**

Teacher Comment: **Look at the third picture. Name this vehicle and describe it to your partner.**

    Student Response: This vehicle is a bus. A bus is a large vehicle that picks up passengers at bus stations and takes them along a regular route. People pay to ride on the bus. It has a large engine to move the weight of many passengers.

Teacher Comment: **What details do you describe to explain that the vehicle in the picture is a bus?**

    Student Response: I described its size, where it goes, how it moves, and what it carries.

Teacher Comment: **Write the word "bus" in the lined spaces.**

• Check students' work. Continue this dialog to discuss students' answers.

Thinking About Thinking

Teacher Comment: **How did you decide which word belonged with each picture?**
    Student Response:
    1. I looked at the details in the picture and named the vehicle.
    2. I looked for the word in the WORD BOX that describes the vehicle.
    3. I wrote the word for the vehicle on the blank.

Personal Application

Teacher Comment: **When is it important to write vehicle names?**
    Student Response: I need to know vehicle names to tell or write about them.

Page 136 - DESCRIBING VEHICLES

LESSON

Introduction
Teacher Comment: **We have described the size of vehicles, what they carry, and whether they travel on land, sea, or air. Some vehicles move fast; some move slowly.**

Stating the Objective
Teacher Comment: **In this lesson you will match the picture of each vehicle to the word "fast" or the word "slow."**

Conducting the Lesson
Teacher Comment: **Name the vehicle in the top picture.**
    Student Response: The first vehicle is a car.
Teacher Comment: **Is a car a fast or a slow vehicle?**
    Student Response: A car is a fast vehicle.
Teacher Comment: **Draw a line from the car to the word "fast."**

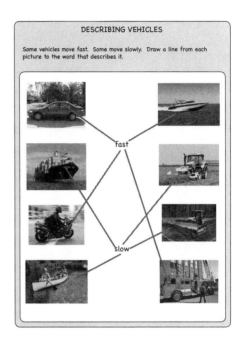

DESCRIBING VEHICLES

Some vehicles move fast. Some move slowly. Draw a line from each picture to the word that describes it.

Teacher Comment: **Name the vehicle in the second picture.**
    Student Response: That vehicle is a cargo ship.
Teacher Comment: **Is a cargo ship a fast or slow vehicle?**
    Student Response: A cargo ship is a slow vehicle.
Teacher Comment: **Draw a line from the cargo ship to the word "slow."**

• Check students' work. Continue this dialog to discuss students' answers.

Thinking About Thinking
Teacher Comment: **How did you decide which word belonged with each picture?**
    Student Response:
    1. I looked at each picture and identified the vehicle.
    2. I decided whether it is a fast or slow vehicle.

Personal Application
Teacher Comment: **When is it important to describe a vehicle?**
    Student Response: I need to describe a vehicle to tell or write about it.

Page 137 - DESCRIBING VEHICLES

LESSON

Introduction
Teacher Comment: **In the last lesson we discussed whether vehicles are fast or slow.**

Stating the Objective
Teacher Comment: **In this lesson you will complete a paragraph that describes a motorcycle. A paragraph is a group of sentences that give much more information about a vehicle than we can say in one sentence.**

Conducting the Lesson
Teacher Comment: **Find the words in the WORD BOX that tell about the motorcycle. Write the words in the blanks.**

• Check students' work.

Thinking About Thinking
Teacher Comment: **What did you pay attention to when you described a motorcycle?**
Student Response:
1. I remembered details about a motorcycle.
2. I looked for the words that tell about a motorcycle.
3. I wrote the words that complete a whole paragraph.

Personal Application
Teacher Comment: **When is it important to describe a vehicle?**
Student Response: I need to describe a vehicle to tell or write about it.

DESCRIBING VEHICLES

Trace each word. Then use the words from the WORD BOX to complete the paragraph.

> **WORD BOX**
> fast, motorcycle, one,
> recreation, small, two, work

A motorcycle
name
is a small   vehicle. It is
size
driven by one   person. It
how many
has two   wheels and can
how many
go very fast   . Some
speed
people drive one to work .
where
It is often used for
recreation   .

Page 138 - PARTS OF A DUMP TRUCK

LESSON

Introduction

Teacher Comment: **To describe vehicles we sometimes need to know the names of its parts and explain how each part is important for the vehicle to work properly.**

Stating the Objective

Teacher Comment: **In this lesson you will think about the parts of a vehicle, what each part does, and explain what would happen if the part were missing or damaged.**

Conducting the Lesson

Teacher Comment: **The word box contains four words for parts of a truck they are "cab," "dump box," "engine," and "wheels." The picture shows that the dump truck is dumping a load of dirt. Which part of the dump truck holds the load?**

Student Response: The "dump box" holds the load of dirt.

Teacher Comment: **Write the words "dump box" on the blank lines in the top box.**

Teacher Comment: **What would happen if the dump box was missing or damaged?**

Student Response: The truck could not carry a load.

Teacher Comment: **Look at the second box. This part holds the driver. What is it called?**

Student Response: The part that holds the driver is the cab.

Teacher Comment: **Write the word "cab" on the blank lines in the second box.**

Teacher Comment: **What would happen if the cab was missing or damaged?**

Student Response: The driver would not have a place to sit and drive the truck.

Teacher Comment: **Look at the third box. This part makes the truck move. What is it called?**

Student Response: The part that makes the truck move is the engine.

Teacher Comment: **Write the word "engine" on the blank lines in the third box.**

Teacher Comment: **What would happen if the engine was missing or damaged?**

Student Response: The truck could not move.

Teacher Comment: **Look at the fourth box. There are ten of these. They let the truck roll from place to place. What are they called?**

Student Response: The part that makes the truck roll are the wheels.

Teacher Comment: **Write the word "wheels" on the blank lines in the fourth box.**

Teacher Comment: **What would happen if the wheels were missing or damaged?**

Student Response: The truck could not move.

Thinking About Thinking

Teacher Comment: **What did you think about in order to describe the parts of a dump truck?**

Student Response:

1. I named the part.
2. I remembered what it is used for.
3. I thought about what would happen if that part was missing.

Personal Application

Teacher Comment: **When is it important to describe parts of a whole vehicle?**

Student Response: I describe the parts of a vehicle to explain how it works and how it is different from other vehicles. I describe the parts to tell a story about a vehicle.

Page 139 - SIMILAR VEHICLES

TEACHING SUGGESTION

Emphasize the wording commonly used to describe similarities. Repeat words that show similarity (both, and, like, similar, resemble, etc.) and encourage students to use them in their responses.

LESSON

Introduction

Teacher Comment: **We have practiced identifying the characteristics and names of vehicles.**

Stating the Objective

Teacher Comment: **In this lesson you will look at a picture of a vehicle and then decide which of three vehicles is most like it.**

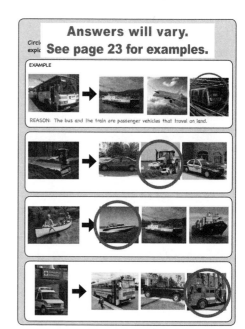

Conducting the Lesson

Teacher Comment: **Name the vehicles in the example.**

Student Response: The vehicles are a bus, a ferry, an airplane, and a passenger train.

Teacher Comment: **You are going to select the vehicle that is most like the first one. Tell your partner all the important things that you know about a bus.**

Student Response: A bus is a very large vehicle that takes many passengers on a scheduled route around the city or across long distances. People pay to ride the bus. The price of the ticket is called a fare.

Teacher Comment: **Which vehicle at the right is most like a bus?**

Student Response: A passenger train is most like a bus.

Teacher Comment: **Notice that a circle has been drawn around the picture of the passenger train. What clues let you know that a passenger train is most like a bus?**
Student Response: Both are land vehicles that carry many passengers around a city or across long distances. People pay a fare to ride the bus or a train.

Teacher Comment: **How are the other vehicles different from a bus?**
Student Response: The ferry is a sea vehicle. The airplane is an air vehicle.

Teacher Comment: **Name the vehicles shown in the second row.**
Student Response: The vehicles are a bulldozer, a car, a tractor, and a police car.
Teacher Comment: **Tell your partner all the important things that you know about a bulldozer.**
Student Response: A bulldozer is a special tractor that crawls on movable treads. It has a blade that is used to move dirt and other materials.
Teacher Comment: **Which vehicle on the right is most like a bulldozer?**
Student Response: A tractor is most like a bulldozer.
Teacher Comment: **Circle the picture of the tractor.**

Teacher Comment: **How do you know that a tractor is most like an bulldozer?**
Student Response: A bulldozer is a special tractor that crawls on movable treads. Both are work vehicles that are driven in fields. Both have a small cab where the driver sits. Both can be used to push dirt.
Teacher Comment: **How are the other vehicles different from a bulldozer?**
Student Response: A car and a police car are automobiles. They are driven on roads and can carry passengers. They do not have special equipment to move dirt.

Teacher Comment: **Look at the third row. Name the vehicles.**
Student Response: The vehicles are a canoe, a motorboat, a ferry, and a cargo ship.
Teacher Comment: **Tell your partner all the important things that you know about a canoe.**
Student Response: A canoe is a small boat that is paddled by two people. It slowly moves along a river or small lake. It is owned or rented by the person that paddles it.
Teacher Comment: **Which vehicle on the right is most like a canoe?**
Student Response: A motorboat is most like a canoe.
Teacher Comment: **Circle the picture of the motorboat.**

Teacher Comment: **What clues let you know that a canoe is most like a motorboat?**
Student Response: Both are small boats that are used for fun (recreation.)
Teacher Comment: **How are the other vehicles different from a canoe?**
Student Response: Both the ferry and the cargo ship are very large boats. They are owned by a government or a large company.

• Young students may not realize that generally a ship is any large boat. However, trying to distinguish between a ship and a boat is probably not useful, since the term "boat" may sometimes apply to a large vessel, such as a fishing boat or a ferry boat.

• Continue this dialog to discuss students' answers.

Thinking About Thinking
> Teacher Comment: **How did you decide which vehicle is most like another?**
> Student Response:
> 1. I recalled the important characteristics of the first vehicle (its appearance, special equipment, etc.).
> 2. I looked for similar characteristics in the other vehicles.
> 3. I selected the vehicle that has most of the same characteristics.
> 4. I checked to see that other vehicles do not fit the important characteristics better than the one I selected.

Personal Application
> Teacher Comment: **When is it important to describe vehicles accurately?**
> Student Response: I need to describe vehicles to describe toys, deliveries, or traffic, or to give directions.

Page 140 - SIMILARITIES AND DIFFERENCES - VEHICLES

TEACHING SUGGESTIONS

- Because young children observe details in the photograph, they may name details that are not characteristic of vehicles of all vehicles of the kind. For example, a student may say that the cargo ship is black, but the freight train is green. Confirm that it is true that in these pictures the vehicles are different colors. Ask whether all freight trains are green. Then explain that we are looking for characteristics that are true for all of this kind of vehicle.

- To reinforce students' responses you may draw a compare and contrast diagram to record their answers. For an example see right. For a blank compare and contrast graphic see the appendix.

COMPARE AND CONTRAST DIAGRAM

BUS   PASSENGER TRAIN

HOW ALIKE?

Both are public transportation vehicles.
Both require that passengers buy a ticket to ride.
Both run on a schedule.

HOW DIFFERENT?
DETAIL

| _larger than a family car_ | _Size_ | _made of many long cars_ |
| _can carry about fifty passengers_ | _Passengers_ | _can carry hundreds of passengers_ |

LESSON

Introduction

> Teacher Comment: **We have described how two vehicles are alike; we compared them. Sometimes we want to know how vehicles are different in order to understand something important about them. When we describe how vehicles are different, we contrast them.**

Stating the Objective

> Teacher Comment: **In this lesson you will look at pictures of two vehicles and compare and contrast them.**

Conducting the Lesson

> Teacher Comment: **The first row shows a cargo ship and a freight train. Write the words "cargo ship" and "freight train" on the blank lines. How are these vehicles alike?**

Student Response: Both are large vehicles that carry heavy loads over long distances; both have large engines to move heavy loads. Both are owned by large companies. People or companies pay a fee for these vehicles to carry large loads.

Teacher Comment: **How are these vehicles different?**

Student Response: The train travels on railroad tracks and the ship travels on large lakes, rivers, or oceans.

Teacher Comment: **Look at the second row. It shows a crane and a dump truck. Write the words "crane" and "dump truck" on the blank lines. How are these vehicles alike?**

Student Response: Both are work vehicles used to build roads, bridges, or buildings. Both have large engines to move heavy loads.

Teacher Comment: **How are these vehicles different?**

Student Response: The crane is used to lift heavy objects. The dump truck is used to haul materials like dirt or stone. The crane only moves around the construction space. The dump truck travels on roads and moves around the construction space. The crane has one large arm that can lift loads high into the air. The dump truck has a dump box that lifts just high enough to dump the load.

Teacher Comment: **Look at the third row. It shows a bicycle and a motorcycle. Write the words "bicycle" and "motorcycle" on the blank lines. How are these vehicles alike?**

Student Response: Both are two-wheeled vehicles usually used to transport one person from one place to another. Both are usually owned by the person who drives them.

Teacher Comment: **How are these vehicles different?**

Student Response: The bicycle is pedaled to make it move. The motorcycle has an engine that makes it move. The bicycle moves only as fast as the person can pedal. The motorcycle can travel as fast as a car.

Answers will vary.
See page 23 for examples.

WORD BOX
airplane, cargo ship, bicycle, crane, dump truck, freight train, helicopter, motorcycle

cargo ship   freight train

crane   dump truck

bicycle   motorcycle

airplane   helicopter

Teacher Comment: **Look at the fourth row. It shows an airplane and a helicopter. Write the words "airplane" and "helicopter" on the blank lines. How are these vehicles alike?**

Student Response: Both vehicles travel in the air.

Teacher Comment: **How are these vehicles different?**

Student Response: The airplane is a large plane that can carry many passengers. A helicopter is smaller than the airplane and can carry only a few passengers. The airplane has two or four engines on its wings. The helicopter has one engine that turns the rotor on top. The airplane moves very fast. The helicopter moves more slowly. The airplane only moves forward and must take off and land on a long runway. The helicopter can move forward and up and down and can land in a very small space. The airplane is used to carry people or cargo over long distances. The helicopter is used to lift people or small loads for short distances. The airplane is used for public transportation or carrying large cargo. The helicopter is sometimes used to help people in emergencies.

Thinking About Thinking
Teacher Comment: **What did you think about to compare and contrast vehicles?**
Student Response:
1. I remembered the important characteristics of each of the vehicles (its appearance, special equipment).
2. I thought about how the vehicles are alike.
3. I thought about how the vehicles are different.

Personal Application
Teacher Comment: **When is it important to compare and contrast vehicles?**
Student Response: I need to describe vehicles to describe toys, deliveries, or traffic, or to give directions.

Page 141 - COMPARING VEHICLES

TEACHING SUGGESTIONS
• Help students recognize and use terms for comparing order – least, most, fast, faster, fastest, large, larger, largest.

• Emphasize the sentence structure that shows comparison. For example, a car can carry <u>more</u> passengers <u>than</u> a motorcycle, <u>but fewer</u> passengers <u>than</u> a train.

LESSON

Introduction
Teacher Comment: **One way that we can describe vehicles is to compare them to other vehicles.**

Stating the Objective
Teacher Comment: **In this lesson we will compare vehicles in order to understand something important about them.**

Conducting the Lesson
Teacher Comment: **We will arrange vehicles from the one that carries the fewest passengers to the one that carries the most. Name the vehicles in the top box.**
Student Response: The vehicles are a car, a motorcycle, and a passenger train.

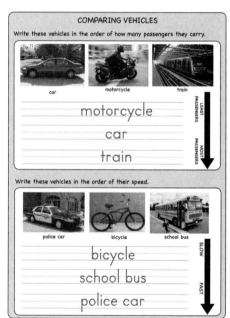

Teacher Comment: **Which vehicle carries the fewest passengers?**
Student Response: The motorcycle can carry one or two people.
Teacher Comment: **Write the word "motorcycle" on the first line.**

Teacher Comment: **Which vehicle can carry the most passengers?**
Student Response: A train can carry hundreds of passengers.
Teacher Comment: **Write the word "train" on the third line.**

Teacher Comment: **Which vehicle can carry more passengers than a motorcycle, but fewer passengers than a train?**
   Student Response: A car can carry more passengers than a motorcycle, but fewer passengers than a train.
Teacher Comment: **Write the word "car" on the second line.**

Teacher Comment: **What do we learn about these vehicles by arranging them in order of the number of passengers they can carry?**
   Student Response: I learned that my family may need to ride different vehicles for trips or for daily transportation.

Teacher Comment: **In the bottom box list the vehicles in order of their speed. Which vehicle is the slowest?**
   Student Response: A bicycle is slower than a bus or a police car.
Teacher Comment: **Write the word "bicycle" on the first line.**

Teacher Comment: **Which vehicle is the fastest?**
   Student Response: The police car can go very fast in emergencies.
Teacher Comment: **Write the words "police car" on the third line.**

Teacher Comment: **Which vehicle is faster than a bicycle, but slower than a police car?**
   Student Response: The school bus is faster than a bicycle, but slower than a police car.
Teacher Comment: **Write the words "school bus" on the second line.**

Teacher Comment: **What do we learn about these vehicles by arranging them in order of the speed?**
   Student Response: I learned to watch out for the speed of these vehicles in traffic.

Thinking About Thinking
   Teacher Comment: **What did you think about when you put vehicles in a particular order?**
   Student Response:
      1. I looked at the pictures and decided which vehicle has the least passengers or speed.
      2. I decided which vehicle has the most passengers or speed.
      3. I decided which vehicle has passengers or speed between the least and the most.

Personal Application
   Teacher Comment: **When is it important to compare vehicles by the number of passengers they can carry?**
   Student Response: I compare passenger vehicles to know what kind can carry my friends or family on different kinds of trips.

   Teacher Comment: **When is it important to compare vehicles by their speed?**
   Student Response: I compare passenger vehicles by their speed to understand how long it will take for different trips and to stay safe when crossing streets by understanding the speed of on-coming traffic.

Page 142 - KINDS OF VEHICLES

TEACHING SUGGESTION

Define types of vehicles (cargo, public transportation, and work vehicles):

Cargo is a load of goods.

Public means "everyone" and transportation means taking things from one place to another. (trans = across, port = move)

A work vehicle is one that a worker drives to work or uses in his or her work.

LESSON

Introduction

Teacher Comment: **Some vehicles haul heavy goods or materials long distances. They are cargo vehicles. Some vehicles carry large numbers of passengers from place to place. Any person can buy a ticket to ride these large vehicles. They are "public transportation vehicles." Some vehicles are used by their owners to go to work or school or for recreation, they are "personal vehicles."**

Stating the Objective

Teacher Comment: **In this lesson you will match vehicles to the group in which it belongs.**

Conducting the Lesson

Teacher Comment: **Name the first vehicle.**

Student Response: It is a cargo ship.

Teacher Comment: **What kind of vehicle is the cargo ship?**

Student Response: The cargo ship is a cargo vehicle.

Teacher Comment: **How do you know that this ship is a cargo vehicle?**

Student Response: I see that the ship is very large. It has stacks of cargo on top. It is so large and expensive that it must be owned by a large company or government.

Teacher Comment: **Draw a line from the photograph of the cargo ship to the words "cargo vehicle."**

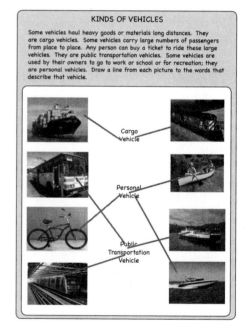

KINDS OF VEHICLES

Some vehicles haul heavy goods or materials long distances. They are cargo vehicles. Some vehicles carry large numbers of passengers from place to place. Any person can buy a ticket to ride these large vehicles. They are public transportation vehicles. Some vehicles are used by their owners to go to work or school or for recreation; they are personal vehicles. Draw a line from each picture to the words that describe that vehicle.

Teacher Comment: **Name the second vehicle.**

Student Response: The second vehicle is a bus.

Teacher Comment: **What kind of vehicle is a bus?**

Student Response: A bus is a public transportation vehicle.

Teacher Comment: **How do you know that this bus is a public transportation vehicle?**

Student Response: I see that the bus is very large and carries many passengers. It is so large and expensive that it must be owned by a large company or government.

Teacher Comment: **Draw a line from the picture of the bus to the words "public transportation vehicle."**

Teacher Comment: **Name the third vehicle.**

Student Response: The third vehicle is a bicycle.

Teacher Comment: **What kind of vehicle is a bicycle?**
  Student Response: A bicycle is a personal vehicle.
Teacher Comment: **How do you know that this bicycle is a personal vehicle?**
  Student Response: I see that the bicycle is too small to carry other passengers. The driver makes it move by pedalling, so it can't carry much weight. I remember a bicycle is usually owned by the person or family that rides on it.

Teacher Comment: **Draw a line from the picture of the bicylce to the words "personal vehicle."**

• Check students' work. Continue this dialog to discuss students' answers.

Thinking About Thinking
Teacher Comment: **What did you think about to name a group of vehicles?**
  Student Response:
    1. I looked at each picture and identified the important characteristics of the vehicle (size, how it is used, how many people it can carry, where it is driven).
    2. I looked for the word that describes other kinds of vehicles that have those same important characteristics.

Personal Application
Teacher Comment: **Why is it important to classify vehicles?**
  Student Response: I need to know the purpose of the vehicle.

Page 143 - A DIFFERENT KIND OF VEHICLE

LESSON

Introduction
Teacher Comment: **We have named types of vehicles.**

Stating the Objective
Teacher Comment: **In this lesson you will identify a vehicle that is not like the others, and draw a circle around it.**

Conducting the Lesson
Teacher Comment: **Name the vehicles shown in the pictures in the first row.**
  Student Response: These vehicles are a bus, a motorboat, a passenger train, and an airplane.

Teacher Comment: **Discuss with your partner how three of the four vehicles are alike.**

Teacher Comment: **How are these three vehicles alike?**

A DIFFERENT KIND OF VEHICLE

Three of these vehicles are the same kind. Circle the vehicle that is different. Then explain your answer to your partner or teacher.

EXAMPLE

REASON: The bus, train, and airplane are public transportation vehicles. The motorboat is a recreation vehicle.

Student Response: The bus, a passenger train, and an airplane all take passengers from place to place. They are transportation vehicles.

Teacher Comment: **Which vehicle is not a transportation vehicle?**
Student Response: The motorboat does not transport passengers; it carries only a few people. The motorboat is usually owned by the driver or the driver's friends or family.
Teacher Comment: **Notice a circle is drawn around the motorboat to show that it is a different kind of vehicle.**

Teacher Comment: **Name the vehicles shown in the pictures in the second row.**
Student Response: These vehicles are a fire truck, an ambulance, a police car, and a freight train.
Teacher Comment: **Discuss with your partner how three of the four vehicles are alike.**
Student Response: The fire truck, the ambulance, and the police car are emergency vehicles.

Teacher Comment: **Which vehicle is not an emergency vehicle?**
Student Response: The freight train is not an emergency vehicle. It carries cargo, not injured or sick people.
Teacher Comment: **Draw a circle around the freight train.**

• Check students' work. Continue this dialog to discuss students' answers.

Thinking About Thinking
Teacher Comment: **What did you think about when you decided which vehicle is not like the others?**
Student Response:
1. I looked at the picture of each vehicle and identified what kind of vehicle it is.
2. I found three vehicles that were the same kind.
3. I identified the vehicle that does not fit that group and explained why.

Personal Application
Teacher Comment. **When is it important to understand how a vehicle may be different from others?**
Student Response. I need to know how a vehicle may be different from others in order to understand how the vehicle is used and to write or tell about.

Page 144 - CLASSIFYING VEHICLES

TEACHING SUGGESTION
Use a class and members diagram like the one in the appendix to record students' answers. A blank class and members diagram can be found in the appendix.

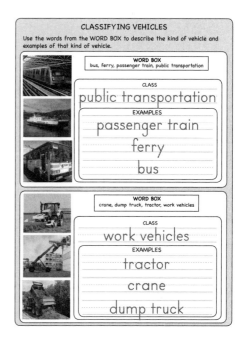

LESSON

Introduction
Teacher Comment: **We have learned about different types of vehicles. When we name different kinds of vehicles, we are classifying them.**

Stating the Objective
Teacher Comment: **In this lesson you will look at pictures of three vehicles and name the class to which they belong.**

Conducting the Lesson
Teacher Comment: **Name the vehicles in the top box.**
Student Response: The vehicles are a passenger train, a ferry, and a bus.

Teacher Comment: **With your partner discuss how these vehicles are alike.**
Student Response: They are all large vehicles that take many passengers from place to place. Passengers pay to ride on them.

Teacher Comment: **What words in the WORD BOX describe all these vehicles?**
Student Response: These vehicles are public transportation vehicles

Teacher Comment: **Write the words "public transportation vehicles" on the line labeled "CLASS."**

Teacher Comment: **Find the names of these public transportation vehicles in the WORD BOX and copy them on the lines under "EXAMPLES."**

Teacher Comment: **Name the vehicles shown in the pictures in the bottom box.**
Student Response: The vehicles are a tractor, a crane, and a dump truck.

Teacher Comment: **With your partner discuss how these vehicles are alike.**
Student Response: They all can be used for doing work. The tractor is used by a farmer to plow his fields, the crane is used by a worker to lift heavy things, and the dump truck is used by a worker to carry materials.

Teacher Comment: **What words in the WORD BOX describe all these vehicles?**
Student Response: They are work vehicles

Teacher Comment: **Write the words "work vehicles" on the line labeled "CLASS."**

Teacher Comment: **Find the names of these work vehicles in the WORD BOX and copy them on the lines under "EXAMPLES."**

Thinking About Thinking

Teacher Comment: **What did you think about to classify these vehicles?**

Student Response:

1. I looked at pictures of the vehicles and named that class of vehicles.
2. I looked for the word that describes the class of vehicles.
3. I looked for the words for examples of that class.

Personal Application

Teacher Comment: **When is it important to classify vehicles?**

Student Response: I classify vehicles to understand their use and to tell or write about them.

Page 145 - CLASSIFYING VEHICLES - SORTING

LESSON

Introduction

Teacher Comment: **We have practiced classifying vehicles.**

Stating the Objective

Teacher Comment: **In this lesson we will sort vehicles into two groups: emergency vehicles and personal transportation vehicles.**

Conducting the Lesson

Teacher Comment: **Name the vehicle in the first picture.**

Student Response: That vehicle is a motorcycle.

Teacher Comment: **Is a motorcycle an emergency or a personal transportation vehicle?**

Student Response: The motorcycle is used for personal transportation.

Teacher Comment: **Write the word "motorcycle" in the box labeled "PERSONAL TRANSPORTATION."**

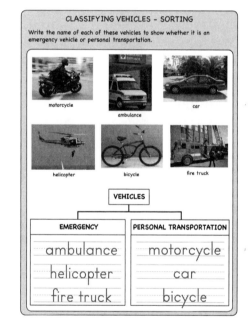

Teacher Comment: **Name the vehicle in the second picture.**

Student Response: That vehicle is an ambulance.

Teacher Comment: **Is an ambulance an emergency or a personal transportation vehicle?**

Student Response: An ambulance is an emergency vehicle.

Teacher Comment: **Write the word "ambulance" in the box labeled "EMERGENCY."**

• Check students' work. Continue this dialog to discuss students' answers.

Thinking About Thinking
Teacher Comment: **What did you think about to sort vehicles?**
Student Response:
1. I looked at each picture and decided whether it is an emergency vehicle or a personal vehicle
2. I looked for a word that describes that class of vehicles.
3. I wrote the word for each vehicle under the word for its class.

Personal Application
Teacher Comment: **When is it important to explain the purpose of a vehicle**?
Student Response: It's important for me to know the purpose of a vehicle to tell or write about it.

Page 146 - MATCH DRIVERS TO THEIR VEHICLES
LESSON

Introduction
Teacher Comment: **We have studied occupations in previous lessons and we have described different kinds of vehicles.**

Stating the Objective
Teacher Comment: **In this lesson you will match a person to the vehicle he or she drives.**

Conducting the Lesson
Teacher Comment: **The first picture shows a pilot. Which vehicle does the pilot drive?**
Student Response: The pilot flies an airplane.
Teacher Comment: **Draw a line from the pilot to the airplane.**

Teacher Comment: **The second picture shows a farmer. Which vehicle does the farmer drive?**
Student Response: The farmer drives a tractor.
Teacher Comment: **Draw a line from the farmer to the tractor**

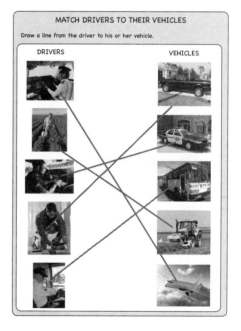

MATCH DRIVERS TO THEIR VEHICLES
Draw a line from the driver to his or her vehicle.
DRIVERS   VEHICLES

• Check students' work. Continue this dialog to discuss students' answers.

Thinking About Thinking

Teacher Comment: **What did you think about in order to match a person's job to the vehicle used in that occupation?**

Student Response:
1. I looked at the details of the driver in the picture.
2. I named that driver.
3. I found the vehicle that he drives.
4. I drew a line from the driver to the vehicle.

Personal Application

Teacher Comment: **When is it important to know what vehicle a worker drives?**

Student Response: I tell the vehicle that a person drives when I describe deliveries, describe traffic, or give directions when using public transportation.

CHAPTER THIRTEEN – THINKING ABOUT PLACES
(Pages 147-164)

GENERAL INTRODUCTION

CURRICULUM APPLICATIONS
Social Studies: Cite the role that places play in providing community needs and services; identify examples of types of places (residences, government buildings, recreational buildings, and stores); identify the key characteristics of various types of places (structure, appearance, ownership, and people who use it)

TEACHING SUGGESTIONS
- Encourage students to identify in their local community where the places described in this lesson are located.
- "Dwellings" or "residences" are abstract concepts for most young children. Dwellings can refer to homes for animals, as well as people; residences refers only to people. Use the terms "dwellings" or "residences" often in these activities and in other contexts and encourage students to do so.
- Teachers may use the graphic organizer at the right for bulletin board displays, student art work, or end-of-unit summary lessons.
- Enlarge and display the list of places on graphic master number 5 in the appendix. Refer to the word list when students discuss, write, or draw each place in order to associate the word with the place.

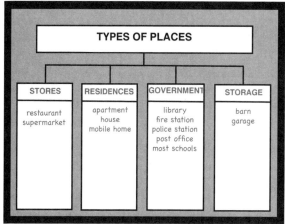

MENTAL MODEL
A mental model outlines the characteristics that one must state to describe or define a concept. After completing this chapter, each student will have applied this mental model to places in the lessons. A mental model helps a student:
- Anticipate what he or she needs to know to understand a new place
- Remember the characteristics of a place
- State a clear definition or write an adequate description of a place
- Explain a place to someone else

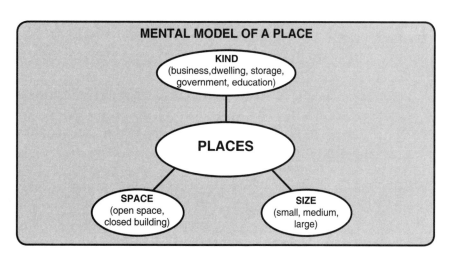

Page 148 - DESCRIBING PLACES

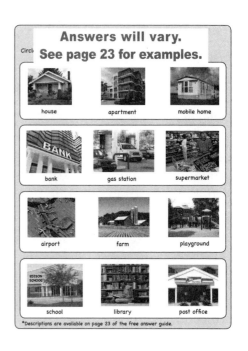

Answers will vary. See page 23 for examples.

house   apartment   mobile home

bank   gas station   supermarket

airport   farm   playground

school   library   post office

*Descriptions are available on page 23 of the free answer guide.

Introduction
Select a familiar place and describe it to the class in three to five sentences.

Teacher Comment: **Name the place I described.**

Teacher Comment: **What clues let you know what place I described?**

Student Response: The size, location, what it is used for, etc., let us know which place you described.

Stating the Objective
Teacher Comment: **In this lesson I will describe a place and you will select it.**

Conducting the Lesson
Teacher Comment: **Look at the places in the first row. This place can be moved on wheels and pulled by a large truck. Some can be as big as a small house. Some people use this place as their permanent home. Other people live in one while traveling or on vacation. What do we call this place? Select the picture that fits the description.**

Student Response: This place is a mobile home.

Teacher Comment: **What clues let you know that the place is the mobile home?**

Student Response: It can be moved. It is a small home that only a few people live in all the time.

Teacher Comment: **Why don't the other places fit the description?**

Student Response: A house and an apartment are too large to be moved.

Teacher Comment: **Circle the photograph of the mobile home.**

Teacher Comment: **Look at the places in the second row. Select the picture that fits the description. This place is used by people who want to cash checks, deposit money in their checking or savings accounts, or borrow money.**

Student Response: This place is a bank.

Teacher Comment: **What clues let you know that the place is a bank?**

Student Response: The word "bank" is on the sign.

Teacher Comment: **Why don't the other places fit the description?**

Student Response: A gas station and a supermarket are stores. A bank helps people with money but is not a store.

Teacher Comment: **Look at the third row. This place and the space around it is where people go to get on an airplane. The large main building is called a terminal. It has large spaces where people buy tickets and give their luggage to airport workers to put on the airplane. It has many long hallways that lead to the door where an airplane is parked. Outside the main building there are long roads called runways. Airplanes roll very fast down the long runways in order to gain enough speed to fly.**

Student Response: This place is an airport.

Teacher Comment: **What clues let you know that the place is an airport?**
Student Response: I see the large terminal building and the long hallway where the airplanes are parked.
Teacher Comment: **Why don't the other places fit the description?**
Student Response: A farm and a playground do not have hallways or airplanes. The barn on the farm is not as large as the terminal on the airport. The playground has no large buildings at all.

• Check students' work. Continue this dialog to discuss students' answers.

Thinking About Thinking
Teacher Comment: **What did you look for when you picked the place that was described?**
Student Response:
1. I listened for and remembered the important characteristics of the place.
2. I found the important characteristics in the pictures.
3. I checked which pictures show those important characteristics.
4. I checked that the other pictures of places don't show those important characteristics as well.

Personal Application
Teacher Comment: **When is it important to describe places well?**
Student Response: It is important to describe places in order to describe trips, to give directions, and to find places.

Page 149 - DESCRIBING PLACES

LESSON

Introduction
Teacher Comment: **In the last lesson we described places.**

Stating the Objective
Teacher Comment: **In this lesson you will match a photograph of a place to its name.**

Conducting the Lesson
Teacher Comment: **Name the place shown in the first photograph.**
Student Response: That place is a barber shop.
Teacher Comment: **What details in the photograph show that it is a barber shop?**
Student Response: The man cutting a boy's hair is a barber.
Teacher Comment: **Draw a line from the photograph of the barber shop to its name.**

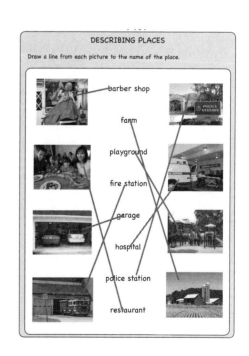

DESCRIBING PLACES
Draw a line from each picture to the name of the place.

barber shop
farm
playground
fire station
garage
hospital
police station
restaurant

Teacher Comment: **Name the place in the second photograph.**
Student Response: That place is a restaurant.
Teacher Comment: **What details in the photograph show that it is a restaurant?**
Student Response: The family is sitting at a table with a meal in front of them. There are other people eating in the background.
Teacher Comment: **Find the word "restaurant" in the list of words and draw a line from the photograph to the word "restaurant."**

• Check students' work. Continue this dialog to discuss students' answers.

Thinking About Thinking
Teacher Comment: **How did you decide which word belonged with each photograph?**
Student Response:
1. I looked at the details.
2. I named the place
3. I looked for its name.

Personal Application
Teacher Comment: **When is it important to find the word for a place?**
Student Response: It is important to find the word for a place to read signs and to understand or give directions.

Page 150 - DESCRIBING PLACES

LESSON

Introduction
Teacher Comment: **We matched the words for some places.**

Stating the Objective
Teacher Comment: **In this lesson you will write the words for places.**

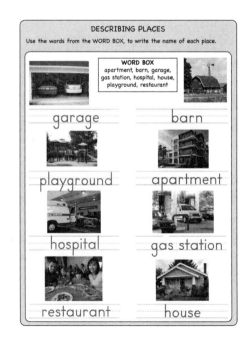

Conducting the Lesson
Teacher Comment: **Look at the first place. Name this place and describe it to your partner.**
Student Response: That place is a garage. It is used to keep cars safe from weather or damage. It also usually stores yard equipment or tools. It is usually attached to the house and is just large enough to hold one or two cars.
Teacher Comment: **Find the word "garage" in the WORD BOX and write it on the blank.**
Teacher Comment: **What details show that the place is a garage?**
Student Response: I see two cars parked inside. A large door opens and closes to keep the cars safe. I see tools stored on the back wall.

Teacher Comment: **Look at the second place. Name this place and describe it to your partner.**

Student Response: That place is a playground. It is a large open space with many things to play on. There are swings, slides, and ladders to climb on. There are benches where children and adults rest. Sometimes there are small, open buildings to play in.

• Check students' work. Continue this dialog to discuss students' answers.

Thinking About Thinking

Teacher Comment: **How did you decide which word belonged with each picture?**
Student Response:
1. I looked at the details in the picture and named the place.
2. I looked for the word in the WORD BOX that describes the place.
3. I wrote the word for the place on the blank.

Personal Application

Teacher Comment: **When is it important to write the names of places?**
Student Response: I need to know the names of places to tell or write about them.

Page 151 - DESCRIBING PLACES

LESSON

Introduction

Teacher Comment: **In the last lesson we wrote the names of places.**

Stating the Objective

Teacher Comment: **In this lesson you will decide whether a place is a public place or a private place.**

Conducting the Lesson

Teacher Comment: **Public places are stores and government buildings where anyone can go to buy things or get government services. Private places are homes or farms that are owned by families. You need the owner's permission to go into a private place. Name the first place.**

Student Response: That place is a mobile home.
Teacher Comment: **Is a mobile home public or private?**
Student Response: A mobile home is private. You need permission to go into it.
Teacher Comment: **Draw a line from the photograph to the word "private."**

DESCRIBING PLACES

Some of these places are public. Anyone can go into a public place. Some places are private. The owner lets only some people go into a private place. Draw lines from each picture to the word that describes that place.

public

private

• Check students' work. Continue this dialog to discuss students' answers.

Thinking About Thinking
Teacher Comment: **How did you decide whether the place was public or private?**
Student Response:
  1. I looked at each picture and identified the place.
  2. I decided whether people needed permission to go into the place.

Personal Application
Teacher Comment: **When is it important to know if a place is public or private?**
Student Response: I need to know whether a place is public or private to know whether I need permission to go into it.

Page 152 - DESCRIBING A PLACE

LESSON

Introduction
Teacher Comment: **In the last lesson we decided whether a place was a public place or a private place.**

Stating the Objective
Teacher Comment: **In this lesson you will complete a paragraph that describes a post office.   A paragraph is a group of sentences that gives us much more information about a place than we can say in one sentence.**

Conducting the Lesson
Teacher Comment: **Find the words in the WORD BOX that tell about the post office. Write the words in the blanks.**

• Check students' work.

Thinking About Thinking
Teacher Comment: **What did you pay attention to when you described a post office?**
Student Response:
  1. I remembered details about a post office.
  2. I looked for the words that tell about a post office.
  3. I wrote the words that complete a paragraph about the post office.

Personal Application
Teacher Comment: **When is it important to describe a place?**
Student Response: I need to describe a place to tell or write about it.

Page 153 - PARTS OF A FARM

LESSON

Introduction
Teacher Comment: **To describe places we sometimes need to know the names of its parts and explain how each part is important for the place to work properly.**

Stating the Objective
Teacher Comment: **In this lesson you will think about the parts of a farm, what each part is for, and explain why each part is important.**

Conducting the Lesson

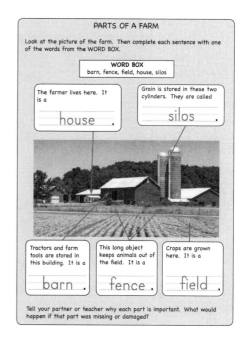

Teacher Comment: **Which part of the farm is where the farmer lives?**

Student Response: The farmer lives in a house on the farm.

Teacher Comment: **Write the word "house" on the blank line in the top box.**

Teacher Comment: **What would happen if the house was missing or damaged?**

Student Response: The farmer could not live there.

Teacher Comment: **Look at the second box. This part holds grain. What is it called?**

Student Response: The part that holds grain is the silo.

Teacher Comment: **Write the word "silos" on the blank lines in the second box.**

Teacher Comment: **What would happen if the silos were missing or damaged?**

Student Response: The farmer would have to store his grain somewhere else.

Teacher Comment: **Look at the third box. This building is used to store farm equipment. What is it called?**

Student Response: That storage building is a barn.

Teacher Comment: **Write the word "barn" on the blank lines in the third box.**

Teacher Comment: **What would happen if the barn was missing or damaged?**

Student Response: The farm equipment would be stored outside where it could be damaged by weather.

Teacher Comment: **Look at the fourth box. This part is very long. It keeps farm animals out of the field. What is this long part called?**

Student Response: This is a fence.

Teacher Comment: **Write the word "fence" on the blank lines in the fourth box.**

Teacher Comment: **What would happen if the fence was missing or damaged?**

Student Response: Animals could come into the field and eat the crop.

Teacher Comment: **Look at the last box. This is where the farmer grows crops. What is it called?**
Student Response: The part that the farm where crops are grown is the field.
Teacher Comment: **Write the word "field" on the blank lines in the fourth box.**
Teacher Comment: **What would happen if the field was missing or damaged?**
Student Response: The farmer could not grow crops or raise animals.

Thinking About Thinking
Teacher Comment: **What did you think about in order to describe the parts of a farm?**
Student Response:
1. I named the part.
2. I remembered what it is used for.
3. I thought about what would happen if that part was missing.

Personal Application
Teacher Comment: **When is it important to describe all the parts of a whole place?**
Student Response: I describe the parts of a place to explain how it works and how it is different from other places. I describe the parts to tell a story about a place.

Page 154 - SIMILAR PLACES

TEACHING SUGGESTION
Emphasize the wording commonly used to describe similarities. Repeat words that show similarity (both, and, like, similar, resemble, etc.) and encourage students to use them in their responses.

LESSON

Introduction
Teacher Comment: **We have learned how to describe places.**

Stating the Objective
Teacher Comment: **In this lesson you will identify a place that is most like another place.**

Conducting the Lesson
Teacher Comment: **Name the places in the example.**
Student Response: The places are a garage, a hospital, a playground, and a barn.
Teacher Comment: **Tell your partner all the important things that you know about a garage.**
Student Response: A garage is a building that is used to protect a car and to store tools and materials.
Teacher Comment: **Which place at the right is most like a garage?**
Student Response: A barn is most like a garage.

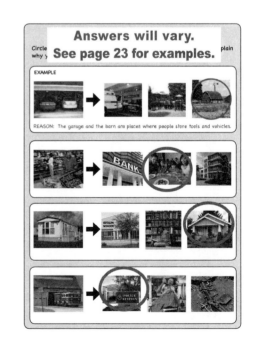

Teacher Comment: **How is a barn most like a garage?**
Student Response: Both are places where equipment/tools are stored.
Teacher Comment: **How are the other places different from a garage?**
Student Response: A hospital and a playground are not storage places. A hospital is an emergency place. A playground is a recreational place.
Teacher Comment: **Notice a circle is drawn around the photograph of the barn to show that it is like a garage.**

Teacher Comment: **Name the places in the second row.**
Student Response: The buildings are a supermarket, a bank, a restaurant, and an apartment building.
Teacher Comment: **Tell your partner all the important things that you know about a supermarket.**
Student Response: A supermarket is the large store where people by food.
Teacher Comment: **Which place at the right is most like a supermarket.**
Student Response: A restaurant is most like a supermarket .
Teacher Comment: **Draw a circle around the restaurant.**

Teacher Comment: **How is a restaurant most like a supermarket?**
Student Response: Both are businesses where food is sold.
Teacher Comment: **How are the other places different from a supermarket?**
Student Response: A bank is a place where people deposit and withdraw money. An apartment is a residence.

Teacher Comment: **Name the places in the third row.**
Student Response: The places are a mobile home, a school, a library, and a house.
Teacher Comment: **Tell your partner all the important things that you know about a mobile home.**
Student Response: A mobile home is a small place where people live. It can be moved on wheels.
Teacher Comment: **Which place at the right is most like a mobile home?**
Student Response: A house is most like a mobile home.
Teacher Comment: **Draw a circle around the house.**

Teacher Comment: **How is a house most like a mobile home?**
Student Response: Both are private places where people live.
Teacher Comment: **How are the other places different from a mobile home?**
Student Response: Schools and libraries are public places; people do not live there.

Teacher Comment: **Name the places in the fourth row.**
Student Response: The places are a fire station, a police station, a barber shop, and an airport.
Teacher Comment: **Tell your partner all the important things that you know about a fire station.**
Student Response: A fire station is a place where fire engines and fire equipment are stored. The firefighters work on the engines and equipment to keep them in good condition. Some firefighters are on duty at all times to answer emergency calls. Firefighters eat and sleep there when they are on duty, but they do not live there.

Teacher Comment: **Which place at the right is most like a fire station?**
Student Response: A police station is most like a fire station.
Teacher Comment: **Draw a circle around the police station.**

Teacher Comment: **How is a police station most like a fire station?**
Student Response: Both are government buildings where vehicles and equipment are stored. Both firefighters and police officers are on duty at all times to answer emergency calls.
Teacher Comment: **How are the other places different from a fire station?**
Student Response: A barber shop is a business. An airport is a large terminal and an open space where airplanes land.

Thinking About Thinking
Teacher Comment: **What did you think about to describe similar places?**
Student Response:
1. I recalled the important details of the first place (its appearance, special equipment, etc.).
2. I looked for similar details in the other places.
3. I selected the place that has most of the same details.
4. I checked to see that other places do not fit the important details better than the one I selected.

Personal Application
Teacher Comment: **When is it important to understand how places are alike?**
Student Response: I need to understand how places are alike to tell or write about them.

Page 155 - SIMILARITIES AND DIFFERENCES - PLACES

TEACHING SUGGESTION
Teachers may use a compare and contrast graphic to record students' answers. See the appendix for a blank graphic.

LESSON

Introduction
Teacher Comment: **We have described how two places are alike; we compared them. Sometimes we want to know how places are different in order to understand something important about them. When we describe how places are different, we contrast them.**

Stating the Objective
Teacher Comment: **In this lesson you will look at a pictures of two places and compare and contrast them.**

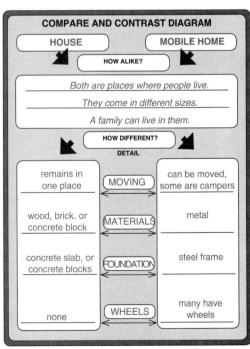

Conducting the Lesson

Teacher Comment: The first row shows a house and a mobile home. Write the words "house" and "mobile home" on the blank lines. How are these places alike?

Student Response: Both are places where people live. Usually they are residences for one family.

Teacher Comment: How are these places different?

Student Response: A house is designed to stay in one place. Houses are made of wood or concrete and sit on a concrete foundation. A mobile home is made of aluminum or metal and sits on a steel frame. It can be moved to a different location at any time. Some mobile homes have wheels and can be pulled by a car or truck and taken on vacation.

Teacher Comment: What characteristics did you pay attention to when explaining how these places are alike and different?

Student Response: I thought about their size and purpose.

Teacher Comment: Look at the second row. It shows a bank and a post office. Write the words "bank" and "post office" on the blank lines. How are these places alike?

Student Response: Both are places where people pay for a service. Customers pay the bank to save or receive money. Customers buy stamps the post office to send letters or packages.

Teacher Comment: How are these places different?

Student Response: The bank is a private business that helps customers save or borrow money. The post office is a government place that mails and delivers letters and packages.

Teacher Comment: Look at the third row. It shows a school and a library. Write the words "school" and "library" on the blank lines. How are these places alike?

Student Response: People go to both places to get information or learn something new. Both use books. Both are usually government places.

Teacher Comment: How are these places different?

Student Response: Most schools serve only children. Students go to school five days a week for nine months of the year. Students spend their time in classrooms. At school students use special books to help them learn to read and do arithmetic. Schools also have small libraries where children can borrow books. Both adults and children borrow books from libraries. The books that they borrow may teach them new information or skills, or they may borrow books for entertainment. People go to the library to borrow or return books, movies and music or to use computers to find information.

Teacher Comment: Look at the fourth row. It shows a farm and a playground. Write the words "farm" and "playground" on the blank lines. How are these places alike?

Student Response: Both are large spaces with equipment.

Teacher Comment: **How are these places different?**
Student Response: A farm is a private business where a farmer grows food or raises animals. It has large fields and buildings to store food and farm equipment. People do not visit a farm unless they know or have business with the farmer. Most children seldom visit the farm. A playground is a public space that families can use whenever they wish. Playgrounds contain swings, slides, and climbing equipment for recreation.

Thinking About Thinking
Teacher Comment: **What did you think about to compare and contrast places?**
Student Response:
1. I remembered the important characteristics of each of the places (its appearance, its use, and special equipment).
2. I matched characteristics that both places have.
3. I thought about how the places are different.
4. I checked to see that I have included all the important characteristics of both places.

Personal Application
Teacher Comment: **When is it important to tell how places are alike or different?**
Student Response: I need to tell how places are alike or different to describe how they are used, or to give directions.

Page 156 - COMPARING PLACES

TEACHING SUGGESTION
Emphasize the sentence structure that shows comparison. For example, a bank is <u>larger than</u> a barber shop, <u>but smaller than</u> a supermarket.

LESSON

Introduction
Teacher Comment: **We have described how two places are alike or different.**

Stating the Objective
Teacher Comment: **In this lesson you will arrange places in order of size or how often you visit them.**

Conducting the Lesson
Teacher Comment: **In the top box you will arrange the places in order of size from smallest to largest. Name the places in the top box.**
Student Response: The places are a barber shop, a bank, and a supermarket.
Teacher Comment: **Look at the size of the places and think about what you know about them. Which place is the smallest?**
Student Response: The barber shop is the smallest.
Teacher Comment: **Write the words "barber shop" on the top line.**

Teacher Comment: **Which place is the largest?**
 Student Response: A supermarket is the largest.
Teacher Comment: **Write the word "supermarket" in the third blank.**

Teacher Comment: **Which place is larger than a barber shop, but smaller than a supermarket?**
 Student Response: A bank is larger than a barber shop, but smaller than a supermarket.
Teacher Comment: **Write the word "bank" in the second blank.**

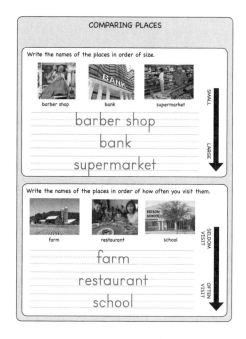

Teacher Comment: **Name the places in the second box.**
 Student Response: The places are a farm, a restaurant, and a school.
Teacher Comment: **You will arrange these places in the order of how often you visit them. Which one do you visit the least often?**
 Student Response: I rarely visit a farm
Teacher Comment: **Write the word "farm" in the top blank.**

Teacher Comment: **Which place do you visit the most often?**
 Student Response: I go to school five days a week.
Teacher Comment: **Write the word "school" in the bottom blank.**

Teacher Comment: **Which place do you visit more often than a farm, but less often than you go to school?**
 Student Response: I visit a restaurant more often than a farm, but less often than I go to school.
Teacher Comment: **Write the word "restaurant" on the second blank.**

Thinking About Thinking
 Teacher Comment: **What did you think about when you put places in order?**
 1. I looked at the pictures and decided which place was smallest or seldom visited.
 2. I decided which place was the largest or most often visited.
 3. I decided which place was in between the size or use of the others.

Personal Application
 Teacher Comment: **When is it important to compare places by size?**
 Student Response: I compare places by size to find them or to describe them to someone else.
 Teacher Comment: **When is it important to compare places by how often we visit them?**
 Student Response: I compare places by how often we visit them to understand how important they are to families or to describe them to someone else.

Page 157 - KINDS OF PLACES

TEACHING SUGGESTION
To reinforce students' responses, you may use a branching diagram to record their answers. For a blank branching diagram see the appendix.

LESSON

Introduction
Teacher Comment: **There are different kinds of places. Some places contain stores that sell things or provide a service; they are "businesses." Some places are owned by the city, state, or national government to provide a service; they are "government buildings." Some places are where people go to relax; they are "recreation places." Some places are where people park their vehicles or store equipment and other belongings; they are "storage places."**

Stating the Objective
Teacher Comment: **In this lesson you will match places to the group in which it belongs.**

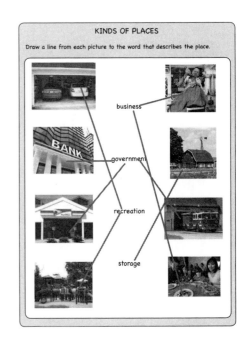

Conducting the Lesson
Teacher Comment: **Name the first place.**
Student Response: It is a garage.
Teacher Comment: **What kind of place is the garage?**
Student Response: The garage is a storage place.
Teacher Comment: **Draw a line from the picture to the word "storage."**

Teacher Comment: **Name the second place.**
Student Response: The second place is a bank.
Teacher Comment: **What kind of place is the bank?**
Student Response: A bank is a business.
Teacher Comment: **Draw a line from the picture to the word "business."**

• Check students' work. Continue this dialog to discuss students' answers.

Thinking About Thinking
Teacher Comment: **What did you think about to name a group of places?**
Student Response:
1. I looked at each picture and identified the important characteristics of the place (its size, its use, who owns it).
2. I looked for the word that describes the kinds of places that have those same important characteristics.

Personal Application
Teacher Comment: **Why is it important to know kinds of places?**
Student Response: I need to know the kinds places to tell or write about it them.

Pages 158 - A DIFFERENT KIND OF PLACE

LESSON

Introduction
Teacher Comment: **We have named different kinds of places, such as businesses, government buildings, recreational places, residences, and storage places.**

Stating the Objective
Teacher Comment: **In this lesson we will identify a place that is not like the others.**

Conducting the Lesson
Teacher Comment: **Name the places in the first box.**
Student Response: The places are a fire station, a police station, a post office, and a barn.
Teacher Comment: **Discuss with your partner how three of the places are alike.**

Teacher Comment: **How are three of the places alike?**
Student Response: The fire station, police station, and the post office are government buildings.
Teacher Comment: **Which place is not a government building?**
Student Response: The barn is not a government building.
Teacher Comment: **Notice that a circle is drawn around the barn to show that it is a different kind of place.**

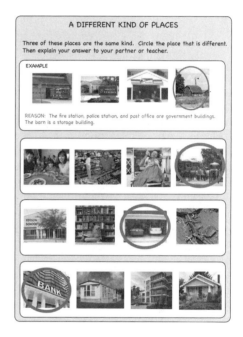

Teacher Comment: **Name the places in the second box.**
Student Response: The places are a restaurant, a supermarket, a barber shop, and a playground.
Teacher Comment: **Discuss with your partner how three of the places are alike.**

Teacher Comment: **How are three of the places alike?**
Student Response: The restaurant, supermarket, and barber shop are businesses.
Teacher Comment: **Which place is not a business?**
Student Response: The playground is not a business.

• Check students' work. Continue this dialog to discuss students' answers.

Thinking About Thinking

Teacher Comment: **What did you think about to decide what characteristics these three places have in common?**

Student Response:

1. I looked at pictures of various places and identified what kind if place it is (size, who lives or works there, usual location, and equipment it houses).
2. I found three places that were the same kind.
3. I found the place that does not fit that group and explain why.

Personal Application

Teacher Comment: **When is it important to understand which place is different from others?**

Student Response. I need to know which places are different from others to describe deliveries, give or understand directions, or explain a particular place to someone that is unfamiliar with it.

Page 159 - CLASSIFYING PLACES

LESSON

Introduction

Teacher Comment: **We have learned about government buildings, such as the post office and libraries. We know that places where people live are called residences. We know that stores are businesses. We know that barns and garages are storage buildings. When we name kinds of places, we are classifying them.**

Stating the Objective

Teacher Comment: **In this lesson you will name the class for each group of places. You will also write the names of the places in that class.**

Conducting the Lesson

Teacher Comment: **Name the places in the top box.**

Student Response: They are a fire station, a post office, and a police station.

Teacher Comment: **How are these places alike?**

Student Response: They are government buildings.

Teacher Comment: **Write the words "government buildings" on the blank marked "CLASS."**

Teacher Comment: **Use words in the WORD BOX to write the names of the places on the lines under "EXAMPLES."**

Teacher Comment: **Name the places in the bottom box.**

Student Response: The places are a supermarket, a gas station, and a restaurant.

CLASSIFYING PLACES

Use the words from the WORD BOX to write the class (kind or group) of each place on the top line. Then write the names of the places on the three lines.

WORD BOX
fire station, government buildings, police station, post office

CLASS
government buildings

EXAMPLES
fire station
post office
police station

WORD BOX
business, gas station, restaurant, supermarket

CLASS
business

EXAMPLES
supermarket
gas station
restaurant

Teacher Comment: **How are these places are alike?**
  Student Response: These places are businesses.

Teacher Comment: **Write the word "business" on the blank marked "CLASS."**

Teacher Comment: **Use words in the WORD BOX to write the names of the places on the lines under "EXAMPLES."**

Thinking About Thinking
Teacher Comment: **What did you think about to name a class of places?**
  Student Response:
  1. I looked at each picture and identified the important characteristics of the place.
  2. I looked for the word that describes that class of places.
  3. I named examples of places in that class.

Personal Application
Teacher Comment: **Why is it important to classify places?**
  Student Response: I need to classify places to tell or write about them.

Page 160 - CLASSIFYING PLACES - SORTING

TEACHING SUGGESTIONS
• Model and encourage students to express the following process for classifying places.
• Use the terms "groups," "types," "kinds," and "classes" to help students conceptualize classification. Encourage students to use these words in their discussions.

LESSON

Introduction
Teacher Comment: **We have classified some places, such as government buildings and businesses.**

Stating the Objective
Teacher Comment: **In this exercise you will sort places into three classes. Some places are residences where people live. Some places are businesses, where people buy things, and some places are places where people store things.**

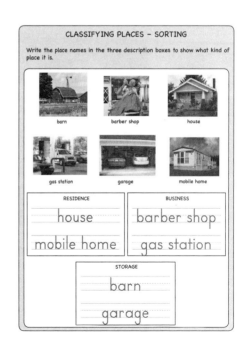

Conducting the Lesson
Teacher Comment: **Name the place in the first picture.**
  Student Response: That place is a barn.
Teacher Comment: **What kind of place is a barn?**
  Student Response: A barn is a storage place.

Teacher Comment: **Write the word "barn" in the box labeled "STORAGE."**

Teacher Comment: **Name the place in the second picture.**
  Student Response: That place is a barber shop.

Teacher Comment: **What kind of place is a barber shop?**
  Student Response: A barber shop is a business.

Teacher Comment: **Write the words "barber shop" in the box labeled "BUSINESS."**

Teacher Comment: **Name the place in the third picture.**
  Student Response: That place is a house.

Teacher Comment: **What kind of place is a house?**
  Student Response: A house is a residence.

Teacher Comment: **Write the word "house" in the box labeled "RESIDENCE."**

• Check students' work. Continue this dialog to discuss students' answers.

Thinking About Thinking
Teacher Comment: **What did you think about to classify places?**
  Student Response:
  1. I looked at each picture and decided what kind of place it is.
  2. I looked for a word that describes that class of places.

Personal Application
Teacher Comment. **When is it important to classify places?**
  Student Response: I classify places to give or understand directions or to explain a particular place to someone who is unfamiliar with it.

Pages 161 - MATCH THE JOB AND VEHICLE TO THEIR PLACE

LESSON

Introduction
Teacher Comment: **We have studied jobs, places, and vehicles.**

Stating the Objective
Teacher Comment: **In this lesson you will match a person's job to the place in which he or she works and to the vehicle that the worker drives.**

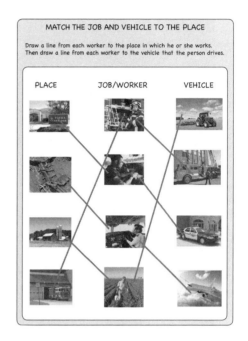

Conducting the Lesson
Teacher Comment: **Look at the first job/worker. In which place does a firefighter work?**
  Student Response: The firefighter works in a fire station.
Teacher Comment: **Draw a line from the firefighter to the fire station.**

Teacher Comment: **Which vehicle does the firefighter drive or ride in?**
  Student Response: The firefighter rides on a fire truck.
Teacher Comment: **Draw a line from the firefighter to the fire truck.**

• Check students' work. Continue this dialog to discuss students' answers.

Thinking About Thinking
Teacher Comment: **What did you think about in order to match a person's job to the place and vehicle used in that occupation?**
  Student Response:
  1. I named the job in the picture.
  2. I found the place in which that person works.
  3. I drew a line from the worker to the place.
  4. I found the vehicle used by the worker.
  5. I drew a line from the worker to his or her vehicle.

Personal Application
Teacher Comment: **When do you need to describe the place in which a person works and the vehicle used by that worker?**
  Student Response: I describe a worker's vehicle and place to describe a family members' job.

Page 162 - FINDING PLACES ON A MAP

LESSON

Introduction
Teacher Comment: **We have studied different types of places**

Stating the Objective
Teacher Comment: **In this lesson you will use a map to find the location of places. A map is a drawing that shows the streets in a town or city. People use the map to locate places and to understand what streets they need to follow to go from one place to another.**

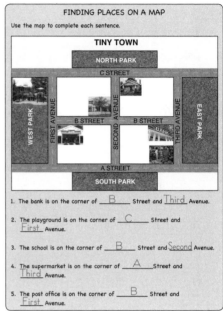

Conducting the Lesson
Teacher Comment: **On the map the streets run across the page and the avenues run up and down. Find the bank on the map. On which street is the bank located?**
Student Response: The bank is on B Street.
Teacher Comment: **Write a "B" on the first blank.**

Teacher Comment: **On which avenue is the bank located?**
Student Response: The bank is on Third Avenue.
Teacher Comment: **Write "third" on the second blank.**

• Check students' work. Continue this dialog to discuss students' answers.

Thinking About Thinking
Teacher Comment: **What did you think about to describe the location of a place?**
Student Response:
1. I found the picture of the place on the map.
2. I found the street where it is located.
3. I found the avenue where it is located.

Personal Application
Teacher Comment: **When is it important to explain where a place is located?**
Student Response: I explain where a place is located to describe deliveries or to give or understand directions.

Page 163 - FINDING DISTANCES ON A MAP

LESSON

Introduction
Teacher Comment: **We have located places on a map.**

Stating the Objective
Teacher Comment: **In this lesson you will use a map to tell the distance between two places.**

Conducting the Lesson
Teacher Comment: **The first sentence asks about home and school. Find the house on the map.**
Teacher Comment: **Find the school on the map.**
Teacher Comment: **The space between two streets is called a "block." How many blocks would a person walk to get from home to school?**
Student Response: The home is one block from the school.
Teacher Comment: **Write a "1" on the first blank.**

• Check students' work. Continue this dialog to discuss students' answers..

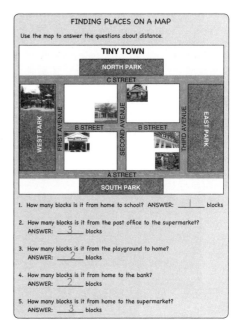

Thinking About Thinking
Teacher Comment: **What did you think about to describe the distance between two places?**
Student Response:
1. I found the pictures of the two places on the map.
2. I counted the blocks between the pictures.

Personal Application
Teacher Comment: **When is it important to explain where a place is located?**
Student Response: I explain where a place is located to describe deliveries or to give or understand directions.
Teacher Comment: **When is it important to explain the distance between places?**
Student Response: I explain the distance between places to give or understand directions and to tell how far a person must walk or drive.

APPENDIX

GRAPHIC MASTERS

The following graphics may be used to produce transparencies. They also may be photocopied for distribution to your class.

1. Word list - FOOD .... page 197

2. Word list - ANIMALS.. page 198

3. Word list - JOBS .... page 199

4. Word list - VEHICLES.. page 200

5. Word list - PLACES .... page 201

6. How are two things ALIKE?... page 202

7. How are two things DIFFERENT?................................. page 203

8. Compare and Contrast Diagram.................................... page 204

9. Kinds of Things.. page 205

10. Branching diagram - 2 branches .... page 206

11. Branching diagram - 3 branches .... page 207

12. Branching diagram - 4 branches .... page 208

13. Comparison Diagram.. page 209

GRAPHIC MASTER 1 - Food list

FOOD

apple	grapes
bacon	ham
banana	lettuce
beans	milk
blueberries	onion
bread	orange
broccoli	peas
butter	peach
cabbage	potato
carrot	rice
celery	salmon
cheese	strawberries
chicken	steak
corn	tomato
eggs	turkey

GRAPHIC MASTER 2 - Animal list

ANIMALS

alligator	goldfish
ant	grasshopper
bat	horse
bee	lizard
blue jay	ostrich
butterfly	owl
camel	pig
chicken	salmon
cow	shark
duck	snake
eagle	spider
elephant	squirrel
fish	turkey
frog	turtle
giraffe	whale
goat	zebra

GRAPHIC MASTER 3 - Jobs list

JOBS

artist
bank teller
bus driver
carpenter
construction worker
cook
dentist
doctor
farmer
firefighter
grocer
librarian
mail carrier
nurse
pharmacist
pilot
plumber
police officer
sales clerk
teacher

GRAPHIC MASTER 4 - Vehicles list

VEHICLES

airplane

ambulance

bicycle

boat

bulldozer

bus

canoe

car

cargo ship

crane

dump truck

ferry

fire truck

freight train

helicopter

motorboat

motorcycle

passenger train

pickup truck

police car

school bus

ship

tractor

GRAPHIC MASTER 5 - Places list

PLACES

airport	house
apartment	library
bank	mobile home
barber shop	playground
barn	police station
farm	post office
fire station	restaurant
garage	school
gas station	supermarket
hospital	

GRAPHIC MASTER 6 - Compare graphic
Use to show how two family members, foods, animals, occupations, vehicles, or places
are alike.

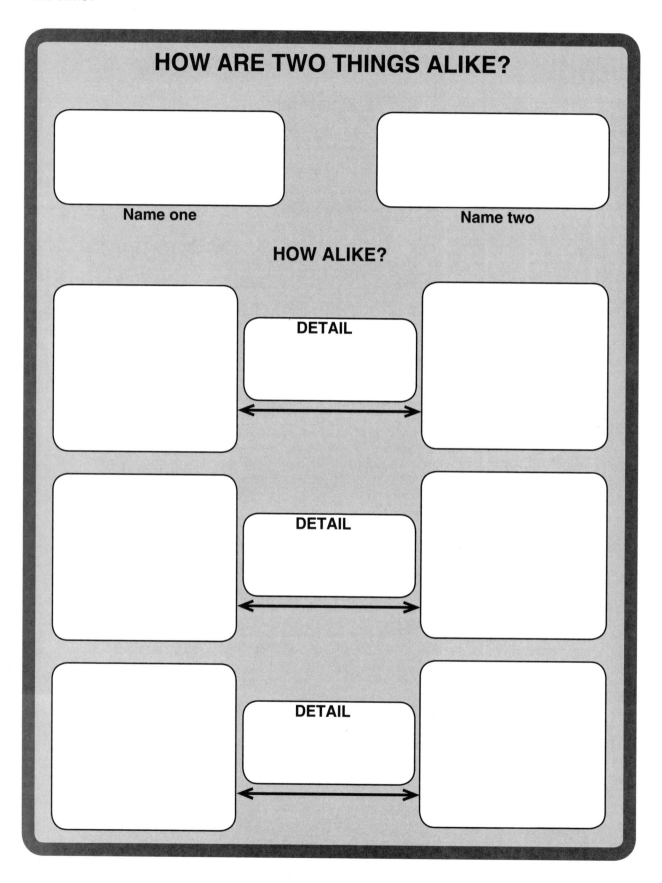

GRAPHIC MASTER 7 - Contrast graphic
Use to show how two family members, foods, animals, occupations, vehicles, or places are different.

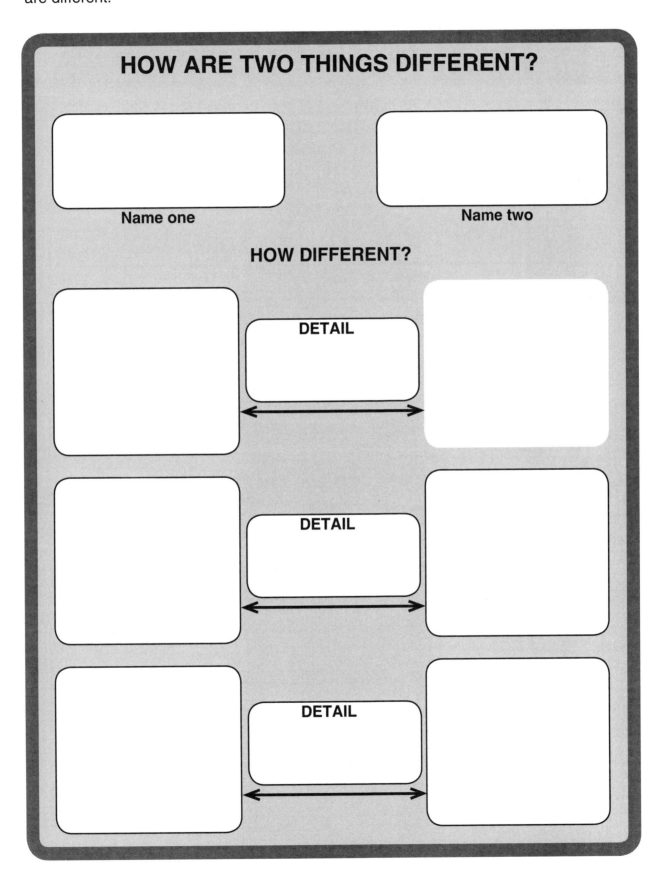

GRAPHIC MASTER 8 - Compare and Contrast graphic
Use to show how two family members, foods, animals, occupations, vehicles, or places are alike and different.

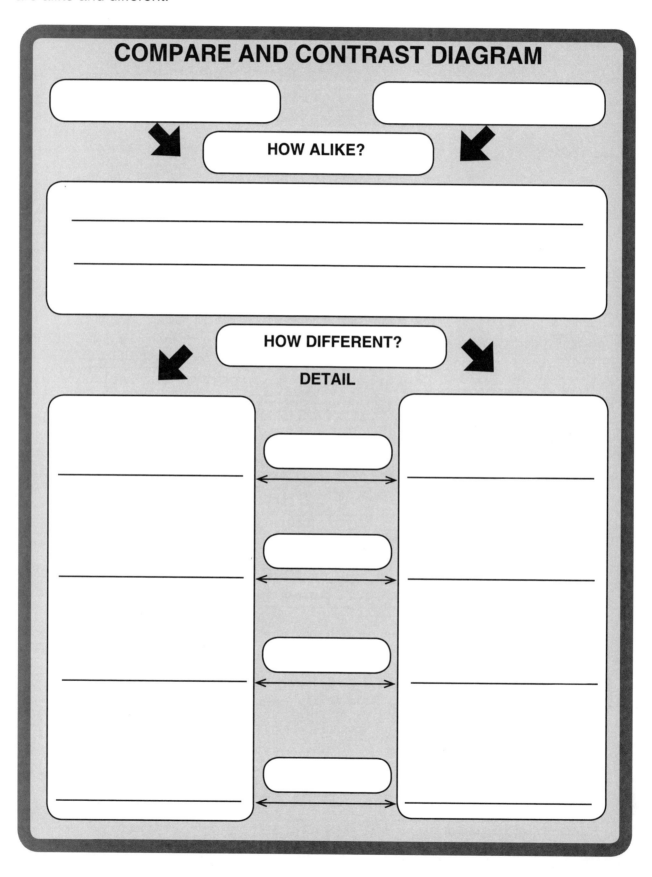

GRAPHIC MASTER 9 - Central Idea graphic
Use to show a examples of land forms, bodies of water, food, animals, occupations, vehicles, or places.

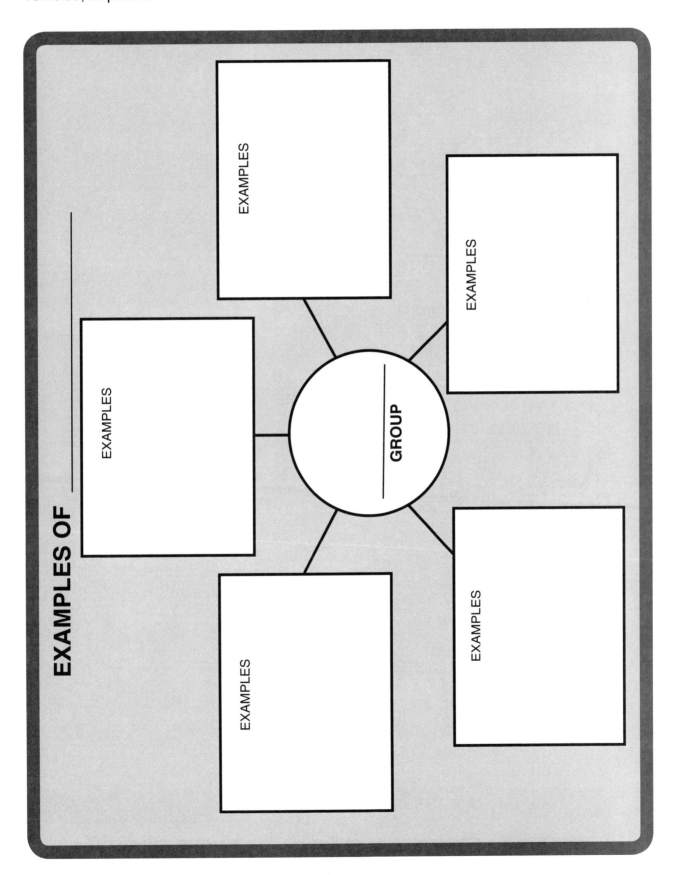

GRAPHIC MASTER 10 - Branching diagram
Use to sort a group into two classes.

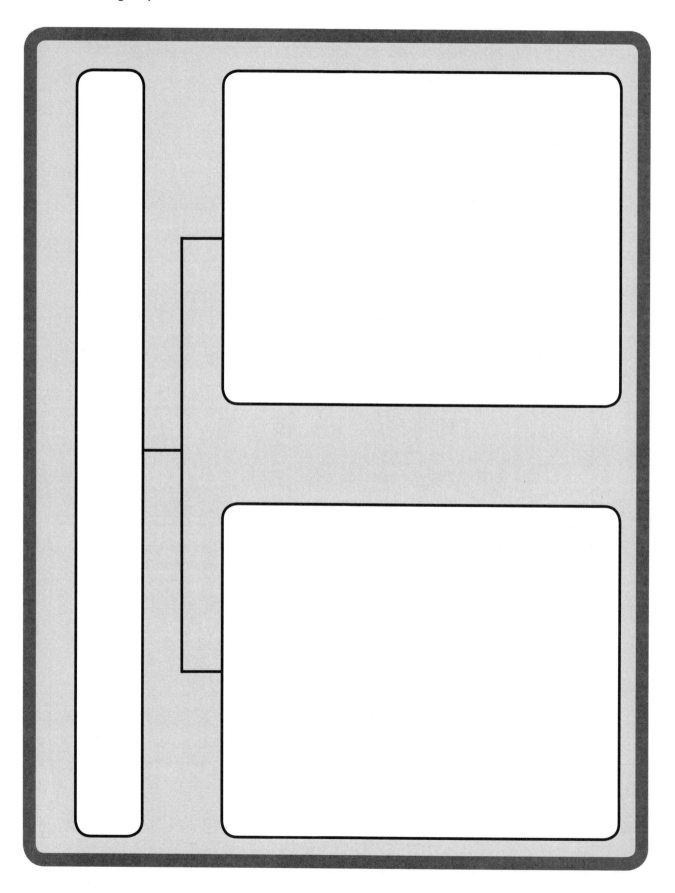

GRAPHIC MASTER 11 - Branching diagram
Use to sort a group into three classes.

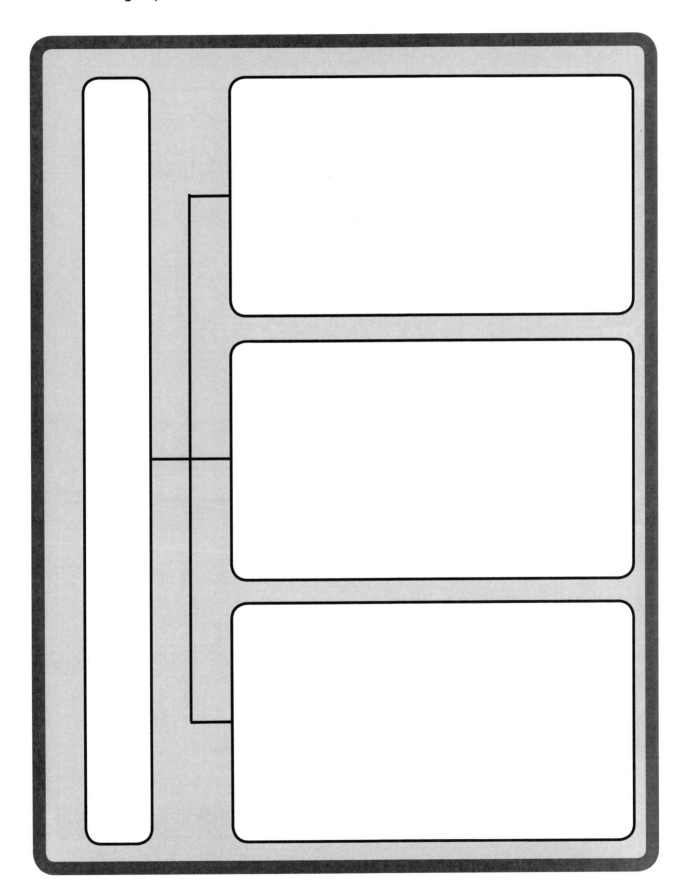

GRAPHIC MASTER 12 - Branching diagram
Use to sort a group into four classes.

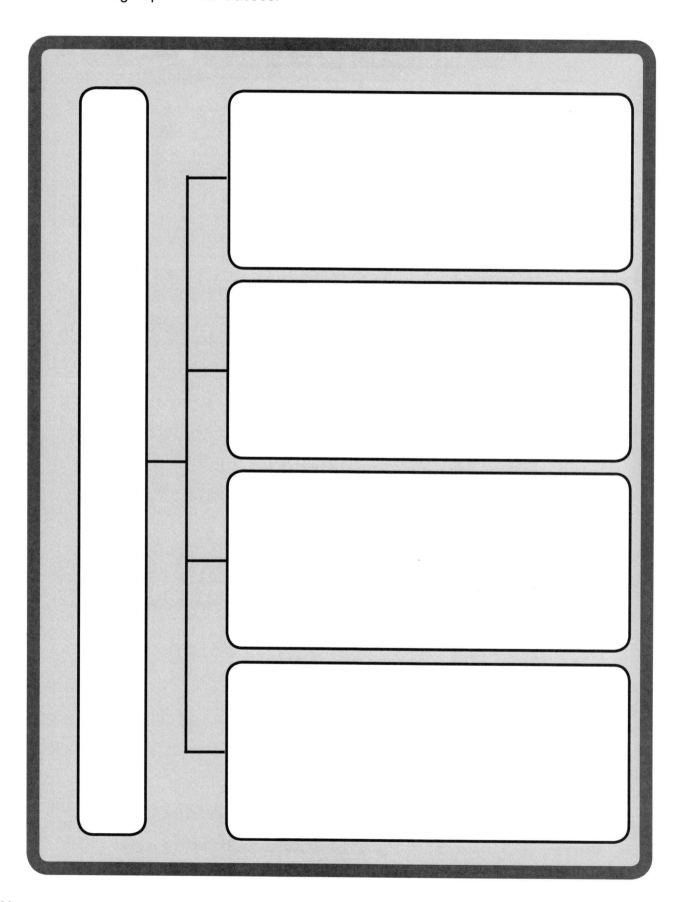

GRAPHIC MASTER 13 - Comparison diagram

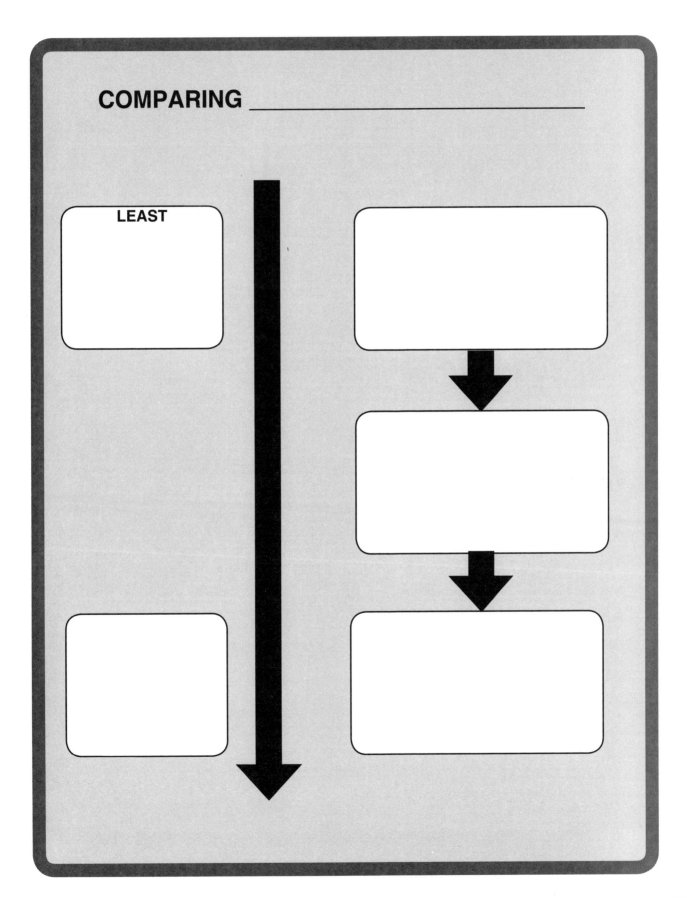

COMPARING _____

LEAST

212